S0-ACV-375

Beyond Sound

ML
3795
.P426
2013

Phillips, Scott L.

Beyond sound.

$24.95

DATE			

BAKER & TAYLOR

·FASKEN LEARNING RESOURCE CENTER

9000084259

84259

Beyond Sound

The College and Career Guide in Music Technology

SCOTT L. PHILLIPS

OXFORD
UNIVERSITY PRESS

OXFORD
UNIVERSITY PRESS

Oxford University Press is a department of the University of Oxford.
It furthers the University's objective of excellence in research, scholarship,
and education by publishing worldwide.

Oxford   New York
Auckland   Cape Town   Dar es Salaam   Hong Kong   Karachi
Kuala Lumpur   Madrid   Melbourne   Mexico City   Nairobi
New Delhi   Shanghai   Taipei   Toronto

With offices in
Argentina   Austria   Brazil   Chile   Czech Republic   France   Greece
Guatemala   Hungary   Italy   Japan   Poland   Portugal   Singapore
South Korea   Switzerland   Thailand   Turkey   Ukraine   Vietnam

Oxford is a registered trademark of Oxford University Press
in the UK and certain other countries.

Published in the United States of America by
Oxford University Press
198 Madison Avenue, New York, NY 10016

© Oxford University Press 2013

All rights reserved. No part of this publication may be reproduced, stored in a
retrieval system, or transmitted, in any form or by any means, without the prior
permission in writing of Oxford University Press, or as expressly permitted by law,
by license, or under terms agreed with the appropriate reproduction rights organization.
Inquiries concerning reproduction outside the scope of the above should be sent to the
Rights Department, Oxford University Press, at the address above.

You must not circulate this work in any other form
and you must impose this same condition on any acquirer.

Library of Congress Cataloging-in-Publication Data
Phillips, Scott L.
Beyond sound : the college and career guide in music technology / Scott L. Phillips.
pages cm
Includes bibliographical references and index.
ISBN 978-0-19-983768-7 (alk. paper) — ISBN 978-0-19-983766-3 (alk. paper)
1. Music—Vocational guidance.   2. Music and technology.   I. Title.
ML3795.P426 2013
780.23—dc23
2012042406

9 8 7 6 5 4 3 2 1
Printed in the United States of America
on acid-free paper

84259

For Kristi, Daniel, Joseph, and Benjamin

Contents

Acknowledgments

ALTHOUGH MINE IS the only name on the cover of this book, there were many people who helped to bring it about. These people deserve recognition for their contributions and I want to offer them my deepest gratitude. I would like to thank Norman Hirschy, my editor at Oxford, for believing in this project and guiding it from inception to completion. I would also like to thank the others at Oxford University Press who worked on the project as well as those professionals who reviewed the proposal and the manuscript. Their insights and enthusiasm were helpful and encouraging.

For allowing me to interview them, I want to thank Fred Bogert, Robert Fernandez, Jim Frankel, Barbara Freedman, Will Giuliani, Peter Lee, Joe Pisano, and Doug Siebum. I am grateful to each of you for sharing your insights.

I would like to thank the faculty members of the University of Alabama at Birmingham Department of Music. I am grateful for their kind support of my professional activities and my career. I am honored and humbled to work with a group of musical professionals who are so devoted to the success of their students.

I would like to thank my academic mentors at the University of Central Florida and the University of Iowa. I am especially grateful for my association with Ken Phillips, whose clear examples of professional scholarship, academic excellence, and kindness are the models for my college teaching career. Thanks to all of the past and present students with whom I have the pleasure of working. Your endless enthusiasm, passion, energy, and creativity inspire me.

I would also like to thank my mother, who taught me the value of hard work, and my father, who made helpful suggestions to the manuscript and who always preached the importance of professional connections.

I express my deepest gratitude to my three sons and my wife. To Daniel, Joseph, and Benjamin, who are avid readers, talented musicians, and who, individually and taken together, are much smarter than I am. I will be forever grateful for your sincere interest in my work, and for your patience and sacrifice as I finished the book. Finally, my thanks and love to Kristi, without whom none of this would have been possible. Your endless proofreading, unfailing support, tireless encouragement, and selfless sacrifice made this book possible.

Foreword

YOU READ ABOUT it every day; the music business paradigm has shifted and the industry has evolved.

It's all quite true that music creation, delivery, marketing, and distribution has changed considerably from what it was for many years. So much of it is now based around what you can individually do on your personal computer rather than what happens within the confines of a recording studio or record label. For instance, when I first started in the recording end of the business, all you needed to do to get a job in a studio was to show up and display an interest. You'd start out sweeping the floor and cleaning the toilets, but the job was yours if you had a good attitude, and you could work your way up to being an engineer or producer from there if you stayed around long enough.

Today you might still start out much the same way, but the technology has evolved to a point where it's beyond what can be learned on the job without some prior training. Once upon a time it was possible to learn the process of recording just by assisting a pro for a period of time and carefully observing what he did. While some measure of that still occurs today, the minimum prerequisites to even get into that position require a level of expertise unprecedented in the history of the industry, and that expertise can only come through education. Where once upon a time it would have been ridiculous for a studio manager to ask what school you attended (since there were no schools for that sort of thing at the time), today that very well may be the first question.

That's why this book is so important if you're looking to enter the music business on any level. Music technology is such an essential part of any musician's toolbox today, that if you don't have at least some tech background, you'll forever be at a disadvantage throughout any career in the industry that you choose to pursue. For composing, songwriting, and even good old fashioned instrument and band practice, having at least some rudimentary tech knowledge can raise your level of creativity, efficiency, and productivity, not to mention your value. If you're aiming for the business side of music, a background in technology allows you to better understand the needs of your clients and coworkers, since they will be bound by that same technology surrounding their music.

While it's difficult to argue how invaluable a solid music technology education can be, the landscape for attaining that education can be confusing indeed. There are so many educational choices available that it's easy to get confused and even discouraged. That's why you need a roadmap to find the training that best suits your career goals, and that's why you need *Beyond Sound*.

Speaking of career goals, as you'll see in this book, there's a lot more to the music business than being an artist, songwriter, recording engineer, or producer, which are the most visible careers of the recorded music business. Scott does an excellent job of providing an outline of a number of different potential career paths that you might not have been previously aware of or considered. It's a much larger industry than initially meets the eye. Even if your career intention is to be a musician, artist, or engineer, that goal may change at some point along the way. It's surprising the number of people who used to be active players or engineers and decided at some point that such a career wasn't for them, causing them to transition into another area of the business. It might not be in the area where you thought you'd end up, but it's in an area still involving music, which can be just as satisfying to the soul (and it might even pay more).

Beyond Sound will also provide a great overview of the different music technology courses available, what the differences between them are, and the qualifying requirements of each. All of this comes in an extremely easy-to-read package that you'll find as enjoyable as it is informative. You'll find some interesting career anecdotes, get lots of advice, and have a clearer idea about your future when you're finished. With that, I join Scott in hoping that this book sets you on the way to a long and fulfilling career in music technology.

Bobby Owsinski
November 2012

About the Companion Website

www.oup.com/us/beyondsound

Oxford has created a password-protected website to accompany *Beyond Sound: The College and Career Guide in Music Technology*. There, readers will find links to professional organizations in music technology, college music programs, and bonus video and audio clips from the interviews in the book. Readers are encouraged to take full advantage of this resource as they explore their future working in the world of music technology and prepare to take their careers *Beyond Sound*.

Introduction

IF YOU LOVE music technology, this book is for you. If you are a college student interested in or currently studying music technology, this book is for you. If you are one of the lucky high school students who has discovered the exciting world of music technology and you want to study it in college, this book is for you. If you are an adult working in an uninteresting and unsatisfying job and you spend most of your free time making and recording music on the computer, this book is for you.

Perhaps you use your laptop, your phone, or handheld device to make beats or loops or songs. Maybe you play in a band and have tried your hand at recording and mixing your own music. Maybe you have volunteered at a church or school or worked at a club running the soundboard.

You may feel like you are the only person you know who is interested in music technology and you might even be hoping you can turn your passion for sound and electronics into a career. But building a successful career in music technology goes way beyond sound. It requires thousands of hours of preparation. It entails an understanding of what jobs in the industry are like and what skills you will need to get them. It demands focused effort developing your musical and technological skills. It takes a good résumé and the right connections to get into the business. And in most cases, to establish a stable career in music technology, it takes a four-year college degree.

Beyond Sound was written to help you take your interest in music technology and turn it into a professional career. It gives definitive answers to the following pressing questions:

"What kind of jobs can I find in music technology?"
"Why is it a great time to work in the world of music technology?"
"Where can I go to study music technology in college?"
"How do I decide which type of college degree is best for me?"

"What is life like for people who work in music technology?"
and
"How do I get started on my music technology career?"

Currently, there are thousands of jobs for qualified music technologists in recording studios, live performance venues, software companies, the video game industry, film and television production, sales and customer service, and education. And as technology develops at an ever-increasing pace, many more jobs are being created, and some of them will be jobs that don't even exist today. Over the course of the next thirty to forty years of your career, the demand for prepared, qualified, and educated music technologists will only increase. *Beyond Sound* will give you the guidance, direction, and advice that will help you join the ranks of the successful music technologists of the future.

Layout of this Book

The purpose of this book is two-fold and the chapters are divided into two sections. Chapters 1–4 will help you prepare for your career in music technology. In Chapter 1 you will learn about the history of music technology and why now is a great time to enter the profession. In Chapter 2 you will learn about the importance of dedicated hard work and commitment as you undertake informal and formal preparations. Chapter 3 presents information about formal education in music technology at the college level. You will learn the difference between various types of degree programs and be presented with information about where these programs are offered. In Chapter 4 you will learn about résumé writing, participation in professional organizations, and networking. You will hear from web designer and handheld app developer Joe Pisano, who gives practical advice on how to use the Internet to give you a leg up on the competition in the job market.

The second section of the book, comprising Chapters 5–10, gives detailed descriptions of the jobs and career paths that are available for music technologists. These chapters also feature interviews with successful professionals who share their advice for starting your career, keeping your job, and finding success.

In Chapter 5 you will learn about jobs in and around the recording studio and hear from engineer, producer, and studio owner Fred Bogert. Several of the albums Fred produced were nominated for Grammy Awards and in my interview with him you will learn about the ups and downs of the recording business and the importance of knowing who you are and what you have to offer.

Chapter 6 describes jobs in the world of live sound production. You will learn what kinds of skills you need to have to work in venues large and small and what life is like if you work at a club, a church, or with a traveling show. Will Giuliani describes his work as the technical director of Oak Mountain Church, with more than 2,500 members and several live shows each week. He discusses the importance of having a diverse skill set, being a lifelong learner, and surrounding yourself with the best people.

In Chapter 7, sound and music for film and television are explored. The many jobs for music technologists in production and postproduction are described. Film scoring mixer Robert Fernandez shares the story of his twenty-four-year career at Warner Bros. Studios, his subsequent success as an independent scoring mixer, his process for scoring films, and his love of movie music.

Chapter 8 presents jobs in digital media, including computer programming, software development, web design, and sound design for video games. Rising Software founder Peter Lee recounts his experiences starting a software title with global distribution as a nineteen-year-old high school graduate. He discusses the constant challenges of responding to customer needs, marketing the product, running the company, managing his family, and still finding time to write code.

In Chapter 9, the booming world of music technology manufacturing is explored and jobs for music technologists in various aspects of sales and service are presented. Jim Frankel discusses his role as the former managing director of Korg USA's educational division, SoundTree. He reflects on the nontraditional career path that led him to this corporate position, the demands on his time required for travel, and on his own secret to success: hard work.

Chapter 10 presents careers for music technologists in education. The necessary preparations for schoolteachers and college professors are described. Technology Institute for Music Educators 2012 Teacher of the Year Barbara Freedman reflects on her career teaching music through technology at Greenwich High School in Connecticut. She outlines the need for music teachers to embrace technology as a means of advocacy for their profession.

The Conclusion points out that while you may choose to take your career in the direction of one of the paths described in the book, there is the real possibility that you may begin your career working in a lot of different areas. Doug Siebum, a recent college graduate and audio engineer living in the Los Angeles area describes how his diverse skills have helped him to stay very busy working in the industry. In the five years since graduation, he has worked in radio, television, film, live sound, corporate venues, and at a 27,000-seat sports arena. His secret? Work harder than everybody else.

Beyond Sound is written for anyone who is interested in building a career in the exciting world of music technology. Whether you want to be a recording engineer, work in a movie studio, design the sounds for video games, manage the sales force of a major music manufacturer, teach music in a school, or take one of the thousands of music technology jobs that will exist in the future, this book will tell you how to make the right preparations to develop the skills you will need for success in this exciting and diverse profession.

This book will give you an intimate and accurate view of the exciting world of music technology to help you learn about, prepare for, and begin a successful career that goes *Beyond Sound*.

1

The Professional Music Technologist

The Music Technologist

In November of 1877, Thomas Edison invented the phonograph at his Menlo Park, New Jersey, Laboratory. He employed a team of inventors, researchers, musicians, engineers, and electricians to refine the phonograph until speech and then music could be reliably recorded and played back. Edison's team was motivated by pressing competition and the hope of financial success. Laboratories led by Alexander Graham Bell, Charles Tainter, Emile Berliner, and others all competed in this emerging and potentially lucrative market. Eventually, huge business empires would be based on recorded sound. These early pioneers may be considered the first modern music technologists, but in a broader sense, music technology has existed as long as there has been music.

The word technology is derived from the Greek *technologia*, meaning the systematic treatment of an art, and can be defined as the practical application of knowledge in a particular area. By this definition, the design and construction of any musical instrument, instructional method, or singing style can be considered music technology.

There are many interesting examples of technological development from throughout the history of music. Here are three:

1. In the year AD 1010, the Benedictine Monk Guido de Arezzo devised a mnemonic system for singing where note names were mapped to parts of the human hand. This system evolved into the solfeggio or do-re-mi method used by singers today. The 1965 Academy Award-winning film and Broadway musical *The Sound of Music* features a scene in which Maria teaches the Von Trapp children to sing using this method.
2. In the early 1730s the composer, organ builder, and musical scientist Johann Sebastian Bach was presented with a new technological development in

keyboard instruments. After playing the instrument he complained to its creator, Gottfried Silbermann, that, "it was too weak in the high register and too hard to play." Due to this criticism, the inventor worked on improving his design for more than fifteen years, at which point Bach gave Silbermann, "complete approval."[1] The new instrument would go on to significantly propel the future musical careers of Mozart, Beethoven, and others. Eventually it would become the most important and universal musical instrument in the world, the piano.

3. During the 1800s music technology provided many developments for symphony orchestras. Builders and designers created new instruments and devised modifications for existing ones. Instruments such as the saxophone, tuba, valve trombone, piccolo, and others allowed music to be performed with a wider range, broader tone color, and greater intensity and speed than ever before.

Although it can be argued that music technology has been around as long as music itself, today, technology usually refers to the recent development of electronic or computerized tools. And although we often refer to this field as music technology, recording, creating, and manipulating nonmusical sounds such as the speaking voice or sound effects requires the same tools and preparation necessary for someone working with musical sounds. As a result, this book will use the following definition—Music Technologist: Any professional who uses electronics and computers as tools to design, create, perform, teach, and record music and sound.

A Little History

From the invention of the phonograph until the present time, music technology's development has been considerable. And while this field is relatively new, its short history has been characterized by constant change. Below are listed some of the most important events, discoveries, and advancements as well as the key people and companies that have shaped the history of music technology from the advent of the phonograph to the present day.

1877, Invention of the phonograph, Thomas Edison
1894, Invention of the radio, Guglielmo Marconi
1904, Invention of the vacuum tube, J. Ambrose Fleming
1915, Invention of the first loudspeaker "Magnavox," Peter L. Jensen
1920, The first commercial radio station broadcast, Frank Conrad

1927, The first feature-length commercial motion picture with synchronized sound, *The Jazz Singer*, is released, Warner Bros.

1927, The first television is patented, Philo Farnsworth

1928, Digital Sampling Theory proposed, Harry Nyquist

1931, Method of stereo recording patented in England, Alan Blumlein

1935, The first magnetic tape recorder, the magnetophone, is demonstrated, BASF/AEG

1939, The computer company Hewlett Packard is founded. Its first product, the HP 200 Audio Oscillator was used by Walt Disney to create sound effects for the 1940 film *Fantasia*, David Packard and Bill Hewlett

1940, Vinyl becomes the material of choice for playback of recorded sound, RCA Victor Company

1946, The first commercially successful electric guitar is marketed, Leo Fender

1947, Invention of the Williamson vacuum tube amplifier, D. T. N. Williamson

1948, The first long-playing records (LPs) are sold, Columbia

1950, The first transistors are designed and patented, William Shockley at Bell Labs

1951, The UNIVAC I computer is delivered to the US Census Bureau. A total of forty-six machines were sold at a cost of more than $1 million each, Remington Rand

1958, Stereo headphones are introduced, KOSS

1963, The compact audio cassette is introduced, Philips

1966, Cars are fitted with 8-track tape players, Ampex and RCA

1971, The first affordable synthesizer, the Minimoog Model D, is marketed, Robert Moog

1975, Nineteen-year-old Bill Gates and twenty-one-year-old Paul Allen create a BASIC interpreter for the Altair 880 computer. Microsoft Corporation is born

1976, Twenty-one-year-old Steve Jobs and twenty-six-year-old Stephen Wozniak found Apple Computers

1977, The Apple II, Commodore PET, and TRS 80 are introduced as the first personal computers for home use. Cost: $500–$700 each, Apple, Commodore, and Tandy Radio Shack

1977, Digital Audio Recordings are demonstrated at the Audio Engineering Society Convention, Thomas Stockham and Soundstream

1978, The first all-digital classical album, *Holst's Suites For Band* by the Cleveland Orchestra, is released and dubbed "The Bass Drum Heard 'Round the World," Telarc and Soundstream

1979, *Bop 'Til You Drop* is released as the first multitrack all-digital album, Ry Cooder and Warner Bros.

1979, The Walkman portable audio cassette player is introduced, Sony

1982, The first CDs are marketed, Philips and Sony

1982, The average personal computer hard drive stores about 20 MB of data

1983, Cassette sales surpass LP sales, RIAA

1988, CD sales surpass LP and cassette sales, RIAA

1988, Finale music notation software is released, Coda Music Software

1989, Sound Tools hard-disk digital recorder is released. Changes name to Pro Tools in 1991, Digidesign

1989, The Sound Blaster PC sound card is released with the ability to play back and record audio samples, Creative Technology

1990, The first digital radio programs are broadcast

1990, Digital Performer, the world's first Digital Audio Workstation (DAW) software for MIDI and audio recording and sequencing is released, Mark of the Unicorn

1993, Logic DAW software is released, Emagic

1995, The MP3 digital audio format is released, Fraunhofer Society

1995, The average computer hard drive stores 1 GB of data

1996, The first Internet radio station, Advice-net.com, begins broadcasts, George Maat

1997, DVD players go on sale in the United States

1998, The first digital 24-bit 48-track recording produced in Nashville, Jonell Polansky

1998, Sibelius notation software is released, Sibelius Inc.

1999, The peer-to-peer file sharing website Napster is released, Shawn Fanning

1999, Digital television recording is introduced, TiVo and Philips

2000, Computer processors exceed 1.0 GHz processing speed, Intel and AMD

2000, The average computer hard drive stores about 20 GB of data

2000, Reason virtual music studio rack software is released, Propellerhead

2001, The iPod is introduced, Apple

2001, Satellite radio is launched, XM and Sirius

2002, DVD sales surpass VHS sales

2002, The average computer hard drive stores 60 GB of data

2008, The iTunes Store sells its 5 billionth song, Apple

2009, US CD Sales decrease by nearly $1.2 billion (22%) from 2008, RIAA

2009, US music download sales increase by nearly $320 million (19%) from 2008, RIAA

2010, The average computer hard drive stores 500 GB of data

Several important concepts can be gleaned from a careful consideration of this timeline. These concepts may not be exclusive to music technology, and some may even seem cliché, but they should be pointed out here in our context, to aid our understanding.

Theories Come Long Before Products

Throughout the timeline, theories describing how an invention could work, or determining how the physical properties of sound might be manipulated, always preceded technological advancement. One example can be seen in sampling theory, one of the most fundamental concepts for music technologists to understand in a digital age. This theory explains why sound must be sampled 44,100 times per second to achieve CD quality audio. It dictates how to build electronic filters that remove unwanted noise from the digitization process. And an understanding of this theory helps an audio engineer decide whether to spend the extra money to purchase recording equipment that provides sampling rates that go far beyond CD quality.

This theory, which has so many implications for today's musicians, was explained by Nyquist in 1928, fifty years before the first digital audio recording occurred. Additionally, most of the capabilities of today's computers were discussed in theory years before the hardware and software were produced to make them a reality. And the timeline contains many other examples of inventions designed in theory years before the actual product was realized. It is true for radio, television, movies, and even the Internet.

This point underscores the importance of a good formal education for music technologists. It is important to understand the software and hardware of today's machines, but it is also important to understand the underlying theories that they operate on, as well as those theories for which inventions and developments have not yet been realized.

Format Change Is the Only Constant

The cliché "change is the only constant," attributed to the Greek philosopher Heraclitus of Ephesus (535–475 BC) certainly holds true for the development of audio and video recording and playback formats. Change in this context has meant improvement on existing products, but it has also meant the unveiling of new products. Examples include LPs, cassettes, videotapes, CDs, DVDs, and MP3s.

The simple knowledge that formats will inevitably change is a valuable survival tool for those pursuing careers in music technology. An ironic example of someone who failed to understand this point was the man considered by many to be the greatest innovator in the modern age, Thomas Edison. By 1914, most of the phonograph industry had gone to pressing recordings using resin discs, but Edison refused, citing the superior sound quality and reliability of his cylindrical design. Despite the advice of his own researchers and developers, Edison continued to produce cylinder recordings long after it was profitable to do so. Eventually the Edison Company converted to resin disks as well, but the refusal to accept the new format almost bankrupted the company.[2]

David Kearns, former CEO of Xerox, recounts a personal experience that illustrated this point for him. "When I was new at IBM, working in sales and taking a management training program in Sleepy Hollow, New York, I came back to my room grumbling about the lack of speed and reliability of the tape drives, and wondered why the engineers couldn't do something about it. My roommate stared at me with a look of total exasperation. 'Boy, you guys in sales are all the same,' he said. 'You remind me of the farmer in 1850. If you asked him what he wanted, he would say he wanted a horse that was half as big and ate half as many oats and was twice as strong. And there would be no discussion of a tractor.'"[3]

The Rate of Advancement Increases over Time

Developments in music technology evolve at an ever-increasing pace. Notice that the phonograph was invented in 1887, but it wasn't until 1940 that the vinyl record became the standard. This means it took more than fifty years of research and market forces to progress from foil cylinders to vinyl records, but only fifteen years to progress from LPs to compact cassette tapes. And while it took twenty years for the cassette to surpass the LP in sales, the CD surpassed the cassette tape and LP in sales only six years after its release. Columnist Philip Elmer-Dewitt, who has followed the development of Apple for nearly twenty years, writes of this "continued acceleration." Speaking of the iTunes store, he states: "It took Apple nearly three years to sell its first billion songs (Feb. 23, 2006), ten months to sell its second billion (Jan. 6, 2007), seven months to sell its third (July 31, 2007), five and a half to sell its fourth (Jan. 15,

2008), and five months to sell its fifth (June 19, 2008)."[4] This ever-increasing rate of change requires music technologists to stay abreast of the latest developments in the field, despite the fact that this task becomes increasingly more difficult as time goes on.

Breakthroughs Create Sonic Booms

Sometimes advancements are so important, they create shockwaves that resonate throughout the entire industry. This concept is analogous to an interesting physical phenomenon that occurs when a fast-moving object approaches the speed of sound. In normal conditions (at sea level and room temperature) sound pressure waves travel in all directions from the source of a sound at about 761 mph. If the source of a sound approaches this speed, the sound waves moving forward lose the ability to outpace the source. As the fast-moving object reaches the speed of sound, it travels at the same rate as the air molecules that are being pushed out in front of it. The waves collect and create a barrier where the air pressure increases exactly in front of the moving object. When enough force is applied to move the object through this barrier, the pressure is broken and the object moves forward, uninhibited by the sound waves. The resultant and sudden pressure change creates a shockwave known as a sonic boom.

This phenomenon can be observed in technological advancements. Sometimes progress reaches a point at which the advances tend to bunch up just ahead of the speed of innovation. Ideas are formulated that push against the barrier until a major breakthrough has the force to push through. The result is a boom in development and advancement that moves forward uninhibited until the next barrier is reached.

In the world of electronics, the transistor was such a breakthrough. In the 1930s and 1940s, researchers in the relatively new field of electronics had created radios, speakers, televisions, and even computers with the new technology of vacuum tubes. But the glass tubes were large, generated a great deal of heat, and were easily broken. Theories for improving electronic devices abounded, but the clumsy glass tubes became the limiting factor. After the advent of the transistor in 1950, electronic devices of all kinds and specifically computers could be made to work faster and be built smaller than was ever thought possible. Transistors have gotten continually smaller and more affordable over the past sixty years, and are the key component in every electronic device in the world. In 2002 Jim Turley, an independent market analyst, made the following estimation and prediction: "About 60 million transistors were built this year just for you, with another 60 million for each of your friends, plus 60 million for every other man, woman, and child on Earth. By 2010 the number should be around one billion transistors per person per year."[5]

Breakthroughs of this magnitude can have an almost immeasurable impact for the development of career opportunities within a profession. Think of the millions of jobs that have been created in the world of electronics and computers since the advent of the transistor.

Breakthroughs in Music Technology

In music technology there have been two major breakthroughs that have cleared the way for considerable growth in this field. In another fifty years, it may be said that these breakthroughs had as great an impact for the professional music technologist as the transistor did for the world of electronics.

The first breakthrough was the advent of digital audio. In November 1977 Jack Renner and Robert Woods, founders of the then-tiny Cleveland, Ohio-based classical label Telarc, heard demonstrations of audio recordings made with Thomas Stockham's 16 bit/37.5 kHz 2-track digital recorder. They were impressed with the sound, but asked Stockham if he could extend the sample rate to accommodate frequencies up to 20 kHz. By January of 1978, Stockham had improved his equipment to record up to four tracks at 50 kHz. On April 4th and 5th, the Cleveland Symphonic Winds, under the direction of Frederick Fennell, recorded what would become the first commercially released all-digital classical album in the United States. The album was released to critical acclaim, and the *World Book Yearbook* for 1978 dubbed it "the Bass Drum Heard 'Round the World." Renner recalled the 1978 recording session this way: "At the sessions, we had writers from every major audio magazine of the time. There was a feeling on the part of all concerned that this was something special."[6] Renner was right. Digital audio had changed the course of music technology forever. Historian Thomas Fine notes, "By the beginning of the 1980s, all major record companies had embraced digital recording in one form or another."[7]

The impact of digital audio moved next to playback format and the Compact Digital Disc's meteoric rise was the result. Initially, only well-funded companies could afford the technology to convert analog to digital, but throughout the 1980s and '90s, the technology became more powerful and less expensive. Software programs for manipulating digital audio such as Sound Tools (eventually Pro Tools), Digital Performer, Cubase, Logic, Sonar, Sound Forge, and Cool Edit Pro began to flood the marketplace.

But the considerable demands for processing speed and hard drive memory required of digital audio kept digital recording out of the realm of many professionals and most amateurs as another barrier to progress was quickly being reached. To be more specific, in 1995, the average computer hard drive could store about one gigabyte of data, but stereo digital audio requires about ten megabytes of storage per minute. That means an entire hard drive at maximum capacity could store less than five minutes of a 24-track recording. Just like the vacuum tube had been the limiting factor to progress before 1950, computer memory and processing speeds were limiting the further development of music technology.

The second breakthrough came in March of 2000 when, within two days of one another, Intel and AMD each released computer processors clocked at 1.0 GHz. At this point computer hard drive capacities were exceeding 25 GB of memory, and suddenly the personal computer could feasibly manage digital audio. No longer was it necessary to enter a recording studio to produce high-quality recordings. And with the widespread use of the Internet, which precipitated not only the dot-com boom of 1999 but also the introduction of peer-to-peer services such as Napster, Kazaa, LimeWire, Morpheus, Aimster, Grokster, and others, the rules of music distribution, and ownership, were being rewritten.

The barriers had been broken, clearing the way for unprecedented growth in music technology and giving the masses the ability to control digital sound. Existing software companies changed their products to make them affordable and accessible for the amateur user, and dozens of new software companies were formed. Digital audio became the standard in film, video games, and over the Internet, and new markets for digital music downloads, audio loops, virtual synthesizers, digital effects processors, and a host of other products were created. Even higher education, one of the slowest institutions to react to societal change, was significantly impacted. Between 2000 and 2010, the number of four-year universities granting degrees in music technology quadrupled, and literally hundreds of courses in music technology were added to university curricula.

Now is the Time

This review of the history of music technology was included here for several reasons. First, someone who is employed in this field should have a working knowledge of its history. Second, a careful look at the development of music technology helps not only to illustrate how careers in this field have evolved over the past 130 years but also identifies current trends and opportunities for today's music technologists. Last, the historical review provides strong evidence that there has never been a better time to enter the professional world of music technology.

Your Career as a Music Technologist

This is an exciting and dynamic field and those who are prepared find that job opportunities abound. There is great demand for music technologists in all aspects of music. Technologists are needed in commercial music, classical music, live music, recorded music, church music, and music education. In entertainment, music technologists are sought after in radio, television, film, and the ever-expanding video game industry. Music technologists are also in demand in computer science, engineering, manufacturing, and business, to design, build, and sell the software, hardware, instruments, studios, and performance facilities used by musicians.

Indeed, careers in music technology are as varied as the people who work in them, but it is nearly impossible to select a music technology career that suites your strengths, skills, interests, and personality without knowing what those careers are like. Furthermore, once you decide which career to pursue, identifying the path to your chosen career can be difficult. Fortunately, the field of music technology is emerging as an independent discipline, and so are clear paths to career success in this field. This book is designed to help you discover those paths and make the necessary preparations for traveling down them.

Notes

1. Christoph Wolff, *The New Bach Reader: A Life of Johann Sebastian Bach in Letters and Documents* (New York: W. W. Norton and Company, 1998), 365–366.
2. Andre Millard, *America on Record: A History of Recorded Sound* (New York: Cambridge University Press, 2005), 132–134.
3. Clayton M. Christensen, *The Innovators Dilemma* (New York: HarperCollins Publishers, 2003), 64.
4. Philip Elmer-Dewitt, "iTunes Store: 5 Billion Songs; 50,000 Movies per Day," *Fortune Magazine* [Online]. June 19, 2008. Available: http://tech.fortune.cnn.com/2008/06/19/itunes-store-5-billion-songs-50000-movies-per-day/.
5. Jim Turley, "The Two Percent Solution," *EE Times* [Online]. December 18, 2002. Available: http://www.eetimes.com/discussion/other/4024488/The-Two-Percent-Solution.
6. Thomas Fine, "The Dawn of Commercial Digital Recording," *ARSC Journal*, 39:1, 7.
7. Fine, "Commercial Digital Recording," 13.

2

Preparing to Be a Music Technologist

KENNETH WAS ONLY twelve years old when he decided what he would do with the rest of his life. The inspiration came as he was watching a beautiful singer on a television show. As the camera shot panned over to a window in the recording studio, Kenneth saw a man behind the desk who seemed to be in charge. In that moment, he resolved to become a recording engineer. For the next several years, all his efforts were focused on achieving this goal, but he had little direction or assistance from his schoolteachers or counselors. They didn't know what was involved in recording and instead encouraged him to pursue a "real job." Through research, Kenneth determined that he should attend the local university and study engineering. When most of his friends left school for the workplace at age fifteen, he stayed to prepare for his exams. The idea of additional schooling wasn't appealing, but he was committed to his dream.

After one particularly difficult day at school, Kenneth decided he had had enough of exams. He opened the local phone book and looked up every record label, radio station, and television station he could find. The next morning he sent letters to many of them. On the following Tuesday, he received a response from a local recording studio asking him to come for an interview. Within a week of the interview, Kenneth left school and began work at the recording studios—in the tape library, earning $8 a week.

The year was 1964. Kenneth held in his hands the master copy of a new recording. The studios were owned by EMI and located on Abbey Road in London, and the recording was "Can't Buy Me Love" by The Beatles. Within three and a half years, at the age of twenty, Ken Scott became The Beatles' primary recording engineer. In addition to working with The Beatles, Ken Scott would go on to record and produce dozens of hits and numerous albums for other artists as well, including David Bowie, Elton John, Pink Floyd, The Rolling Stones, and many others. Today, Ken Scott may be considered one of the most important, influential, and successful engineers and producers in the history of recorded music.

Ken's story is an inspiring one for anyone hoping to work in the exciting world of recorded music, and you may think that if this kind of success can come to a sixteen-year-old boy who had nothing more than a dream, it can certainly come to you. But in 1964, getting a job in the recording industry was radically different than it is today.

Still, there are some important lessons to be learned from Ken's experience. First, he decided what he wanted to do and stuck to it. When his schoolteachers didn't know whom he should contact, he made the contacts himself. He accepted a job with a low salary (even for 1964) because it put him in a position that would get him close to people doing what he wanted to do. And, finally, and perhaps most importantly, he was profoundly and inexplicably lucky.

Most successful music technologists today are experienced musicians who play multiple instruments with years of formal and informal training. The majority have studied at universities in music, or computer science, or engineering, or business. Nearly all belong to professional networks and organizations. And while luck may be an important factor in success, one simply cannot build an entire career on luck alone.

In his book *Outliers: The Story of Success*, author and social observer Malcolm Gladwell dispels the myth that the super-successful were simply lucky (he cites Bill Gates, Steve Jobs, and even The Beatles as examples). He claims that their success can be attributed to various environmental factors and at least 10,000 hours of personal dedicated hard work and preparation.[1] To put this overwhelming number in perspective, at 10 hours a week, it will take you 20 years to reach 10,000 hours of work. It can also be achieved in 20 hours a week for 10 years, 40 hours a week for 5 years, or 80 hours a week for 2 ½ years. I don't wish to take the Gladwell 10,000-hour rule too far or promise you that if you put in 10,000 hours of preparation you are guaranteed to be super-successful. However, it should be clear that forging the path to your career will require many hours of preparation (probably thousands), and it is never too late—or too early—to start.

There is a cliché that goes, "Luck favors the well-prepared." In my own career and in those of people whom I respect, I have found this to be true. Interestingly, it was also true for the young Ken Scott.

Let's take a closer look at Ken's story. At first glance it may appear that he was simply in the right place at the right time. But there is more to this story than just luck. Ken loved to listen to music when he was young. Although his family wasn't musical, there was a wind-up gramophone in the spare bedroom of his house and he spent hours listening to recordings on old 78-rpm records. When Ken was twelve, his parents gave him a Grundig TK 25 tape recorder for Christmas. He spent untold hours listening to the radio and recording the music on the simple reel-to-reel tape recorder. In reflecting on this early recording experience, Ken states, "I had no idea how much fun playing with that recorder would be, and lucky for me, that fun is still the driving force in my life even to this day."[2]

Once he was employed at EMI, Ken worked hard and absorbed all he could. In the tape library, he learned how the studio cataloged recordings and the information that was required on each tape. Within a few months he was promoted to assistant engineer and worked as a "button pusher," literally pressing the Record, Play, Stop, and Rewind buttons while observing the recording process during hundreds of sessions. He was soon promoted again and became a "cutter" or mastering engineer, and eventually, at just twenty years old, he was promoted to engineer. Ken's first session as engineer was with The Beatles working on tracks for the album *Magical Mystery Tour*. He reflects, "I can remember very little about the session except that I was almost paralysed (sic) with fear, which probably would have happened on just about any session I'd been given, but add on top of that that this was the biggest bloody band in the world and those long hours were an exercise in terror."[3] In Ken's case, luck had favored the well-prepared. By the time he sat down behind that console while The Beatles played in EMI Studio Number 2, he had thousands of hours of preparation under his belt.

Consider what preparation you have made for your own career. Think about how many hours a week you spend now, or have spent thus far, preparing to become a music technologist. Have you spent those hours focusing on the right things? The purpose of this chapter is to teach you what you can and should be doing with your hours of preparation to become a successful music technologist.

Musical Preparation and Skills

Young people interested in music technology often ask, "Do I need to be able to play an instrument?" The answer is "Yes." This doesn't mean that you need to be a concert pianist, an orchestral soloist, or an opera singer to make it as a music technologist. On the other hand, just being able to play an instrument is not enough. A more complete answer is that you have to be a musician. To be successful in this field, you will need to be able to converse with musicians, understand musical elements, and read music. Even if your specific interests lie in computer programming, or electrical engineering, you will find greater success in a music technology career as an experienced musician.

Some people develop their musical skills through formal music training; in schools and through individual instruction. Some people's musical skills develop in a less formal setting—while playing in a band with friends in the garage or basement, or by listening to music or attending concerts. Both kinds of musical experiences can be important as you develop the skills you need to become a well-rounded musician.

Formal Musical Preparation

Many people have their first opportunity for formal training in their elementary school, middle school, or high school years. Participating in the school band, orchestra, or chorus may be where you learned to read music and understand the basics. You may have also taken private lessons on your band or orchestra instrument. Perhaps you have taken piano, guitar, or voice lessons outside of your school education. All of these experiences are helpful as you learn the basics of music reading and performing. They also help build the skills necessary if you intend to study music at the college level (see Chapter 3).

If you choose a college major in music, you will be required to take lessons on your instrument of choice, participate in musical ensembles, and study music theory and history. Depending on your skill level and instrument, you may also be eligible for considerable financial assistance through scholarships. As a college music major, you will be immersed in music learning and have numerous broad and rich musical experiences.

But even if you choose to major in some area other than music, you should still make it a point to participate in musical activities such as musical ensembles and lessons. It may surprise you to learn that at most universities, non-music majors comprise the majority of students in musical ensembles. Even at universities with large music programs and hundreds of music majors, there are often ensembles specifically for nonmajors and many do not require an audition.

Today's universities offer a wide range of musical experiences and music schools are becoming increasingly diverse. In addition to traditional ensembles such as band, orchestra, and choir, many schools offer guitar, world music, and other nontraditional ensembles. The University of Texas at Austin's Butler School of Music boasts more than forty different musical ensembles, including the Brazilian Ensemble, Early Music Ensemble, Hispanic Caribbean

Ensemble, Javanese Gamelan Ensemble, Mariachi Ensemble, South American Music Ensemble, and the Svaranjali Ensemble, in which students study and perform music from India. Capital University in Columbus, Ohio, offers MU 345: Rock Ensemble, a university-sponsored rock band.

As interest in college music technology has increased, more and more universities are offering technology-related music ensembles as well. Princeton University in New Jersey and Stanford University in northern California sponsor PLOrk and SLOrk, respectively (Princeton/Stanford Laptop Orchestra). Other schools may sponsor a MIDI Band, and at the University of Alabama at Birmingham, I direct the Computer Music Ensemble. Participation in college music ensembles, traditional or otherwise, is an important part of formal music training.

In addition to teaching you music, participation in school music activities and music lessons instills self-discipline, encourages a healthy work ethic, and develops a capability for working with people in group settings—all of which are great life skills that will help you in any career path.

Informal Musical Experiences

Music is such a significant part of everyday life that you may not realize some musical activities you regularly participate in might actually prepare you for your career. These activities can include listening to music, making music with your friends, singing in a church choir, writing songs on your guitar or at the piano or using your laptop, and going to concerts, shows, and clubs. The truth of the matter is that to become a musician one must spend some serious time living with their music. This can't be done only in the piano studio or choir classroom. Real musicians eat, sleep, and breathe their music; music is not a passion that works 9 to 5. This idea is summarized in a conversation I had with Andre Millard. A historian, musician, and author of several books about the history of recorded sound, Millard expressed his desire that more young people understood the importance of just living with their music. He quipped, "I hope the spirit of John Lennon will live on…every time a teenager skips school to spend an afternoon thinking, and strumming a guitar."

Musical Skills

Whether through formal schooling or informal musical experiences, all musicians need to listen to music. They also need to read music and be able to perform on an instrument. Additionally, keyboarding skills are critical to the success of any musician.

Listening

The most basic musical activity is listening to music. Music listening can have a powerful influence on people's lives. Researchers in the fields of music cognition and perception as well as music therapy have looked carefully at the impact of music listening on the intelligence, mental processing, and health of individuals. Considerable research has also been done in the field of music education. My own doctoral research indicates that children who listen to music in the home are more likely to participate in musical activities in school.[4] They are also more likely to take music lessons or participate in other organized musical activities. Listening to music also develops one's musical preferences and tastes. In learning music, listening is an important part of understanding different styles, genres, and musical traditions. As a music technologist, having a broad understanding of various musical styles can be a great asset, whether you are recording in a studio, running the sound at a live venue, or selling microphones to music stores.

Music was always a part of my home as a child. I would load my parents' console-style record player with their cast recordings of Broadway musicals. My siblings and I often ran around the basement singing along to Robert Preston as the Music Man, Zero Mostel as Tevye, Julie Andrews as Maria von Trapp, and Frank Sinatra as Nathan Detroit. My parents also had records by Neil Diamond, Barbra Streisand, Peter, Paul and Mary, and other artists that we listened to constantly. Even now, the Statler Brothers' 1978 album *Christmas Card* is required listening at Phillips family events each holiday season. During my teenage years, the radio was often on in our home. On Sunday afternoons we would use blank cassette tapes to record songs from the local radio stations. We would even call and make requests, then listen, our fingers on the record button after every commercial break and at the end of every song to see if our request was being played next. These listening experiences from my early life had a powerful impact on my participation in music throughout my teenage years, into college and eventually throughout my career.

Reading Music

Music is truly a unique language, and it is one in which you must be fluent if you want to work in this field. You must be able to not only read music, but understand its fundamental elements, such as scales, chords, rhythms and simple harmony.

Your music reading skill may depend greatly on your musical experiences. Most people are introduced to the basics of musical notation during their elementary school years. If you joined the school band in fifth or sixth grade, or if you played a string instrument as part of a string program for young people, you learned to read music in tandem with learning your instrument, and probably learned to read music on either the bass or treble clef. If you were a member of a choir, you may have been exposed to reading sheet music, although a great deal of choral music is taught by rote and repetition, so your understanding of the music may be somewhat limited. If you took piano lessons, you were introduced to both the treble and bass clef in the grand staff. If you are a guitar player and took lessons at the local music store, or taught yourself to play, you may not have learned traditional notation but may have learned to read tablature notation.

Of these experiences, learning to play the piano is particularly helpful because it exposes students to the grand staff. More will be discussed on the importance of piano skills later. But no matter how you started learning music, you will need a solid grasp of written music and its fundamentals to be successful. If you choose to major in music at the college level, you will be required to develop these skills through the music theory courses, ensemble participation, and private and group lessons. You will need some familiarity with these skills before college if you intend to be accepted as a music major. If you choose another major, such as computer science, film, or electrical engineering, a college minor in music is highly recommended. If you do not pursue formal music participation in college, you will need to develop these skills on your own. Taking piano lessons from a local piano teacher is a great way to learn the basics of printed music. Also, you can study music theory by purchasing a college music fundamentals or music theory textbook and learning the information on your own. *Tonal Harmony* by Stefan Kostka and Dorothy Payne is one of the most widely accepted music theory textbooks in college classrooms. An understanding of the first four chapters, "Fundamentals," is a great start.

Performing

The ability to perform music is a basic part of musicianship. Most public school music programs are based on performance as a vehicle for learning music. If you have participated in a school choir, band, or orchestra, you have undoubtedly been on stage or on the field and performed dozens of times in front of hundreds, and perhaps thousands, of people. If you choose to be a music major in college, you will perform many more times. Formal musical performances are fundamentally different than other musical experiences. They require a level of preparation that is far greater than that required to play in your home or for your music teacher. These performances evoke emotions of pride, exhilaration, euphoria, anxiety, fear, and a sense of accomplishment. They become a badge of honor and an unspoken bond among all musicians and put you in a "club" with them, so to speak. If you haven't been or aren't a performing musician, you simply won't be in the club and it will be more difficult to work with those people who are.

Performance is a standard part of all college music programs. Most programs require students to participate in large and small ensembles. Depending on the focus of the major and the school requirements, some may require solo recitals as well. These can be great experiences that you will remember throughout your career. Outside of school activities, find other opportunities to perform, such as weddings, clubs, and shows. Join a band or form your own. Most of my music technology students at the university are members of multiple bands and gig regularly at various clubs and events in the area. This can also be a great way to use your skills to start making some money. Oftentimes, an added benefit of a paid performance is an increased sense of pride.

The Keyboard

Keyboard skills are valuable for professionals working in any area of music technology. There are many reasons for the piano's universal usefulness to musicians. First, the piano is one of the few instruments that can effectively play almost every pitch in the range of human hearing. Also, the architecture of its keys clearly displays the half and whole steps that make up music's fundamental building blocks. The accessibility of its keys to the human hands makes it one of the few musical instruments that allow a single musician to create the harmonic and melodic parts of the music simultaneously. Recent music technology makes keyboard skills even more useful. Keyboard synthesizers are so versatile and flexible that they can be played to create any instrument from horns, to strings, to drums. Being able to sit down at the keyboard and play a melodic line, a bass part, or the chords from a lead sheet is essential. And, as mentioned earlier, keyboarding and music reading skills go hand in hand.

I am not alone in my thinking on this. Evidence of the universal acceptance of the importance of piano skills can be seen in the fact that the degree requirements of almost every university music program in the world require that a student pass a piano proficiency exam before graduation. The following is an example of the requirements for such an exam:

SAMPLE PIANO PROFICIENCY EXAMINATION REQUIREMENTS
The student is expected to demonstrate proficiency in the areas of sight-reading, performance, technique, and related functional skills including transposing and improvising simple accompaniments.

1. Sight-reading of song arrangements and/or simple solo piano literature such as a selected example from Chapter 5, pages 195–219 in *Progressive Class Piano* by Elmer Heerema.
2. Perform a solo selected from the following list or from repertoire of comparable difficulty (memorization optional): J.S. Bach, *Little Preludes*; Clementi, *Sonatinas*; Schumann, *Album for the Young*.
3. Perform two patriotic songs: "America" and "The Star-Spangled Banner." Music may be used.
4. Demonstrate proper technique while playing: all major and harmonic minor scales, two octaves in parallel motion, hands together; all major and minor arpeggios, two octaves, hands together.
5. Perform accompaniment improvisations (see *Progressive Class Piano*).
6. Transpose a simple accompaniment or song at sight (see *Progressive Class Piano*, Chapter 5, pages 195–204, for examples).
7. Play the progression I–IV–I 64–V7, I hands together in all major and minor keys.

The College Music Audition

Almost all of the college music technology programs, and many of the music business, music industry, and commercial music programs considered in the next chapter require students to pass a musical audition for admittance. To improve your chances of success, you should prepare carefully for this audition. It may seem very overwhelming to think that you will have to sit in a room facing three or more music professors and sing or play your instrument for them. However, knowing what to expect and how best to prepare can not only alleviate your fear, but can also give you a great deal of confidence. Having watched hundreds of prospective music students in auditions, I can tell you that careful preparation and self-confidence can not only spell the difference between acceptance and denial, but can also improve your chances of receiving scholarship money.

What to Expect

College music auditions are a relatively simple process and usually only take about ten minutes. Each school may have slightly different requirements, and you should check with them well before the audition, but most will ask you to do the following:

1. Play or sing two short pieces of contrasting nature
2. Sight-read a short passage of music
3. Instrumentalists will be required to know the major and minor scales and will be asked to play a couple of them, usually at least two octaves with arpeggios.
4. Vocalists will be asked to sing a few exercises with someone at the piano in order to determine their voice range, hear their tone quality, and assess their vocal strength and agility. Vocalists will also likely be asked to sing back short phrases played on the piano to determine the accuracy of their ear and intonation.

In addition to these requirements, most professors will want to spend a few minutes talking to you to get to know you better.

Selecting Your Music and Sight-reading

The two pieces you choose to perform should be from the standard classical repertoire for your instrument. The term "contrasting nature" means that the two songs may contrast in tempo, style, or dynamics. This does not mean that you should perform one classical piece and one selection of popular music, or a song you have written. Pick two pieces that you can perform well at the audition. It is better to perform an easy solo well than to perform a difficult solo poorly.

If you play a traditional school band or orchestra instrument, you can select two contrasting etudes from one of the various methods books, or solos from the standard repertoire. If you are unsure what this means, you can ask your school director for suggestions. They will likely be more than willing to suggest pieces and may even volunteer to help you prepare. Pianists can ask their piano teacher what would be appropriate. Vocalists should perform simple art songs or classical solos. There are many good books available at your local music store, and the series of books entitled, *The First Book of Soprano Solos* (also available for alto, tenor, baritone, or bass) is a great starting place. Any of the songs in these books or books like them will work perfectly. Again, if you are in school choir, your director may help you with this. If you are not in school choir and have not taken vocal lessons before, you may want to hire a voice teacher for a few months leading up to the audition. Most university music programs, professional and community orchestras, and music stores can provide you with names of qualified teachers whom you can contact.

If you learned to play the guitar, bass, or drums as a member of a local band, you can still audition for a college music technology program. It is likely that you taught yourself to play and are a pretty good musician, but you may not read music and may not be familiar with any classical music for your instrument. Music stores offer lessons in guitar, bass, and drums, and most will begin by helping you learn to read music. You should start taking lessons at least a year before the audition process. Guitarists should ask the teacher to help them learn two simple classical etudes, as well as scales and arpeggios. Drummers can learn to play traditional percussion patterns for snare drum and keyboard instruments. Bass players can learn basic jazz progressions, scale patterns, and simple solos.

Since sight-reading will likely be a part of the audition process, you should practice this skill on your instrument, just as you practice your scales and rudiments. You can practice playing new pieces of music or select songs that you may have skipped in your lesson or methods books. Another great source of sight-reading material for most musicians (except the piano) is a sight-singing book. Examples include *Music for Sight Singing* by Robert Ottman and Nancy Rogers and *Progressive Sight Singing* by Carol Krueger, but there are many of these types of books on the market to choose from. They are written for use in college aural skills and ear training classes, and the exercises are designed to become progressively more difficult in both melody and rhythm throughout the book. This can be great material for preparation in sight-reading for voice as well as for band or orchestra instruments. Whether using a sight-singing book, or other material, each time you practice, you should follow the same procedure:

1. Take a few seconds to look at the material. Determine the time signature, key signature, and starting and ending notes.
2. Quickly sing through the example in your mind, scanning for any difficult leaps, rhythms, or fingerings (if you are an instrumentalist).
3. Prepare to sing or play the passage, taking a deep breath.
4. Play or sing at a slow but consistent tempo. If you make a mistake, keep going and stay in time. If you get lost, skip to the next logical measure and continue.

5. Be confident throughout. Don't shake your head if you make a mistake, don't start over, and don't apologize.

Day of the Audition

The audition day is an important one, and you will likely be nervous. However, if you are well prepared, the confidence you feel will be a great help. Get a good night of sleep the night before and don't go to the audition on an empty stomach. You should dress professionally and look your best. Arrive early to the audition location to ensure you are in the right place. If possible, you may visit the location on a day before the audition and walk through the motions, and even play or sing in the room to boost your comfort level. You will be given a warm-up location and time. Take advantage of this warm-up and make sure you are ready to go. If you are performing with an accompanist provided by the school, you will be given a chance to work with him or her as part of your warm-up time. The accompanist will want to help you succeed and will try to play at a tempo and using dynamics that you are comfortable with. Be kind, respectful, and professional as you rehearse.

When the time comes for your audition, enter the room with confidence. Greet each of the judges with a smile. You will likely perform first, then speak with them for a few minutes. Relax and do your best as you perform your selections. When you sight-read, follow the same procedure you did in practice. After your performance, answer questions respectfully and honestly. However, you do not need to divulge what other schools you are applying to or whether this school is your first choice. Remember that scholarships are used to attract desirable students. Stating that you have already decided to go to their school may reduce the amount of scholarship money they will spend to attract you. They may ask if you have any questions and you should have several prepared. You may ask about notification of decisions, about the program, perhaps about a particular faculty member, or the department. You should not ask if they thought you did well or how many students they are accepting. At the end of the audition, kindly thank them for their time. You may also wish to follow up with an e-mail or a card thanking them for their consideration. If you are well prepared, the college music audition can be a very positive and lucrative experience.

Technological Preparation and Skills

In discussing technological preparation for a career in music technology, we can again make the distinction between formal and informal experiences.

Most young people today have considerable informal experience with technology. As computer access has become widespread in the past twenty years, most people already possess the basic skills that at one time needed to be taught in schools. Sometimes it is even said that kids today are "hard-wired" with computer skills. Of course there is nothing special about the brain of a person born in the last twenty years that predisposes them to be able to use computers. It is simply a matter of environment. By the time they begin middle school, America's young people don't have to be shown how to use the computer to find something on the Internet, or to write a report in a word processing program. Most can be introduced to a new computer program or video game and figure out the basics of using it within a couple of hours. The computer is simply a tool we all use, and it is no more foreign to today's young people than a butter churn would have been to children growing up on the American prairie in the 1850s.

Nonetheless, there are still a lot of specific ways that music technologists need to use the computer. These skills may vary significantly depending on what area of music technology you choose to pursue, and specifics will be addressed in the later chapters of this book. However, there are some basic technology skills and proficiencies that all music technologists should possess to be successful. Recently, a significant research study conducted by Peter Webster and David Williams revealed the kinds of things a student of music technology should know and be able to do.[5] Their findings are summarized here:

Know:

The difference between analog and digital sound

The difference between Audio and MIDI files

The frequencies of pitches in the audible spectrum and the frequency range of various instruments

The pitches associated with the overtone series and how they impact live and recorded performances

The impact of sampling rate and bit depth on a digital audio file

The copyright laws applicable to recorded and print music

The proper use of microphones and their placement with common instruments for use in live and recorded sound

The difference between dynamic and condenser microphones and the use of phantom power

The common uses of XLR, RCA, ¼", ½", USB, and MIDI cables

The proper use of mic level, line level, instrument level, and speaker level signals

The use of compressed and noncompressed digital audio formats including wav, mp3, aif, and m4a

Do:

Music Notation:

Create a musical score for an instrument including accompaniment with expressions and articulations and observing proper conventions of musical notation

Digital Audio:

Set up a digital music workstation including a computer, audio interface, MIDI controller, and speakers

Use software to generate synthesized sounds

Download audio from the Internet

Remove audio from a CD

Burn audio onto a CD

Audio Recording:

Create an audio recording using digital means and be able to save and distribute the file in an appropriate format

Make timeline edits on an audio recording

Perform basic editing tasks such as creating fades, removing noise, equalizing, and adding reverb with an audio recording of a performance of the major instrument

Live Sound Reinforcement:

Connect microphones to a mixing board and a mixing board to speakers

Adjust trim, EQ, pan and output to appropriate levels

Mac versus PC

Most people develop a preference for one computer operating system or another. Whether you have more experience using a Mac or a PC, you should be comfortable with both if you want to make a career in the music technology world. Most recording studios and universities use Macintosh computers for audio editing and education, but PCs dominate the programming and consumer market. If you have a PC and can't afford to buy a Mac, go to the local library, or university, or ask a friend if you can work on their Mac just long enough to become familiar with the interface. There is very little difference between the two platforms, and most people can easily become familiar with whichever platform they don't know. You don't want to find yourself on a job interview, or the first day at an internship, asking someone how to save a file on the computer. Each semester my Computer Music I class is full of PC users who have never touched a Mac. By the second week of the semester, they are all comfortable with the Mac platform. In my office at the university, I have a PC on one desk and a Mac on the other. I use both all the time and suffer no ill effects from switching between the two.

Notes

1. Malcolm Gladwell, *Outliers: The Story of Success* (New York: Little, Brown and Company, 2008).
2. Ken Scott and Bobby Owsinski, *Abbey Road to Ziggy Stardust* (Los Angeles: Alfred Music Publishing, 2012), 3.
3. Scott and Owsinski, *Abbey Road*, 28.
4. Scott L. Phillips, *"Contributing Factors to Music Attitude in Sixth-, Seventh-, and Eighth-Grade Students,"* (Ph.D. diss., University of Iowa, 2003, Iowa City, IA).
5. Peter Webster and David Williams, *"Music Technology Skills and Conceptual Understanding for Undergraduate Music Students: A National Survey"* (Richmond, VA: Paper presented at the Association for Technology in Music Instruction National Conference, 2011).

3

Studying to Be a Music Technologist

AS MUSIC TECHNOLOGY has evolved and expanded over the past forty years, the study of music technology at colleges and universities has also evolved. Although most academic institutions of higher learning are slow to create and embrace new programs, the ubiquitous use of technology in the creation, performance, and education of music has led to expanded opportunities to study music technology in colleges all across the United States. Additionally, many trade schools, art schools, and "pro" schools offer instruction and even courses of study in music technology software and hardware without offering a college degree. And while a college degree may not be required to build a successful career in music technology, it can be one of the best ways to develop the skills necessary for career success. Before spending the years and thousands of dollars required to earn a college degree, it is important to determine what college program is the best fit for your skills and experiences and which one will best prepare you to embark on your career.

Differences among Programs

Not all college music technology programs are the same. Of course, one could argue that this is true of any college program. Harvard's Law School, for example, is considered by many people to be *better* than almost any other: its students have higher average entrance scores, its graduates have higher paying jobs, and its teachers are among the most respected law professors in the world. But music technology programs vary not only in quality, but also in content. A graduate of any reputable law school can pass the Bar Examination and become a practicing lawyer. But there is no "Bar Exam" for music technology. And while this book outlines the kinds of things a music technologist should be able to do, there isn't an accepted body of knowledge or mandated skill set that college programs are required to teach to their students. Schools and programs may even be accredited by diverse accrediting agencies (see Box 3.1). In most cases, programs have emerged independently from one another, with little consideration to how other schools structure their degrees.

BOX 3.1

Accreditation

Accreditation is a word often bantered about in the academic world, but what does it mean? In an effort to achieve accountability and ensure consistent quality from one university to another, independent nongovernmental agencies certify, or accredit, universities and their programs of study. These agencies are recognized by the US Department of Education and work to ensure that all universities follow similar guidelines, provide similar offerings, and comply with established standards of current educational practice. There are national, regional, and content-specific agencies. Some examples of accrediting agencies include NEASC (New England Association of Schools and Colleges), MSCHE (Middle States Commission on Higher Education), NWCCU (Northwest Commission on Colleges and Universities), and ACICS (Accrediting Council for Independent Colleges and Schools). All of these independent agencies have similar goals and objectives. SACS, the Southern Association of Colleges and Schools, is the accrediting agency for institutions of higher learning in an eleven-state region in the Southeast United States. On its website, it states:

"The Commission's mission is the enhancement of educational quality throughout the region and it strives to improve the effectiveness of institutions by ensuring that institutions meet standards established by the higher education community that address the needs of society and students. It serves as the common denominator of shared values and practices among the diverse institutions in Alabama, Florida, Georgia, Kentucky, Louisiana, Mississippi, North Carolina, South Carolina, Tennessee, Texas, Virginia…that award associate, baccalaureate, master's, or doctoral degrees."[1]

In addition to university-wide accreditation, programs of study are often accredited through discipline-specific agencies. NASM, The National Association of Schools of Music, evaluates and accredits university music programs. Of course, not all music technology programs are housed in schools of music and many are not evaluated by NASM. Some programs belong to business, engineering, or computer science departments and may be accredited by those disciplines' accrediting agencies. The audio engineering technology degree in the Mike Curb College of Entertainment and Music Business at Belmont University, for example, is accredited through AACSB, the Association to Advance Collegiate Schools of Business. On its website, it boasts that it is "the only AACSB International accredited Music Business program in the world."[2] At many smaller colleges and two-year institutions, music technology programs are not accredited independently, but are simply accredited as part of the college-wide accreditation.

Music technology is a multifaceted field that is fundamentally focused on music, but it is also related to engineering, computer science, physics, business, communications, theater and film, and the visual arts. As a result, various schools that offer music technology may actually prepare students to do different things. Furthermore, a program may have been created at one college in response to student interest. Another college may have founded a music technology course of study as a result of faculty members' particular experiences or skills. Some schools have even created music technology programs as a response to market pressures, to pursue new revenue streams, or as a result of geographical location (as illustrated in Box 3.2). Finally, music technology is an expensive and ever-changing discipline, and programs vary in how well they keep up with the latest developments. All of these issues are things to consider as you try to determine which school is right for you.

BOX 3.2

How Geography Can Build a Program

UNC Asheville's department of music started a music technology program in 1983 due, in part, to its proximity to Moog Music, the electronic music company founded by synthesizer pioneer Robert Moog. Moog is located less than two miles from the University's music building. The relationship has been mutually beneficial. UNC Asheville students can complete practicum experiences at Moog, and over a dozen Moog employees are UNC music technology graduates.[3]

Unfortunately, researching music technology degree programs is more challenging than it would be if you were seeking a degree in a more common field like economics, or psychology, or biology. There are several reasons for this. First, while music technology offerings are expanding, still a relatively small number of colleges and universities offer them. In 2009 a review of the 640 university music programs accredited by the National Association of School of Music (NASM) revealed that only forty-two schools offered degrees in music technology.[4] There may be as many as sixty NASM schools with programs today, but many of these are not even listed as technology programs in NASM's directory. Second, not all music technology programs are called by that name. If you were to do a Google search for music technology programs, you may get a few hits, but titles such as sound technology, audio recording, music industry, and even music business may be used to identify degree programs that are very similar to those in music technology. Third, there are differences among types of degree programs. Schools can offer music technology degrees as bachelor of arts, bachelor of music, bachelor of science, and bachelor of fine arts degrees.

To illustrate the diversity of music technology programs, let's consider a few examples of programs around the United States. I teach at the University of Alabama at Birmingham, where we offer a BA in music technology. Duquesne University, in Pittsburgh, Pennsylvania, offers a BM in music technology and students select a track in performance, composition, or sound recording. At the California Institute of the Arts in Valencia, California, the program is a BFA in Music Technology: Interaction, Intelligence, & Design. The popular music technology degree programs at Indiana University-Perdue University Indianapolis (IUPUI) award a BS degree housed in the School of Engineering and Technology. The Georgia Institute of Technology's Center for Music Technology in Atlanta belongs to the School of Architecture but shares professors from the areas of music, computing, engineering, design, and business. Belmont University in Nashville, Tennessee, offers a BA in music technology in their School of Music, and a BS in audio engineering technology in the Mike Curb School of Entertainment and Music Business. And at the University of Hartford, in Connecticut, The School of Music offers a BM in music production and technology, while the College of Engineering Technology and Architecture offers a BS in audio engineering technology and a BS in acoustical engineering and music. Is it any wonder that students interested in music technology may find the task of researching college programs to be a little overwhelming?

The purpose of this chapter is to help you learn how to research and explore college programs in music technology. You will find out what programs are offered, how programs are named, the difference among types of bachelor degrees, and how to find out more information about each program.

Finding Music Technology Programs

The first step in researching college programs is to find out what programs are being offered. Various organizations such as the Audio Engineering Society (AES), the Music and Entertainment Industry Educators Association (MEIEA), and the NASM maintain lists of college programs, but the information provided in these directories is far from comprehensive and is often incomplete. Appendix A contains a listing of more than 180 college and trade school programs that are currently offered in the United States in music technology, sound technology, audio recording, music industry, and music business. This is the most complete listing of music technology and music business programs ever compiled. Programs are listed by institution name, degree title, degree type, and by state for easy searching. This list of programs is provided as a resource while you consider where you might attend college. The list is also posted on this book's companion website at www.oup.com/us/beyondsound, with a search feature and with links to each program. As new programs are created, they will be added to the website.

What's in a Name?

Once you identify a college program, the next step is to look at its name. There is some rhyme and reason behind the names used to identify university courses of study. These labels are not always used consistently, and may not tell the whole story, but they give us a good place to start. Fortunately, in most cases, there is a correlation between how a program is named and what kind of degree is offered.

Traditionally, the bachelor degree is designed to provide students with two kinds of education. First is a broad and general education in various academic areas. This aspect of the college degree is usually referred to as general education or the core curriculum. The second aspect of the college degree is the student's major. This part of the degree program focuses a student on their specific area of interest. Often, the relative number of major courses, general education courses, and elective courses that make up a program, in addition to the content of those courses, determines the kind of bachelor degree an institution grants.

There are four distinct types of bachelor degrees offered in music technology. While each of these types of degrees will be explained in greater depth later in this chapter, with examples of specific school programs, a definitional understanding of each is useful. The four degrees can be defined as follows:

Bachelor of Music (BM)

The BM degree is considered the professional music degree. Entrance to the program is generally based on a highly competitive audition process. Courses in the BM degree focus primarily on music subjects, with about 60 percent of the degree's total coursework being completed within the major, 20 to 30 percent completed in general education, and 10 to 20 percent completed in electives.

Bachelor of Fine Arts (BFA)

The BFA degree is considered a professional performance degree. Entrance to the program is generally based on a highly competitive audition process. Courses in the BFA degree focus primarily on music subjects, with an emphasis on performance. About 60 percent of the degree's total coursework is completed within the major, 20 to 30 percent completed in general education, and 10 to 20 percent completed in electives.

Bachelor of Arts (BA)

The BA is a liberal arts degree. Entrance to the program is generally based on an audition process. Courses in the BA degree focus primarily on general education with the addition of a relatively small major of music subjects. About 40 percent of the degree's total coursework is completed within the major, 40 percent completed in general education, and 20 percent completed in electives. Often a minor course of study is also required.

Bachelor of Science (BS)

The BS degree is considered the professional science degree. Entrance to the program may or may not require a music audition. Courses in the BS degree focus primarily on science subjects, with about 60 percent of the degree's total

Table 3.1. Semester Hour Requirements for Bachelor
Degree Programs

Degree	Major	General Ed	Electives
Bachelor of Music	70–85	30–45	0–20
Bachelor of Fine Arts	70–85	30–45	0–20
Bachelor of Arts	40–50	45–60	18–32
Bachelor of Science	70–85	30–45	0–20

coursework being completed within a music major, augmented with courses in math and technology. General education occupies 20 to 30 percent of the degree and 10 to 20 percent of the courses are completed in electives, usually based on engineering, computer science, electronics, or physics.

Table 3.1 summarizes the semester hour requirements for each of these four types of degree programs. Most bachelor degree programs require students to complete a total of 120 to 132 credit hours to graduate.

A Major in Music Technology

When considering music technology as a major, it is important to realize that only a portion of the music classes will be completed in music technology. The rest of the major classes will be in music history, music theory, private and group instrument or voice instruction, and performance ensembles. For someone going to school for four years to earn a degree in music technology, learning that you may take as few as two or three classes in the subject may be quite surprising. But remember, the courses in music theory, history, and ear training, as well as the experiences taking lessons and performing with an ensemble will all prepare you for your career as a music technologist. And, in addition to these required courses, most degree programs also offer additional electives, as well as a semester-long music technology internship or project. Some offer participation in electronic or computer music ensembles that allow students to incorporate skills acquired in music technology courses through live performance.

Conventional wisdom may assume that if a student gets a BM, BFA, or BS degree, with up to eighty-five hours in the major, they will take a lot more music technology classes than if they were to get a BA degree with only forty hours in the major. However, this is simply not the case.

Table 3.2. Average, Median, and Range of Required Music Technology Courses in the Majors of Fifty-five Selected Bachelor Degree Programs

Degree	Average	Median	Range
Bachelor of Music (n=24)	7.25	7	3–10
Bachelor of Fine Arts (n=3)	9.33	12	4–12
Bachelor of Science (n=13)	6.31	6	4–10
Bachelor of Arts (n=15)	4.65	5	2–8

Table 3.2 shows the results of a comparison of fifty-five selected music technology programs. On average, BM degrees provide about three more music technology classes than BA degrees, but when considering the range of courses offered at various schools, it can be seen that some BM degrees offer as few as three music technology courses, while some BA degrees offer as many as eight.

Often the differences in various kinds of music technology degrees have little to do with the music technology courses that are required. In fact, some universities (Stetson University and Capital University, for example) offer both a BA and a BM degree, and the music technology course requirements are identical for both. Virginia Tech offers two BA options in music technology, one with a 50-hour major, and one with a 78-hour major, but both share the same music technology courses. The University of Michigan offers a BM, BS, and BFA in music technology, but the music technology course requirements are nearly identical for each. The main difference among the various degrees lies in the number of music courses that must be taken as part of the major, whether science or technology courses are part of the major, and the level of traditional musicianship that must be demonstrated.

Now that we have laid some groundwork, let's explore each of these degree programs in a little more depth and consider some specific schools. The names of some of the programs vary, but all of the programs in the following sections will be considered music technology programs, in that they offer music technology-specific courses within the framework of a college music major.

Bachelor of Music in Music Technology

The bachelor of music is considered the professional music degree. A professional degree means that the course of study is designed to prepare someone to work professionally in the field of choice. The BM at most institutions requires a competitive audition demonstrating a high level of musical skill and previous experience for entry into the program. Once accepted, students will pursue a rigorous course of musical study that includes music theory, ear training, history, applied instrument or voice instruction, and ensemble participation. The typical core of the music major in a BM degree usually consists of the following elements:

> 4–6 courses in music theory
> 4 courses in ear training (aural skills)
> 3–4 courses in music history
> 8 semesters of participation in a music ensemble
> 6–8 semesters of applied lessons on an instrument or voice
> 1–2 semesters of conducting
> Senior recital, internship, or final project
> For the BM in music technology, 3 to 10 additional courses in music technology will be required to complete the major.

Table 3.3 lists universities that offer bachelor of music programs in music technology. For each program, the number of required music technology courses is listed, as well as the final project or internship, and the option to participate in a music technology performance ensemble.

Bachelor of Fine Arts

In the United States, the bachelor of fine arts degree differs from the other types of bachelor degrees because the major courses focus more heavily on performance and practical application. This is true of BFA degrees in the visual arts, dance, and theater and film, where the BFA is a common offering. In music technology the BFA is a relatively new degree and only three universities in the United States currently offer it. Like the BM and BS, the major in the BFA program occupies 60 to 70 percent (or more) of the courses in the degree. And like the BM, students will be exposed to a strenuous musical education requiring an audition and a high level of musical performance on some instrument. But as there are so few BFA programs in music technology, and they vary in their approach, it is difficult to make generalizations about them. Instead, they will each be described here.

The California Institute of the Arts, located 30 miles north of downtown Los Angeles, offers the bachelor of fine arts in Music Technology: Interaction,

Table 3.3. Bachelor of Music Programs

University and Location	Music Tech Courses	Project/ Internship	Performance Ensemble
Bachelor of Music			
Berklee College of Music, Boston, MA	10	Project	No
Capital University, Columbus, OH	8	Internship	Yes
Duquesne University, Pittsburgh, PA	8	Internship	Yes
Florida Atlantic University, Boca Raton, FL	5	Project	No
Georgia State University, Atlanta, GA	7	Internship	Yes
Jackson State University, Jackson, MS	10	Internship	No
Mansfield University, Mansfield, PA	5	Internship	No
Missouri Western State, Saint Joseph, MO	7	None	No
New York University, New York, NY	8	Internship	Yes
Oberlin College, Oberlin, OH	5	Recital	Yes
Stetson University, Deland, FL	6	Project	No
University of Central Missouri, Warrensburg, MO	5	Internship	No
University of Hartford, West Hartford, CT	5	Internship	No
University of Michigan, Ann Arbor, MI	10	Thesis	Yes
University of Montana, Missoula, MT	3	Project	No
University of Nebraska at Omaha, Omaha, NE	7	Project	Yes
Wayne State University, Detroit, MI	6	Internship	No

(Continued)

Table 3.3 (Continued)

University and Location	Music Tech Courses	Project/ Internship	Performance Ensemble
Bachelor of Music in Sound Recording Technology			
Brigham Young University, Provo, UT	10	None	Yes
DePaul University, Chicago, IL	10	None	No
Ithaca College, Ithaca, NY	8	Internship	No
Lebanon Valley College, Annville, PA	8	Internship	No
Shenandoah University, Winchester, VA	9	Internship	No
Texas State–San Marcos, San Marcos, TX	10	Internship	No
University of Massachusetts— Lowell	7	Internship	Yes
University of Memphis, Memphis, TN	10	Internship	No
Bachelor of Music in Sound Engineering Arts			
William Paterson University, Wayne, NJ	10	Internship	No
Bachelor of Music in Recording Arts and Sciences			
Johns Hopkins University, Baltimore, MD	10	Internship	No
Bachelor of Music in Audio Production			
University of Denver, Denver, CO	5	None	No

Intelligence and Design. The degree consists of a strenuous musical education, similar to a BM degree, and requires an audition. The general education requirements make up a very small portion of the total degree, and there are extensive offerings in music technology. At least twelve courses in music technology are required for the degree, but as many as twenty can be taken. The courses include everything from basic music technology, to instrument building, to robotics, to live performance. Hands-on interaction, musical creation, and performance are a major part of the degree. CalArts' BFA in music technology is quite similar to BFA degrees in other disciplines.

The University of Michigan offers three music technology degrees through the Department of Performing Arts Technology in the School of Music, Theatre and Dance: A BM in music and technology, a BS in sound engineering, and a BFA in performing arts technology, music concentration. All three degrees require music courses similar to a BM. The BFA shares the same required music technology courses as the other two degrees, but allows for additional music technology electives focused on multimedia and visual arts. The department describes the BFA as follows: "The Bachelor of Fine Arts in Performing Arts Technology, Music Technology Concentration is designed for students who possess demonstrated interest in producing art forms that integrate images, sound, and music using computer technology."

The BFA in music and audio technology that is offered at The City College of New York in Manhattan is structured very similarly to a bachelor of music degree. The balance of core music and music technology courses to general education courses is nearly identical to a bachelor of music degree.

Table 3.4 lists universities that offer bachelor of fine arts programs in music technology. The number of required music technology courses is listed, with details regarding final projects and performance ensembles.

Table 3.4. Bachelor of Fine Arts Programs

University and Location	Music Tech Courses	Project/ Internship	Performance Internship
Bachelor of Fine Arts in Music Technology: Intelligence, Interaction, and Design			
California Institute of the Arts, Valencia, CA	12	Project	Multiple
Bachelor of Fine Arts in Performing Arts Technology, Music Concentration			
University of Michigan, Ann Arbor, MI	12	Thesis	Yes
Bachelor of Fine Arts in Music and Audio Technology			
City College of New York, New York, NY	13	None	No

Bachelor of Arts

The bachelor of arts degree seeks to expose students to academic breadth across disciplines and is less concerned with depth in the major area. This is often referred to as a liberal education. According to the Association of American Colleges and Universities:

> Liberal Education is an approach to learning that empowers individuals and prepares them to deal with complexity, diversity, and change. It provides students with broad knowledge of the wider world (e.g., science, culture, and society) as well as in-depth study in a specific area of interest. A liberal education helps students develop a sense of social responsibility, as well as strong and transferable intellectual and practical skills such as communication, analytical and problem-solving skills, and a demonstrated ability to apply knowledge and skills in real-world settings.
>
> Today, a liberal education usually includes a general education curriculum that provides broad learning in multiple disciplines and ways of knowing, along with more in-depth study in a major.[5]

While you may wonder how a degree that provides so few classes in the major can adequately prepare a student for their career, it is good to consider the philosophy of liberal education outlined above. Some in favor of a liberal education feel strongly that a college degree should not prepare a student with specific job-related skills at all, but instead should train the student in life skills that will be beneficial in any profession.

The BA in music technology is often listed as an emphasis, or concentration of that school's BA in music. The basic music major in a BA program usually consists of the following elements:

2–4 courses in music theory
2–4 courses in ear training (aural skills)
2–3 courses in music history
6–8 semesters of participation in a music ensemble
4–6 semesters of lessons on an instrument or voice

To these requirements, courses in music technology are added. Usually two to six courses may be offered, and then a final project or internship in music technology.

This type of degree program can be a great option for the aspiring music technologist. Although only a few courses are offered in the specific technical aspects of music technology, students are exposed to many different fields and are free to explore other areas that interest them. The professional world of music technology is very diverse, and students with broad intellectual interests and a wide range of experiences can be very successful. Additionally, this kind of program is a great preparation for the student considering graduate school after college.

In recent years, more BA programs in music technology have been added to college catalogs than other types of music technology degrees and there may be several reasons for this. Because the BA, by its very nature, requires so few classes in a major, and since most liberal arts colleges already offer a BA in music, an emphasis in music technology can be added to the curriculum with relative ease. Also, liberal arts colleges usually have fewer students and faculty members and are generally much more flexible from a curricular standpoint. As a result, courses of study can be added to the curriculum more quickly. Additionally, liberal arts colleges may be independent private colleges that are not accountable to a state board of regents, and thus the process for curricular change may be more streamlined. Table 3.5 lists universities that offer BAs in music technology.

Bachelor of Science

The bachelor of science degree is listed here last, because an understanding of the other kinds of degree programs is helpful before looking at the BS in music technology. The bachelor of science is considered a professional degree, and as such, the major in most BS programs comprises about 60 percent of the total degree. This is similar in size to the major in the BM degree. However, the music offerings in the BS in music technology are usually more similar in size and scope to those required as part of the BA in music. Generally, a basic set of music courses will be offered as part of the major in a BS program. The remaining coursework in the major consists of classes in the sciences. Usually 20 to 40 percent of the degree consists of courses in electronics, computer science, engineering, or physics. Students who are successful in these programs often have strong math and science skills, as well as musical ability and experience. Examples of schools that offer this type of BS degree in music technology include the University of Miami, Indiana University-Purdue University Indianapolis, and the State University of New York at Fredonia. These programs prepare students to work in the world of

Table 3.5. Bachelor of Arts Programs

University and Location	Music Tech Courses	Project/ Internship	Performance Ensemble
Bachelor of Arts in Music Technology			
Capital University, Columbus, OH	8	Internship	Yes
Clemson University, Clemson, SC	8	Internship	No
Fort Hays State University, Hays, KS	3	Internship	No
Keene State College, Keene, NH	3	Internship	No
Montana State University, Bozeman, MT	6	Internship	No
Plymouth State University, Plymouth, NH	4	None	No
Radford University, Radford, VA	5	None	Yes
Salisbury University, Salisbury, MD	7	Internship	No
San Francisco State, San Francisco, CA	3	None	No
St Mary's University of MN, Winona, MN	6	Internship	No
Stetson University, Deland, FL	6	Project	No
Transylvania University, Lexington, KY	2	Internship	No
Trevecca Nazarene University, Nashville, TN	4	Internship	No
University of Alabama at Birmingham	6	Internship	Yes

(*Continued*)

Table 3.5 (Continued)

University and Location	Music Tech Courses	Project/ Internship	Performance Ensemble
University of Alabama at Huntsville	3	Internship	No
University of Montana, Missoula, MT	2	None	No
Virginia Polytechnic Institute, Blacksburg, VA	5	Internship	Yes
Bachelor of Arts in Music Industry and Technology/Recording Arts			
California State University, Chico, CA	6	None	No
Bachelor of Arts in Sound Recording Technology			
Delta State University, Cleveland, MS	5	Internship	No
University of New Haven, West Haven, CT	5	Project	No

music in computer programming and engineering, electronics, acoustics, and manufacturing.

However, more than any other kind of bachelor degree considered here, the offerings in BS programs vary considerably from one to another. The bachelor of science programs in music technology offered at some universities bear a striking resemblance to the typical BA degree. Examples of these schools include La Sierra University, Stevens Institute of Technology, Evangel University, and California University of Pennsylvania. The bachelor of science programs at other schools are very similar to the bachelor of music. Examples of these schools include Kent State University, Northeastern University, and Ball State University. And in some cases, the BS seems to be a catchall degree for a program that offers a broad approach. The College of St. Rose, for example, requires 128 hours to graduate, consisting of 41 hours in general education, 42 hours in basic music, 17 hours in music technology, 16 hours in commercial music, and 12 hours in music business, and no additional hours of computer, electrical, or physical science. Table 3.6 lists universities with bachelor of science programs.

Table 3.6. Bachelor of Science Programs

University and Location	Music Tech Courses	Project/ Internship	Performance Ensemble
Bachelor of Science in Music Technology			
California University of Pennsylvania, California, PA	6	Internship	No
College of Saint Rose, Albany, NY	4	Internship	No
Evangel University, Springfield, MO	4	Internship	No
Indiana University-Purdue, Indianapolis, IN	4	None	Yes
Kent State University—Stark, Stark, OH	9	Internship	No
La Sierra University, Riverside, CA	7	None	No
Northeastern University, Boston, MA	6	None	Yes
State University of New York, Fredonia, NY	5	Internship	No
Stevens Institute of Technology, Hoboken, NJ	6	None	No
University of North Carolina, Asheville, NC	6	Internship	No
Bachelor of Science in Music or Audio Engineering			
University of Harford, Harford, CT	7	Project	No
University of Miami, Coral Gables, FL	7	None	No
Belmont University, Nashville, TN	10	Internship	No

(Continued)

Table 3.6 (Continued)

University and Location	Music Tech Courses	Project/ Internship	Performance Ensemble
Bachelor of Science in Music Media Production and Industry			
Ball State University, Muncie, IN	8	Recital	No
Bachelor of Science in Music Recording Technology			
Hampton University, Hampton, VA	7	Recital	No
Bachelor of Science in Sound Engineering			
University of Michigan, Ann Arbor, MI	10	Thesis	Yes

Other Degree Programs

The focus of this book is the field of music technology. To this point, college programs that specifically prepare students in music and technology have been discussed. However, in the academic world, the terms music business, music industry, and commercial music are also used to describe programs that may offer useful preparations for the aspiring music technologist. College programs in these areas may include some courses in music technology, but courses in these majors often focus on the creation, distribution, negotiation, promotion, and marketing of commercial music. They often include a significant number of courses in business management, accounting, and the legal aspects of the music industry. Courses may also include song writing, music publishing, and the history of rock and roll. There are BM, BFA, BS, and BA, as well as BBA (bachelor of business administration) and BPS (bachelor of professional studies) degrees offered in music business and industry. Different from the music technology programs considered previously that each required a basic level of traditional musical preparation and education, these programs vary significantly in the kind of musical education they offer and the amount of musical preparation they require. Some programs (especially BM and BA degrees) require at least a basic core of music classes. However, others may require no music courses at all and may be well-suited for students interested in the world of music technology but who have limited musical skill or experience. Also, some of these programs are housed in Schools of Music and music departments, but others belong to business schools, colleges of engineering, or communications departments.

This text will not consider these types of college programs here, but they are listed in Appendix A. Your understanding of music technology programs will help you if you chose to consider attending a program in music business, music industry, or commercial music.

Trade Schools and "Pro Schools"

There are companies that have created training programs in music technology and have given themselves the name "schools." These schools specialize in specific technical training related to the entertainment business and do not usually lead to a college degree, although more and more are offering bachelor degrees. Courses of study are offered in music production, post production, video production, and specific software platforms such as Adobe, Pro Tools, Avid, and others. Students pay by the course, and often complete some kind of certification at the culmination of the coursework. These kinds of schools are usually most successful in large entertainment markets, such as Los Angeles, New York, and Nashville, where scores of young people try to fulfill dreams of successful careers in the entertainment industry. Examples of these kinds of schools are Video Symphony in Burbank, California, and Future Media Concepts in Manhattan. The Art Institutes are a trade school chain that has forty-five locations around the United States. Trade schools are recommended for professionals wanting to start a new career, or get additional training, or for adults who have been unsuccessful at college, but not for young people as a replacement for a college degree.

Beefing up Your Degree

Four years is a long time to be in college, but careful planning can help those years become an even more effective preparation for your career. Music technology is a very diverse field, but if you know what you want to do, you can customize your education to prepare for it. Almost all bachelor degree programs allow for a certain number of electives or a minor as part of the degree. And, at many institutions, there is no additional charge to take courses once you reach a full load. I'm not suggesting that you spend eight years in college, or that you extend your college career at all, but you can take advantage of college far more than most people do. For example, let's suppose your goal is to work in the recording industry as a recording engineer. After reading this book, you will realize that many recording engineers go on to have their own studios, become producers, or at least are self-employed for much of their careers. A bachelor degree in music technology or audio engineering will be a good preparation, but why not get a minor in business management while you are there? If you are interested in programming and the computer side of music technology, a minor in computer science nicely supplements your music degree. If you are interested in working in the world of radio or television, a minor or elective classes in communications or broadcasting is a great idea. And if you are interested in being involved in the sound and music of movies, courses from the film school are invaluable. Students with significant prior music experience may even choose to major in one of these areas, and minor in music or music technology.

Notes

1. Southern Association of Colleges and Schools, *Mission Statement of the Commission* [Online]. Available: http://www.sacscoc.org/documents/Mission-Statement.pdf.

2. Belmont University College of Business Administration, *"Accreditation"* [Online]. Available: http://www.belmont.edu/business/accreditation.html.

3. Paul Clark, "The Sound of Science" *UNC Asheville Magazine* [Online], 3:2 (Fall/Winter 2011). Available: http://www3.unca.edu/magazine/archives/vol4no1/feature1.html.

4. Scott L. Phillips, *"A Survey of Music Technology Programs in the United States"* (Portland, OR: Paper presented at the Association for Technology in Music Instruction National Conference, 2009).

5. Association of American Colleges and Universities, "What is a 21st Century Liberal Education?" [Online]. Referenced March 23, 2012. Available: http://www.aacu.org/leap/what_is_liberal_Education.cfm.

4

Starting Your Career as a Music Technologist

YOUR MUSIC TECHNOLOGY career begins once you get that first job. Most often, one job leads to another, one opportunity to another, one person to another, and before you know it, you have built a career doing what you love. That first big job can be the gateway that opens the path to your career. But to land that job you will need to have some real-world experience, to make connections with the right people, and to be able to effectively show them what you are capable of. Internships can be a great place to get some work experience and start laying the groundwork for that first job. Also, participation in professional organizations, trade shows, and conferences may provide great opportunities as you start to build your network of professional contacts. Being able to write an effective résumé will also help you get started in your career, by giving employers an overview of your knowledge and skills. Finally, it is important to remember that geography can have an impact on the kinds of jobs you are able to find. Moving to a different location may be necessary for you to pursue and follow your chosen career path.

Internships

One of the best opportunities for the aspiring music technologist is to participate in an internship program. Many recording studios, television and radio stations, movie studios, live performance venues, churches, music technology manufacturers, and software developers offer internship programs. The position of intern is not a glamorous one. Interns are often asked to perform the most boring, unimportant, and mundane tasks, and are the lowest man on the totem pole at any job location. They may work between twenty and forty hours a week or more and are often paid very little, if at all. Most college programs in music technology require an internship as part of the educational experience, but even if you study at a college where an internship is not required, or you are not currently a college student, you can still participate in many internship programs.

Why You Should Complete an Internship

There are several reasons why an internship is so important. First, the internship allows you to see and work in the real world of music technology. College classes are a major aspect of your training, but real-world experience helps you put theory into practice. Real-world experience also looks good to future employers. Years ago, before college education was as common as it is today, anyone learning a trade would spend years apprenticed to a tradesman. That system of side-by-side training is long gone in a formal sense, but the internship allows you the opportunity to work alongside professionals in your chosen area of music technology and really see what their lives are like. An internship may help you determine for sure if this is what you want to do with your life.

Second, internships introduce you to people in music technology. Making connections with people will be key to your success. Take advantage of this opportunity by getting to know everyone you can. Find out how they got started in the business, spend time learning about them and their careers, and determine what they like and don't like about their work. Find out who they know and look for opportunities to be introduced to people within their network of professional contacts.

Third, internships allow other people to learn who you are. This is essential if a full-time position opens up at your internship location, but even if they can't hire you, the people who work with you in your internship will be able to speak to your skills and qualifications. They will make great references as you apply for other jobs. Because of this, it is important that you always behave as an ideal employee during your internship experience. This means displaying a positive attitude at all times, no matter what menial tasks you are asked to perform. You must act professionally in the way you talk and dress. You should arrive early and stay late, be reliable, keep commitments, take initiative, and always do your best work.

How to Secure an Internship

The first step is finding what internship opportunities are available. Your college career center or department internship advisor likely has established relationships with various internship locations. This is a natural place to start, and often these can be great opportunities. But you shouldn't feel limited by the locations arranged and approved by your college program. You need to spend time researching companies, studios, manufacturers, and venues that employ people who do what you want to do for a living. Find out who offers internship programs and determine what you need to do to apply. If you want to work in a recording studio, learn all you can about studios that offer internship programs. If you want to design sound for video games, research the internship programs of all the companies who make video games. Remember that the best opportunities may require you to move to another city. Expanding your geographic possibilities may considerably increase your options. If you are a full-time college student, a summer internship may be a good option, allowing you to work temporarily in another city, and returning to your college in the fall.

Once you determine where you would like to intern, contact that location to apply. Try to determine the best person at the organization to receive your materials. In some cases, there may be a personnel department that handles interns. A well-placed, professional phone call can often yield good information as to the application process and the best contact person. Sometimes the application process involves no more than talking to the right person and explaining to them your interests and skills. Other times, however, the process is more formal. Many internships at large companies involve an online application process. Make sure you fill out all information completely and accurately. Also, pay close attention to the calendar. Some application deadlines may be set out as much as a year before the internship begins.

After you have made contact and submitted your application materials, you can follow up with the internship location by phone or e-mail to thank them for considering you. You can also inquire about their hiring timeline. You don't need to be pushy, but you should find out all you can about their selection and notification process.

Securing a good internship can be a time-consuming and tedious process. Depending on the competitiveness of the internship program and the size and reputation of the companies to which you are applying, you may need to apply to dozens of internships before you land one (Box 4.1). But remember, a great internship can help you make great connections, and the better your connections are, the better your job prospects will be.

BOX 4.1

A True Story

Andrew Hyde was a junior in college majoring in music technology. More than anything else, Andrew wanted to complete an internship in sound design for video games. He consulted with his college advisor, who contacted a few people in his professional network, but to no avail. With no real prospects near his hometown, he searched the Internet for internship opportunities. He also borrowed a book in the college library about video game sound design that had a listing of companies in the back. He broadened his scope to include companies that specialized in other kinds of sound design, such as software synthesizer programmers, multimedia companies, and others. Over the course of the next 18 months he applied to dozens of internships all over the country. Many companies never responded, and others sent rejection letters. Although it was discouraging, Andrew looked at each rejection letter as a badge of honor, feeling that each was taking him one step closer to his big opportunity.

At one point, Native Instruments, the German software and hardware company, responded to his application saying they didn't have an internship for him but thought his skills were well suited to creating synthesizer presets for a new product they were working on. They paid him to create several presets, which gave Andrew some sound design experience and a little money, but he still hoped to land that perfect internship.

A few months before his internship semester was to begin, the university's engineering department contacted the music technology director looking for someone to help create sounds for a new three-dimensional virtual environment called the VisCube. The VisCube was a revolutionary training lab where engineers solve mechanical problems, architects test the structural integrity of buildings, and doctors perform and practice virtual surgeries. Knowing of Andrew's interest in sound design, the music technology director contacted him and arranged a meeting with the engineers and programmers.

Andrew took a position as an unpaid intern for the engineering department creating sounds for the VisCube environment. He spent four months working harder than he ever had before, designing sounds, learning computer programming techniques, helping the engineering department write grants to fund future sound design tools, and impressing the faculty and programmers he worked for. After the internship ended, the VisCube project received a major grant and Andrew was hired to work full-time as lead sound designer.

Andrew's diligence, dedication and initiative helped him to secure a valuable internship that propelled him into his first full-time job as a sound designer. And while the internship didn't come through the avenues he had expected, his hard work was rewarded.

Building Your Network of Professional Contacts

An internship can be a great way to get to know other music technologists and potential employers, but there are many other ways to get to know professionals in the business. Too often people overlook the importance of establishing a network of professional contacts, especially in the early stages of their careers. Belonging to professional organizations, going to trade shows, attending conferences, and simply contacting professionals you admire are all good ways to begin to build your network of contacts. Young professionals and college students who become engaged in the professional activities of their discipline will find they have a considerable advantage when it is time to find a job.

Professional Organizations

Almost every profession sponsors an organization in which its members can interact, communicate, advocate, share ideas, and develop and disseminate research pertinent to their field. Every music technologist should budget a few hundred dollars each year to become a member of the professional organizations relevant to his or her field. Most professional organizations even offer college students special membership rates and benefits, or encourage the formation of college chapters specifically designed to help students interact with their professional community. Membership in these organizations is often required to participate in educational programs, conferences, trade shows, and chapter meetings. These events are ideal places to build your professional network. Below are several examples of some of the best-known and most successful professional organizations for music technologists. Information regarding membership and each group's activities is readily available on their respective websites.

AES: Audio Engineering Society (www.aes.org)

International organization of audio engineers, creative artists, scientists, and students that promotes advances in audio engineering and disseminates new knowledge and research. Student memberships and chapters are available.

ADJA: American Disc Jockey Association (www.adja.org)

Professional organization for DJs. Establishes a professional code of ethics and helps to advertise members' services.

ATMI: The Association for Technology in Music Instruction (www.atmionline.org)

National organization of college and university music technology teachers. Student memberships are available.

ESA: The Entertainment Software Association (www.theesa.com)

Serving the business and public affairs needs of companies that publish computer and video games for video game consoles, personal computers, and the Internet.

IGDA: The International Game Developers Association (www.igda.org)

A nonprofit membership organization serving individuals who create video games. Its mission is to advance the careers and enhance the lives of game developers by connecting members with their peers, promoting professional development, and advocating on issues that affect the developer community. Features a special audio development and implementation interest group.

MEIEA: The Music & Entertainment Industry Educators Association (www .meiea.org)

Professional organization of colleges offering music industry programs. Membership is open to schools, teachers, and practitioners.

NAB: The National Association of Broadcasters (www.nab.org)

National organization of radio and television broadcasters. Membership is available to broadcasters and broadcasting companies as well as manufacturers and resellers of broadcasting products.

NAfME: National Association for Music Education (www.nafme.org)

The professional organization for public and private school music teachers of grades PreK–12 as well as college music education programs. Student memberships are available and most universities with music education programs sponsor student chapters.

NAMM: The National Association of Music Merchants (www.namm.org)
International organization established to help music manufacturers and retailers work together to produce and market musical products. Membership is restricted to employees of music manufacturers or retailers. Holding a job at a music retailer can get you access to this organization and its activities.

PLASA: The Professional Lighting and Sound Association (www.plasa.org)
The international professional organization for those in the live sound and lighting industries. Student membership is free to students whose school is an organizational member.

SPARS: The Society of Professional Audio Recording Services (www.spars.com)
An organization of large and small recording facilities and independent engineers and producers. Student memberships are available.

TI:ME: Technology for Music Education (www.ti-me.org)
An international organization of music teachers established to encourage the use of technology in music teaching, primarily at public and private schools in grades K-12. Student memberships are available.

Trade Shows and Conferences

Attending trade shows and conferences is one of the best ways to meet people in your profession, and it is a lot of fun. While these two types of events are similar, they each have a slightly different focus.

Trade Shows

Trade shows focus on providing manufacturers and retailers with a venue in which they can sell products directly to a specific target audience of consumers. Companies pay a fee to be included in the show and receive a booth location on the exhibit floor as well as mention in the program and the opportunity to advertise in the materials related to the show. Trade shows are usually open to the public, and an inexpensive ticket can be purchased for admittance. Some trade-only shows are closed to the public and open only to manufacturers and resellers within an organization. Examples of this kind of show include those sponsored by NAB and NAMM (see Box 4.2).

Conferences

A professional or educational conference seeks to provide information and to disseminate new knowledge. Workshops and informative sessions dominate the schedule of events and presenters and facilitators are often leaders in their fields or representatives of companies or organizations. These presenters are either invited or chosen through a competitive selection process. Conferences are usually presented by a sponsoring professional organization and registration (which can range from $75 to $400) is usually limited to members of that organization. Organizations such as ATMI, CMS, NAfME, SPARS, AES, MEIEA, and others all sponsor such conferences. Many conferences today feature a trade show aspect, with an exhibit hall where retailers

---

BOX 4.2

The NAMM Show

The National Association of Music Merchants puts on a massive event each January in Anaheim, California. The NAMM Show, founded in 1901, is a trade-only event open exclusively to the employees of exhibiting music manufacturers and retailers. It is the largest music product show in the world, with more than 95,000 attendees from ninety countries. The show provides a vital venue for exhibitors to show off new products and resellers to make future purchasing decisions.

At the 2012 show, Behringer, a division of MUSIC Group IP Ltd., won the coveted "Best in Show" award for "Companies to Watch." MUSIC Group's senior vice president of Marketing, Costa Lakoumentas, commented on the importance of the NAMM show:

"We've been in business for 23 years, and I can tell you, NAMM has never been more relevant to our business than it is now. This is still the center of the universe for musical instruments, for pro audio. This is where we meet buyers from around the world, we have an opportunity to network, and we recruit people here. If you're in pro audio…if you're in the music industry business, you need to be at NAMM."[1]

can demonstrate and sell products to conference attendees, but the exhibit hours are usually limited, so as not to detract from the educational focus of the conference.

Make the Most of Your Visit

If you spend the money to go to a trade show, or to join an organization and attend a conference, you should take full advantage of the opportunity. Remember that while you may find some great new gear to buy, and you may learn a new skill or technique, the most valuable thing you can do is expand your professional network. Try not to spend the time hanging out with your friends or in your hotel room. At a trade show, go to the booths of the companies that interest you. Learn about their new products, meet the people who work there, and even find out if they have any internship or job opportunities available for which you might be qualified. At a conference, attend sessions presented by people who do what you want to do or work where you want to work. Stay after the session and introduce yourself to the presenter. Try to get their business card and exchange contact information. You can even send them an e-mail a few weeks after the conference to thank them for their presentation. Professionals may meet hundreds of people at a conference, but the personal connection you make, followed up with a sincere e-mail, can make your meeting with them memorable. Most professionals are glad to spend time with students who show interest and enthusiasm for their field.

The Résumé

It is critical that you are able to effectively convey to a future employer just what you can do and how well you can do it. Creating an effective résumé is an important step for getting that first job. There are many places where you can get advice on résumé writing. The career advisement center at most universities will have extensive information on preparing a résumé and a career counselor will often sit down with you and help you to create and polish yours. Additionally, there are many good career building websites that offer résumé tips and tricks. Unfortunately, however, the information that you get from a career counselor or from the Internet won't address specific things you should consider when putting together a résumé in music technology. The following are a few ideas for showing off your music technology skills and experience in your résumé.

Do Your Research

Spend some time researching the best format and layout for your résumé. While most résumés contain similar sections of contact information, work experience, educational experience, and so forth, how you present these sections may vary considerably depending on the type of job you are applying for and your level of experience. For example, if you are applying for a job in customer support, you will want to highlight your people skills near the top of the résumé, but if the job you are looking at is in software programming, people skills may be less important, and software skills should appear first. Likewise, if you have a strong educational background related to music technology, but little employment experience in the business, you may wish to use a skills-based listing highlighting what you can do instead of where you have worked.

Include a Technology Skills Section

Make sure you include a section on your résumé that describes your skills and experience working with technology. You may want to break these up into applicable subcategories of hardware, software, operating systems, programming languages, networking experience, and web authoring. Even if these skills are listed as part of your employment or educational experience, having them in a separate section allows the reader to see, at a glance, your relevant skill set.

Provide Enough Detail

While brevity is important in any résumé, you should give detailed descriptions of the kinds of things you know how to do. Remember that the people reading your résumé will be familiar with the computer programs, interfaces, and hardware you use. If you hold a recognized certification, you should list that as well. The following are three examples of possible résumé entries for the same individual:

Ineffective: Proficient in Pro Tools.
More effective: Able to use Pro Tools for recording, sequencing, editing, and mixing of audio and MIDI tracks. Familiar with the appropriate use of plug-ins to create EQ, reverb, compression, phase, and other effects.

Most effective: Pro Tools Operator Certification with four years' experience in a professional recording environment. Skills include recording, sequencing, editing, and mixing of audio and MIDI tracks. Experienced with proprietary and third-party TDM, RTAS, and VST plug-ins, including Bomb Factory, McDSP, Waves, Antares, and others.

List Musical Skills and Experience

Don't forget that this is *music* technology. Many times, potential employers are musicians and may be hiring you to work with musicians. Depending on the job, this may not need to be a lengthy section of your résumé and it doesn't need to include too much detail. However, you should at least indicate that you know how to read music and list instruments you play and legitimate musical groups you have been a part of. You never know when an employer may take a chance on a fellow tuba player, for example.

Geography

Music technology is a field that leads to many different kinds of careers. As pointed out previously, there are music technologists in recording, live sound production, broadcasting, software development, manufacturing, retail sales, and education. And while a music technologist can build a career almost anywhere (you can always open a recording studio in your hometown), geographical considerations related to music technology jobs may help you as you are starting and building your career.

The Big Three

Some claim that to have a successful career in music technology, you have to live in New York, Los Angeles, or Nashville. It is true that due to the historical factors related to the development of live and recorded sound in New York, the film industry in Los Angeles, and the establishment of country music in Nashville (see Box 4.3), there are more music, television, and movie studios, more publishers, more live venues, more record labels, and lots of opportunities in these three cities. But to say that they are the only places one can build a career is to seriously oversimplify the geography issue.

BOX 4.3

Country Music and Nashville, Tennessee

Music technology played a key role in launching country music to national prominence and establishing Nashville as one of "The Big Three." In the early 1950s, American radios began to tune in to performances of a new kind of music and entertainment originating from the Ryman Auditorium in Nashville, Tennessee. The Saturday evening show, called "The Grand Ol' Opry," featured music and comedy acts from such performers as Eddy Arnold, Ernest Tubb, Roy Acuff, Minnie Pearl, and the man known as "The Hillbilly Shakespeare," Hank Williams. The all-American sounds of Country and Western, Bluegrass, and Honky Tonk music originated from radio station WSM in Nashville. The secret to the widespread reception was a powerful radio transmitter operated by the station that allowed its signal to be heard nationwide. Stars of the Opry stage soon built recording studios on what would become known as Music Row. Before long, Nashville took its place as one of the three powerhouses in the music industry. A 1953 article in the US Chamber of Commerce newsletter, *Nation's Business*, titled "Country Music Goes to Town" stated, "What brought this homely music out of the backroads (sic) and into great popularity nationally—and now internationally—was radio in general and in particular station WSM.... Through country music, Nashville is now a phonograph-recording center comparable to New York and Hollywood."[2]

Population

Part of the reason there are so many opportunities in New York and Los Angeles has to do with the sheer size of the population in these two metropolitan areas. The 2010 US Census indicated that 31,725,946 people lived in the New York and Los Angeles metropolitan areas.[3] The same census showed that the US population is nearly 310 million, meaning that more than one in ten Americans lived in or near one of these two cities. While there may be many opportunities in these cities, however, there is also a great deal of competition. Competition is not necessarily a bad thing for the industry and the professionals who survive and thrive in these areas have to be very good at what they do. Frank Sinatra may have said it best in "New York, New York" when he sang, "If I can make it there, I'll make it anywhere." Some have even suggested

that experience in New York, Los Angeles, and Nashville or a secondary market like Austin, Atlanta, Miami, San Francisco, Chicago, or Detroit can give
a music technologist a certain degree of clout that will work as a competitive
advantage if they move to a smaller market.

Profession

Depending on the kind of career you choose to pursue, you may discover that
it is necessary to move to another part of the country. Below are some suggestions about a few specific career paths, but you may need to do more research
to determine where the best opportunities can be found related to the area of
music technology that most interests you.

Live Sound

Entertainment hot spots can be great locations for music technology jobs. Of
course, New York is the capital of live entertainment, with Broadway, many
large performance venues, and thousands of smaller clubs. The Los Angeles
area features an active nightlife as well, but there are other areas around the
country where live entertainment is also big business.

In 1976 the television show *Austin City Limits* was first aired on public
broadcasting stations and highlighted the live music scene of Austin, Texas.
The show originally featured regional musicians and their music, but has since
expanded to include many national and international stars. The live music
scene in Austin has thrived over the course of the more than thirty-five years
since the show's first broadcast, and the city even trademarked the phrase,
"The Live Music Capital of the World." *Austin City Limits* is still produced
each week and is the longest-running television music program in history.[4]
The success of the television show boosted the already vibrant live music
scene in Austin and currently, more than two hundred live music venues and
numerous annual music festivals provide opportunities for thousands of live
sound engineers.

Tourist destinations are great places to find live sound jobs, and Las Vegas
and Orlando are two of the most popular. In addition to the big-budget live
shows at the hotels and theme parks, both cities feature a significant nightlife
of entertainment where sound engineers are in demand.

Branson, Missouri, located more than 1,200 miles from New York, 1,600
miles from Los Angeles, and a three-and-a-half hour drive from the near-
est international airport, has become a tourist Mecca, featuring dozens of
live entertainment acts. In 1991 a special feature on the television program

60 Minutes described the booming live theater district. At that time there were twenty-two live theaters in Branson, and today there are more than twice that many.[5]

Education

One advantrage to the education profession is that there are teaching jobs everywhere. For public secondary schools, however, research has shown that there is a higher concentration of music technology teaching jobs in the northeastern United States, followed by the southeastern US, the Midwest, and then the western US.[6] The research on this is still in the initial stages, and new music technology classes and programs are being formed at schools all around the country each year, but this information may be helpful when thinking about where you might find secondary teaching jobs in music technology. For college teachers, the idea of moving to another location for a job is simply an accepted part of the profession. When looking for a college job in music, it is not uncommon for a teacher to apply for jobs all around the country. The *Chronicle of Higher Education* and the College Music Society's Music Vacancy List are the most frequently used resources where universities post their availabilities.

Manufacturing and Retail

With the ease and relatively inexpensive cost of modern transit and communication, and with the consumer's passion for online shopping, a music manufacturer or retailer can locate almost anywhere and market to the entire world. As a result, jobs with various manufacturers or retailers are spread all across the country. Information on the location of these companies' corporate offices can often be found on their websites.

Using the Web to Advance Your Career

Joe Pisano has developed websites, social networks, and handheld apps for communities of musicians for the past ten years. He is the creator of the website mustech.net and is a partner and cofounder of A.P.S. Development, LLC. In the following interview, he describes ways that young people can use Web 2.0 resources to market themselves and make professional connections.

SP: What is Web 2.0?

JP: The best way to understand Web 2.0 is to relate it to Web 1.0. A lot of people think that it's two different broadband technologies, but it's not.

PHOTO 4.1 Joe Pisano

It is a framework for presenting information. Web 1.0 would be a website, back in the old days, like seven years ago, where you would put information up on the web that people could read. You could bookmark it, and later you could come back, but it was a way to input information to be disseminated over the Internet. Web 2.0 adds a collaborative element to that. Now, not only can I read it, but I can also talk about it. Now I can share and have a conversation about that particular piece. One very clear example of Web 2.0 is the website SoundCloud.com. SoundCloud.com allows you to very easily upload audio, and then that audio can be embedded, it can be shared, but what a lot of people don't realize, is that as that audio plays, you can comment on it in real time. Your comments literally show up in real time. The advent of Web 2.0 opens up the community for collaboration: collaborative composition, collaborative recording, and in some cases collaborative performing.

SP: How do RSS feeds fit into this?

JP: This is one of the amazingly cool things about 2.0 technology that is a fundamental paradigm shift in information. In Web 1.0, we had to go out and find the information, and then we would have to keep returning to that particular site to see if the information had changed. Web 2.0 flipped that. Now, by subscribing through RSS feeds or even email alerts, or embedding things on your own website, information can now come to you. That's the fundamental shift. When I first started musictech.net, I started to put information out that was sharable with others. We started to share each other's information online, and we would cross-pollinate. We began to create a conversation, and thus we were able to get better information out about what we were doing on the web. We created a focal point of information around which people of like interests could gather and learn from each other. The site started out with a trickle. In the beginning, if I would get ten to fifteen people to visit my blog in the course of a day, that was pretty exciting because that meant that in the course of a week, I might reach fifty to a hundred people. Today, the stats on mustech.net are such that I will have 800 to 1,500 unique hits a day. That doesn't count the 2,500 people who subscribe to the RSS feeds. It has become a destination on the web.

SP: How can a young person use the web to help them advance their career?

JP: There are a couple of things. First, they can learn about SEO, Search Engine Optimization. This refers to the techniques used to make your information on the web receive the most hits and attention. If they have a website, they can use these techniques to become more visible. There are several good books written on this and tons of web resources. But people aren't going to become SEO masters in a short period of time, so it can take some time and effort to develop that.

A second way has to do with social networking. Social media like Facebook can shortcut the process a little. If somebody has something to say, and they put it on Facebook and people can see it, that word spreads pretty fast. Before we had social media, you could spend a ton of money on advertising and publicity, or you could build up your voice in the wilderness of the Internet hoping that someone was paying attention. The beauty of social media now, is that you can get into a group on Facebook, join some living, breathing social media community, and if you have something to say, you have a platform now that you never had before. You have direct access to an intended audience. For example, you can spend a lot of money for a Google ad. That ad may be seen fifty thousand times before it's clicked. Your return on the investment of a Google ad may be very small. If someone says something on Facebook in one of these groups, it becomes a personal recommendation to the readers in the group.

SP: So if someone uses the web and social media correctly to get to know people in the industry, to build a small business or to market themselves, they can really create a lot of buzz.

JP: Absolutely. Anybody who is building their career has to be able to navigate these waters. I have created websites for a lot of people, but my own website, musictech.net, has had an enormous impact on my visibility as a musician and a music technologist. There can be no doubt about that. Because of the visibility of my site, many people and organizations have noticed me. My intention was to start a conversation, and I did, but it also brought me great professional visibility.

SP: Do you think aspiring music technologists can use these web-based tools to advance their careers as well?

JP: For someone with musical skills, the more they are able to navigate today's web environment, the more successful they are going to be. There is no doubt about it.

SP: Thank you, Joe.

Notes

1. Costa Lakoumentas, "A Must-attend Trade Show," *The NAMM Show* [Online]. Available: http://www.namm.org/thenammshow/2013.

2. Robert K. Oermann, "Grand Ole Opry: The Show that Made Country Music Famous," *Official Website of the Grand Ole Opry* [Online]. Available: http://www.opry.com/about/WhatIsTheOpry.html.

3. Paul Mackun and Steven Wilson, "Population Distribution and Change: 2000 to 2010," *2010 Census Briefs* (March 2011). Volume C2010BR-01, pp. 1–12.

4. Austin City Limits, "History of ACL" [Online]. Referenced July 7, 2012. Available: http://acltv.com/history-of-acl/

5. Branson/Lakes Area Convention and Visitors Bureau, "A Branson History" [Online]. Referenced July 5, 2012. Available: http://www.explorebranson.com/about/branson-history.

6. Rick Dammers, *"Technology Based Music Classes in High Schools in the United States"* (Minneapolis, MN: Paper presented at the Association for Technology in Music Instruction National Conference, 2010).

5

Music Technologists in the Recording Studio

WHEN YOU ENTER the control room of a professional recording studio, it is like entering a whole new world. You notice that the dim lighting is accented with tiny green, red, and yellow lights flashing and blinking on the equipment, while other hues emanate from the lava lamps. A couple of people may be sitting quietly or speaking softly on a plush couch at the back of the small but comfortable room. A waist-high cabinet rack spans the width of the center of the room and houses dozens of pieces of audio hardware and a patch bay that would make a telephone operator blush. On the cabinet's tabletop, recent copies of *Mix Magazine* and *Rolling Stone* lay open next to a few Cokes and a box of cookies. Near the front of the room, an engineer sits comfortably at the massive console, while a producer paces the floor behind him and calls out occasional orders. The console's faders border a sea of knobs, dials, and buttons. Sound waves appear as multicolored tracks on the computer screens in the center of the console and music pulses from one of the sets of speakers at the front of the room. A picture window that appears to be half a foot thick adorns the front wall, and through it you can see the source of the music: a band with guitar players, a drummer, a bass player and a singer, all performing for an audience of microphones.

For many people who are interested in the world of music technology, there is nothing more glamorous than the idea of working in a recording studio. Inside the studio is where all the magic happens: hits are produced, deals are made, stars are born, and mortals are immortalized. In the studio, highly skilled engineers, producers, managers, and musicians work with expensive equipment and use the latest technology to produce hits—and to make millions! Often, when I talk to young people considering working in music technology and ask them what they want to do for a career, they say, "I want to work in a studio" or "I want to be a producer."

But working in a recording studio can also mean long hours and late nights. It can mean staring at a computer screen and listening to the same drum track or guitar riff for hours. It can mean patiently working with hundreds of people who will never be stars, who will never produce hits, and who will never make millions. Those people lucky enough to build their career around the workings of the recording studio learn to take the good with the bad, but before you put all your eggs in this basket, you should know what it is you are signing up for. This chapter will introduce you to the world of the recording studio. You will learn what work and life are like for the people employed by studios. And, if after learning about life in the studio, you decide it is the career path for you, you will be able to pursue the kinds of musical and technological preparations necessary in order to succeed.

Careers in the recording studio include audio engineers, studio managers, producers, and studio owners. In small independent studios, one person may fill all of these roles, while large commercial studios may employ dozens of people. Each role is important and necessary to ensure the success of the studio.

Recording Engineer

The job of the recording engineer is to oversee the technical aspects of the recording process. In the 1960s assistant engineers were classified as tape operators and dubbed the "button pushers" from their responsibility to push the record and pause buttons on the tape machines. Today's recording engineers still push the record and pause buttons, but they also do a lot more. They are responsible for the entire path the sound takes from the musician to the recorded media. This includes understanding microphones and microphone placement, patching and routing the signal, the use of preamps, outboard hardware, and the recording console, and the proper setup and use of both analog and digital recording equipment, including tape machines and computer hardware and software. Additionally, recording engineers are largely responsible for tastefully incorporating equalization, reverb, delay, and compression, as well as other audio effects into the recording. Engineers must have the experience to be able to mix multiple instruments on a recording and balance their levels, and to detect and solve rhythmic and intonation problems. Simply put, a good audio engineer needs to know what sounds good and how to achieve it. Both technical and musical skill and experience are required to be a successful audio engineer.

Additionally, studio engineers must be exceptionally good at working with people – from the members of an up-and-coming band full of dreams for their future, to the grandmother who wants to record her piano playing for posterity; from the demanding producer for whom nothing is ever good enough, to the studio manager who controls the work schedule. People skills are every bit as important as musical and technical skills in the recording studio.

Some engineers are self-employed, working by the hour in multiple studios, while others may work full-time at one studio. A band or an artist may even prefer a specific engineer and bring them in to any studio in which they record.

Specific Technology Skills Required

Hardware:

Digital and Analog Mixing Consoles: able to route audio through console channels, set input and output levels, control panning, EQ, and onboard effects, record and edit automation, select and control playback monitors and talkback function, manipulate transport controls

I/O, Sync, Word Clock, and Audio Interface units: able to set up and route audio and MIDI to these devices, manipulate settings, troubleshoot problems

Patch Bays: able to manage signal flow with proper routing, understand normalled-through, and half-normalled configurations and the use of multi jacks

Analog Tape Machines: able to load, enable tracks, record, overdub, punch in and out, and scrub

Preamps and Direct Boxes: able to set levels and use properly

Outboard EQ, Compression, Reverb, and Delay units: able to manipulate settings to achieve desired effects

Synthesizers: familiar with common models and brands, especially those owned by the studio, able to select and modify patches and programs, able to route directly or through an amplifier

Microphones: familiar with common models and brands, especially those owned by the studio, understand the distinction between and proper use of dynamic and condenser mics, know effective mic selection and placement techniques for all instruments and for amplifiers

Speakers, Monitors, and Headphones: familiar with common models and brands, especially those owned by the studio, able to route signal, adjust levels, and use effectively

Mac and PC computers: able to save, manage, and transfer files, effectively use software (see below), connect to audio interfaces and hardware devices

Software:

Pro Tools: able to route audio signals, manage I/O and word clock settings, integrate with hardware devices, set up tracks, perform all recording and editing tasks

Logic: able to route audio signals, manage I/O and word clock settings, integrate with hardware devices, set up tracks, perform all recording and editing tasks

Audio Effects Plug-ins: able to effectively use RTAS and AU plug-ins for effects processing, familiar with common settings for instruments and voice appropriate to various musical styles

Suggested Education and Training

College Degree: BM, BA, BS, or BFA in music technology, audio engineering, or commercial music

Experience recording and working with live sound. This could include time at a college or university studio, a home studio, or a professional studio

Internship working in a professional recording studio

Studio Manager

The manager sees to the day-to-day operations of the recording studio. He or she is responsible for booking and scheduling the studio as well as for collecting payments and paying bills. The manager is responsible for equipment maintenance, facility issues, and the hiring and firing of studio personnel. Often the studio manager is also responsible for publicizing and advertising the studio, directing studio events, working with artists and their managers and producers, and overseeing the general operations.

Specific Technology Skills Required

The studio manager should be familiar with the hardware and software of the recording studio. Many studio managers have experience working as engineers, or assisting the engineers in the studio. Additionally, managers should be familiar with clerical and accounting software.

Suggested Education and Training

> College Degree: BM, BA, BS, or BBA in music technology, music business, music industry or commercial music, or a degree in business management, arts management, or marketing with a minor in music or music technology
>
> Experience with clerical and accounting software and tasks
>
> Skilled at using social networks, public relations avenues, and advertising campaigns
>
> Experience in the recording studio

Producer

The job of the producer is to oversee all aspects of making an album; they are literally responsible for producing records. They find the talent, select the songs, hire the studio, oversee the recording, arrange distribution, promote the album and the talent, and finance the entire process. The producer has the most to gain from an album's success, but also risks losing the most. In the corporate world of huge record labels, teams of people may work together to accomplish all of these tasks, and an executive producer oversees them, but there are hundreds of smaller labels where a single producer is responsible for making it all happen.

Specific Technology Skills Required

The producer does not need to have the same level of technical ability that the recording engineer needs. However, the producer should be very familiar with hardware and software of the recording studio and should know how it can best be used to make the music sound great.

Suggested Education and Training

> College Degree: BM, BA, BS, or BBA in music technology, music business, music industry or commercial music, or a degree in business management, arts management, or marketing with a minor in music or music technology
>
> Experience writing contracts and hiring and managing people
>
> Skilled at using social networks, public relations avenues, and advertising campaigns
>
> Experience in the music business working for a record label or recording studio

Building the Career

Getting a job working in a recording studio is a matter of building up experience, working hard, chasing after the dream, and making the right connections. Few recording studios will go to the local college to interview graduating seniors at a job fair. More than almost any other profession, people are hired to work in a studio because someone knew them or was familiar with their work. This can be true if you aspire to be a recording engineer, a studio manager, or a producer.

So how do you make these connections? One way is through the teachers at your college or university. Often audio recording teachers are former or current engineers and are well connected to the recording community in your area. You may also make connections during your university internship program. During the internship you should work with professional engineers who are connected to others in the recording world. Find out who they know, and take opportunities to use these connections to widen your network of professionals. Outside of college, join the local chapter of the Audio Engineering Society and attend its meetings. These are great opportunities to meet studio personnel. Find out if members of the organization know what studios are hiring, or where positions are opening up. Go to clubs where live music is performed and get to know the audio engineers. Studio engineers often moonlight in live venues and these can be good places to network. Look up the engineers who worked on the music that you listen to. Contact them via e-mail and tell them how much you like what they do. Ask them questions about their careers and get to know them, and let them get to know you. Students are often surprised at how willing other engineers are to share information with people interested in the profession. Become involved in online chat groups, and professional social networks.

Becoming a record producer requires years of experience in the music industry. Producers often work their way up through the ranks of a record label or a recording studio to the point where they have the experience to oversee the entire process. Students do not leave college and get jobs as record producers, although people with experience in the recording industry can go back to college to bolster their skill set in preparation for becoming a producer. Producers are keen at making relationships and working with people. They are astute financiers and effective managers of people, time, and money. The music industry can be a competitive and cutthroat business, and long-term success for a producer is based on survival of the fittest. Of the careers considered in this section, the producer can be, by far, the most lucrative, but it also carries the greatest risk and is the most difficult to attain.

Finally, be willing to move. No matter how qualified you may be, if there are only two studios in Fargo, for example, the job prospects are going to be very limited. You may need to move to a larger market where the studios, professional organizations, and networks are a lot larger. If you have your heart set on living in Fargo, move away for a little while, get some experience, make some money, and then move back and open your own studio.

Studio Ownership

Owning your own recording studio can be an exciting prospect for the professional music technologist. Many successful studios, especially in smaller markets, are independently owned by recording engineers and producers. The prospect of controlling your own schedule, owning you own equipment, and running your own business can be very exciting. Opening your own studio can be a tempting option, especially when you are first getting started. However, with limited experience and little money, it can be difficult to build up the kind of equipment and reputation it will take to get the new studio off the ground. Most new studios are founded by engineers and other music professionals who have years of experience in the business and the support of wealthy business partners.

In small independent studios, the owner may take on all of the roles in the studio, including recording engineer, studio manager, and producer. In some cases, a separate manager will be hired if the owner does not want to deal with the more routine aspects of the studio, but wants to focus on the role of recording engineer, or producer. In some cases, a wealthy businessman will purchase a studio as an investment but will not be directly involved in the studio's activities. In this case, managers, producers, and engineers may be hired to manage the operations of the studio.

When opening a new studio, no matter what your level of experience or funding, wise business practices must be observed for survival. New studios require the purchase of equipment, the designing and building of specialized rooms, and the hiring of personnel. All of these things can be very expensive, and trying to run a whole studio on $75–$100/hour rates can result in very slim profit margins. As in any business, high volume and low overhead are the simple secrets of success, so the one thing that is guaranteed is that the more work you can do yourself, the more money you can make. For this reason, the

PHOTO 5.1 Fred Bogert

better prepared you are in terms of musical, technological, and business skills, the better your chances of success.

Interview with a Professional: Fred Bogert, Producer, Studio Owner, and Digital Recording Pioneer, Louisville, KY

SP: Please start, if you would, by telling me a little bit about your career as a producer.

FB: My career as a producer was circumstantial and it evolved in a phenomenal nature. I didn't start out intending to be that. Basically over the years, when I would work with people on projects as a studio vocalist, studio musician, studio engineer, I would do more and more work for the clients and take a greater and greater part in decision making on projects. I was helping with project development, artist development, composition, arranging, that kind of thing, just because it's such a passion for me and I really enjoy doing it.

So I would be proactive in doing those things, and finally I reached the point where I started to get frustrated because the clients would take away this wonderful work, and I'd only get paid for some part of what I did. I didn't feel that I was being acknowledged for the size of my contributions.

I was sharing those frustrations with somebody one day, not in a legal sense, but in a creative sense, and they said, "Well, Fred, what you're doing is what a producer does, so why don't you call yourself a producer?" So just declaring myself to be a producer was essentially the last thing that happened in the process.

SP: Were you working as a recording engineer at the time?

FB: Recording engineer has been the common thread through the whole thing. But I found that I had a natural inclination to use my time in the studio in a creative way to express myself musically. The clients that came in and benefitted from my musical perspective and the forces that I could bring to bear as a musician, we ended up having really good, strong relationships, and their careers almost always blossomed as a result of that, and so did mine.

There was a gentleman that I met, a singer songwriter guy, named Jeff. I saw him perform and I said, "Wow Jeff, you're really good. I'd like to have you come to the studio and I'll produce some recordings of you." So I did, and they came out really good, and he really liked them. Well, two or three days later I get a call from John Prine's manager, who had an office across the street from my studios in Nashville. And he said something like, "Hey, this is Al Bunetta and you did the work on this guy, Jeff, and I really like the recordings. I want to find out who you are." So I made an appointment and went over to his office and sat down across the desk from him. He said, as I remember, "Okay. So who are you?" I said, "Well, my name's Fred, and I like music, and I like this and that, and blah, blah, blah." After about five minutes he said, "Okay, that's enough. You don't even know how to tell people who you are. I'll give you a little hint if you're going to stay in the business. If you can't tell people in one sentence who you are, nobody's going to want to have anything to do with you. I think you have a lot of talent, and I love these recordings, but I've got no use for someone who doesn't even know who he is."

Of course that stung, but it was one of the coolest things anyone's ever done for me. I spent a week doing negative surgery. "I'm not this, I'm not that." I decided not to market myself primarily as an engineer, because engineering was just the vehicle for my preferred work as a producer and composer. It's like saying you're really a racecar driver, but you do a lot of mechanic work. I don't want people to think of me as a mechanic. So what do I do? I allow myself three things. I tell people, "My name's Fred Bogert. I'm a producer, composer, and performer of music." And that's it. And wow, it's been really wonderful. He was right. He was absolutely right.

SP: How important was your musicianship in being successful as a producer?

FB: Critical. Beyond critical. I can't say enough about it. It's the elephant in the room that nobody talks about, but it's the elephant that's carried me through my entire career. When there were decisions to be made, when there were problems to be solved, in all these different categories: what kind of guitar should we use, is the guitar in tune, are the chords matching with what the piano's playing, is the singer singing in a way that matches what the story and lyrics imply, is the orchestration too thick, are the strings being recorded correctly—all of those things are addressed by musicianship. There are millions and millions of little decisions to be made. Early in my career, when I hadn't developed the reputation so that people walked in comfortable with me in a leadership position, I would be so frustrated by watching groups of people standing around trying to make these choices. The answers, to me were so obvious. I'm not saying I was always right, or any of that, but they just couldn't find consensus, couldn't make choices. When these little problems would come up with the music, and it would be such a glaring thing to me I had to tell myself, "Shut up, Fred. Don't say anything."

SP: But as a musician, you knew.

FB: Oh yeah.

SP: And the other people without the musical background…

FB: Would be trying to solve musical problems from a perspective of politics and power and all of that. After I established myself, and the projects I produced, etc. started being nominated for Grammys, I was like, "You know what, to heck with it. I feel in my heart that I know what's right in these situations and I'm not going to keep my mouth shut anymore. I'm credentialed enough, I've got enough of a track record, I'm comfortable enough in who I am and what I do, that if somebody disagrees with me, I'm fine with that." And there were times when it was just the right thing to say, and times that people would get really mad.

I finally learned to say to clients "I want you to realize that when you're working with me, I'm not ever going to hesitate to bring options to the table, with the understanding that you as the client are going to be the one to sign off on the decision." I won't hesitate to say, "The vocalist needs to be louder at that spot, the dynamics are not pushing enough in the chorus—you need to push harder, and your pitches are a little low, I want you to be more athletic about it." And to have the client understand that they don't have to worry if they want to say, "No, I don't want to do that.

I want it to be soft and gentle." They've been exposed to the information and they're paying for the session, so that's fine.

SP: How did you get into the recording industry? How did your career evolve?

FB: I went to the University of Miami School of Music and that was when I made the choice to go into music. I'd also been accepted at Florida State University in Painting and Sculpture. The difference between the two was that whenever I did something musical, I wanted to do more of it, right away. When I would paint or sculpt and I would finish something, I didn't want to do it again for a while. It was a draining experience, but music would always make me want to do it more and more.

So I decided to try this music thing until I got tired of it, and then I'd do something else. That was in 1970. After one year at the University of Miami School of Music I said, "Holy mackerel! This is who I am and I'm pumped: job market here I come."

So I went looking for work in the Miami studio scene, as a bass player. I couldn't find anything and ran out of money. I was living on somebody's back porch, which is not a big deal in Miami, and hanging out with the music community. I met up with T.K. Productions in Hialeah. It was an R&B "black" studio: Betty Wright, Carla Thomas, you know. It was just what they would call "race records" back in those days. I knew somebody who worked there as a bass player, so I knew I wasn't going to get work doing that, and one day I'm walking out of the studio, and Steve Alaimo, one of the producers, said, "Hey Fred, isn't that your name? Sorry man, bass is not going to happen, but can you help us find a piano player? We have to find somebody for a session this afternoon and I don't know what we're going to do." Now at the University of Miami School of Music they make you study piano, so I knew my way around. My musicianship has always been really strong, I guess that's my talent, so as far as knowing the architecture and structure of music and all that stuff, it was a no-brainer. Well, I thought I had enough keyboard skills so I said, "I've been playing forever." I lied my way onto the session, thinking, "what have I got to lose? I'm not working now."

They liked it, so they had me do another, and they liked it, and they had me do another, and they liked it. So I worked just as an independent contractor, you know, young kid about 21, doing studio stuff. Eventually I got frustrated with the things I mentioned before. There were days when there would be three or four producers in the room and we'd be getting nothing done. We got paid by the song, so there were days that I'd be in the studio, in that sort of tense, high-pressure situation of having to have the right lick at the right time with a bunch of people arguing in the control room and I'd be there for ten or twelve hours and make 15 dollars. It eventually got to be too much and I just couldn't do it anymore so I moved up to Fort Pierce and went from playing hard core, early R&B, to playing hard core Okeechobee country music. I played in enough bands and did enough things that people would hear me and say, "Hey, you're really good, we want you to come play with us." And one thing led to another.

SP: What were you playing in those bands?

FB: That was all piano. And my skills came back to me. I had had to take lessons when I was a kid. I hated taking lessons as a kid. Nobody in my family knew that I was going to be a musician, or wanted me to become a musician at all, but those years helped to get my physical skills strong enough that I could do it. And the University of Miami School of Music, God bless them, they really pushed me hard. And I've got some pretty strong natural talent, so it all came together and I grew really fast.

In 1974 I went on the road as a music director, which is a fancier sounding position than it really was. I was with a Vegas-style show band, and I really enjoyed that; got to see the country. When that band broke up a year later, an agent met me backstage and said, "Listen, I don't want to lose you. If you'll put another band together I'll book you." I said, "Ok, I want to travel the country, and I want to be booked all the time. If you'll meet my terms, I'll meet your conditions." And he did, and I did, and so for the next two years I did not have a mailing address. We bought and converted a school bus and we were one of those lounge lizard bands that traveled to Wyoming, Idaho, and everywhere else and it was a real magical time for me. And talk about getting chops, if you're playing and singing four and five hours a night, four, five, six nights a week, you're going to learn your trade. So I did that until I came off the road in 1977 and went back to Florida.

I set up a music studio when MIDI came along. I imagined the way that a studio could be, where the process did not dictate the flow of the creativity, but where it was the other way around. All the proprietary, expensive, big, cumbersome, difficult studio gear just never lined up for me. MIDI started to show me that creativity could control the process, and the idea of sequencing and tone generators, and all that stuff was very exciting. I was one of the first users of the Yamaha TX816, the rack synthesizer with eight DX7's. I mean, I went to town with my little primitive computer, designing voices for it and building virtual orchestras, and I was doing that stuff in 1985. It just made sense to me. So that evolved into a little studio where I synchronized that with an 8-track Tascam. The players and musicians and people that I knew, some of whom were Tanya Tucker and Gary Stewart, would come and do some little development projects there and that eventually led to my move to Nashville.

When I moved my family up there, I told my wife that the reason it was time for us to move to Nashville was because we didn't have to. I could live anywhere in the country and do what I was doing. I had enough of a client base, I was strong enough in what I did, I was playing solo piano and the wedding band stuff and making a decent middle class income. But I thought, "I'll never know what I can really do and who I really am, unless I go to the big leagues. I'll never know if I can hit unless I go stand in Yankee stadium and have Vida Blue wind up and throw a couple to see if I can hit 'em."

That was the next 15 years. It started in '92 and was done in '06. It was cool.

I discovered hard disk recording in '91 when I was still in Florida and it blew my mind. I wasn't looking for it; I was up in Connecticut to buy a used 24-track reel-to-reel for my studio. When I walked in the studio that I saw in the paper, a representative from Spectral Synthesis was there that day to demonstrate the first multi-track hard disk platform that was available. So I was just looking over these guys' shoulders and watching, and I'll never forget it. It was like looking for your date and walking in and seeing Marilyn Monroe. It was just like, "Oh my God!" And when he finished his presentation, he asked if any of us had any questions. I said, "Yeah, I've got a question for you. I'm Fred Bogert, I'm from Fort Pierce, Florida. Would you sell me one of those?" So he did, and I bought one. And it was something else. Looking back on it now, I think, "Holy goodness gracious."

SP: Do you remember, how much did it cost?

FB: Oh, I can tell you exactly. It cost $24,000. And it was 8 channels, and they did it with PCI cards, so the computer wasn't doing the work. All of the cards were the dedicated processors—huge busses and all of that stuff. The hard drives were Barracudas in their own bays; each drive was in a box about the size of a shoebox. They were 760 megs, and cost $1,500 a piece.

What happened was I found an investor, and it just so happened that the investor said, "I hear you're going to Nashville, and I think you can do it. I think it's a no-brainer. How deep are your pockets?" I said, "What are you talking about?" He said to me, "Get what you need, and go up there and give it your best shot and don't worry about the money stuff." And I thought, "Oh boy, here we go."

So, I went to Nashville and again we set up the studio and I started working. I reopened the old RCA Studio C, which was this little place in the old RCA Building; a small two-room studio where they used to do remixes and overdubs. It was in pretty good shape and nobody was using it. I got a pretty good lease on it and I thought it would be perfect. I didn't understand why in my first year there I was swamped. I mean, I'm not a big marketing guy, I'm terrible at that stuff, and I'm very naïve as far as those kind of power and politics things go, and yet, these really important people are beating a path to my door. I finally asked this one guy what was going on. He said, "People aren't coming here for the studio, they're coming here for you. You're a good fresh new talent, people are enjoying working with you, and they want to see what you can do. But the other thing is, what in the world is this stuff that you've got? Nobody's ever seen anything like it. Half the people that are coming in here are getting lessons. They're willing to hire you and pay you for a session just to watch you do this." That's where "Frediting" was born.

SP: So the way you were working with digital audio was so novel, it became known as "Frediting?"

FB: Right. And I didn't realize it was groundbreaking. I didn't know what they were talking about because it was meaningless to me. I had found a way to record that, for the first time in my life, made sense to me. I guess it would be like Andrew Wyeth discovering watercolors after being frustrated with oil paints all his life. When I recorded digitally, I didn't even have to think about the process. Everything went along smoothly, and I just got lost in it. We would come out the other side and my clients would say, "Wow, I think that was one of the most wonderful recording experiences I've ever had." My reaction was, "It was? I didn't mean it to be." Or sometimes people would say, "Where are the tapes in here? This really sucks! Why are you doing that? I don't understand this at all. I'm very uncomfortable with this." I'd say, "You are? I'm not in a position to present another option, so if this isn't working for you, I apologize."

SP: There *are* other studios in town.

FB: There's only about 400, that's right. I'll never forget one day when I was having lunch with a really famous songwriter who became a good friend of mine. We'll leave him unnamed, but I was saying to him, "Man, this town is the most beautiful town. Everybody is so nice." And he said, "Yeah, it'll be that way for a while. That's how you know how far up the ladder you are. Once you start getting near the top, just be careful. Keep your wits about you. It'll all change." And it did. The good news was that it meant that I was becoming successful enough to be perceived as competition for the major powers. The bad news was that I was becoming competition for the major powers. And once I got to that level, I wanted nothing to do with any of the crap. I just wanted to make good music and have a good time earning a decent living in the music business.

The year 2000 was a rough year for me. A lot of really tragic personal losses on many levels, and it just happened to coincide with the turning of the millennium. People really close to me passed away, and relationships ended. I lost the studios, my ability to maintain a staff, I lost the investor, I lost all that stuff, and needless to say, it was one of those dark times. It just knocked the chalks out of everything that I had. So I closed down the studios, took all the stuff that I still owned to my house, and in the downstairs of the house I built a little private studio.

I kept doing what I could do, and did the best that I could. Within ten months, I got the first Grammy nomination. I remember getting on my knees on the back deck after I hung up from the phone call and saying, "God, thank you for not being subtle." Sometimes you need a nice big lollypop telling you that you're going to be ok—that it's going to be fine. Sure enough, as soon as I dropped the idea that I was really important, and as soon as I stopped hanging out in that environment, I went back to my core love of music. I love to work in a purely creative environment and I love to share that with people who are willing to pay me to work with them. As soon as I went back to that really simple model, I realized I didn't want to look back.

I enjoyed my time on Music Row. There are some really fine folks in the music industry there who still inspire me. And, of course, I made enough fancy moves and knew enough fancy people that I can still cook up a big batch of name-drop soup to get a call answered if I have to. And it feels great that at this point I can own my life, I can own my career. I know who I am based on all the times that I've run into walls, and I have the scars that I'm happy to have, because it keeps me from making those mistakes again. That's why I consider myself successful. I'm still alive and I still do what I want to do. I don't think that there's anything else that matters.

SP: So what does it mean to be a producer?

FB: There are a lot of people who may not call me a producer, even though that's what I am. To most people who look at the industry from the outside, the producer is the guy that gets the deals and drives the Cadillac and gets the bling and goes to the parties, and there are a lot of producers that that's exactly what they are. I have worked with a lot of really good producers like that who are not one-tenth the musician that I am. But in that definition of a producer, I am not one-hundredth of the producer that they are. Executive producers, for instance, have nothing to do with the creative side of it at all. They're bankers. An executive producer is saying, "I'm paying for this so it has to get past me, I want it to be good." But all you're going to do is to bring them the final product and play it and hope they'll say they like it. So instead of that, I'm the kind of producer who is responsible for working out the real focus of the artist's or project's musical message from start to finish. That involves a lot of in-the-trenches work with musicians and their performance, followed by mixing and editing. It's very hands-on, and that's something I love about it.

SP: And for the people who want work in the industry, are there are a lot of opportunities?

FB: Tons. Tons. I would say look at the whole music industry like a pie. We have engineers, we have promotion people, we have label people, we have A&R people, we have songwriters, artists, studio musicians, roadies, road managers, and we have them all in the pie. Now serve yourself a piece of pie. Where would it be? Where's the one that makes you say, "To the heck with the rest of it."

SP: And how can they prepare for it?

FB: Here's what I recommend for Joe Shmo from Cocomo. Somebody says they want to be in the music industry and there's all those pieces of the pie, but before we get to the pie, you're going to need some keyboard skills. You're going to need to know how to find your chords on the keyboard, and you're going to need to know functional diatonic harmony. You need to know basic classical structure and be able to identify those things, and a little bit of Solfége, and a little bit of formal analysis. You're going to need to know the circle of fifths, and the language of western music. And the reason is, that anybody can say they want to be an engineer, but when 100 engineers show up, and they are as good as you, or better, but you know music, you'll get the job.

SP: So it requires more work than showing up with a pair of hands and a dream?

FB: Sure. That's the educational part of it. And get a liberal arts education so you know how to talk like an educated human being. That's really important.

SP: Speaking of talking with other people, how important is it to be able to work with people in this industry?

FB: There is nothing more critical at all in the whole wide world. I once heard it defined this way: The purpose of a liberal arts education is to teach you how to B.S. at a cocktail party. It's funny, and it's crass, but it's totally true. It's the closest one-sentence definition that I've ever heard for why you should bother to get that paper. Along the way you're going to learn enough about the background of the knowledge of western civilization and social trends and skill sets, language, communication, so that when somebody meets you, maybe you're not going to show them that piece of paper, but they're going to know that they are talking to an educated human being.

I didn't finish my degree until I was forty, but I got a lot of college education when I was younger, and it saved my tail time after time after time. When a person in a position of fiscal responsibility is working on a creative project, there's a lot of financial risk involved. They want to deal with people that they can trust and understand and communicate with. People who are responsible and have high integrity. There is no better reason. And it's critical. I would require that of anybody who is interested in the arts. And it's even more important than it is in other things. You can get a two-year trade degree in repairing tractors and they don't care if you can speak in complete sentences, they just want the tractor fixed. If you can do that, they're going to pay you by the hour. But in the arts, it's way too entrepreneurial. You've got to at least engage them in conversation, and have some meaningful degree of knowledge base so that they feel comfortable talking with you.

SP: I thought what you said about Nashville was really interesting. We talk about New York, LA and Nashville, and you said you wanted to prove to yourself; you wanted to see how far you could go. Do you think, in this day and age, somebody can have a career in the business without being in one of those three cities?

FB: In a heartbeat. I do. I make a really decent middle-class income, and I'm nowhere near any of them. Now I've been to them, which helped, but remember what I was saying, I went to Nashville making a decent middle-class income, and I think the best time to go to Nashville is when you don't need to. Because that's when you are least at risk for being abused and exploited and thrown out, and there's a lot of that that goes on in all three of those cities, in all three of those markets.

SP: When you hire young people to work with you, what kinds of things are you looking for?

FB: Attitude. Attitude first, and talent next. If the puzzle piece that's missing with them is positive attitude, then you can have a lot of talent, but it's never going to happen with me. I can't work with someone who I know is not anywhere near as committed to being there as I am, so attitude is number one.

SP: Describe what attitude means.

FB: Attitude means to be proactive about helping and serving, so that if we have a 9 am session, that person is going to be there at 8:45 asking what they can do to help. And they're not thinking, "What am I getting out of this? I'm tired. I'm bored. What are we doing next? Why isn't this entertaining me?" If they have that attitude I just say go away. Sometimes when I work with people I talk about the difference between creativity and consumerism. I won't have somebody work with me or for me who is there as a consumer. If you're there as a creator, we'll find common ground, and it'll work, and everybody will serve and grow, and all of that stuff, but if you're there to have it serve you, then you're going to have to pay me by the hour.

SP: How does someone break into this business?

FB: Keith Moon, the drummer for The Who, got his job because he wanted to play with them, and so they were playing at a club with another drummer, and during the break, he took the drummer outside and beat the crap out of him, and then came in and said (in his best Keith Moon British accent), "Hey, your drummer can't play with you. You gotta find a new drummer. I play drums. Let me play with you." I don't think that's a good methodology, but you have to beat your way into this business.

That's why I recommend apprenticeships. What I would say to somebody that really wants to do it, whether it's engineering or production, or playing in the studio, or whatever. I would say, go to college, if you don't have a lot of money, first two years go to community college, and get an AA degree, then a bachelor's is a good idea. Then take what money you would spend for more college to become a teacher, or graduate work, take that money and put it in a fund, go to Nashville, New York, Los Angeles, Orlando, Minneapolis, Atlanta, Chicago. There's a bunch of places like that. Live in a cheap place, feed yourself, have ten, fifteen, twenty thousand dollars in the bank, and instead of putting that money into more school, live off of it. Then, go to the parties, go to the places, join AES, join all these networking organizations, and do everything you can to be among these people. Go to the studio, sweep floors, work for nothing. Show them that you want it and sooner or later, one of these places is going to remember that you were the one that wanted it.

SP: Is that any different today than it was 20 years ago?

FB: No. It's no different. Bach did it. Remember when Bach walked 25 miles to go pump the pedals on Dietrich Buxtehude's organ? That's exactly what that was all about. Absolutely. So that hasn't changed in forever.

The opportunity is going to be there, but it's going to be close to where the opportunity comes from. You've got to get under that tree so that when the apple falls, it hits you on the head. And you've got to be ready when it does. I call it God's own spotlight. God's own spotlight is this focused light of opportunity that's buzzing around all over the place and it'll eventually hit you. When it does, you've got five seconds to do that dance. If you've prepared your dance and you're ready to go, then you can say, "I'm the one!" And if you do what I did with Al Bunetta and say, "I really like life man, it's really cool," the world says, "Next!" and you're left wondering where the spotlight went.

I came out of the University of Miami as a bass player. I have never made my living since as a bass player. Building a music career is about the journey. It's about the adventure.

SP: Thank you very much.

FB: You're welcome, Scott.

6

Music Technologists in Live Sound

IN THE PROFESSIONAL world of music technology, if the recording engineer's job is the most glamorous, the live sound engineer's may be the most exciting. The live sound engineer is responsible for making sure that concerts, theater performances, live shows, clubs, dance parties, and church services sound great. They possess many of the same skills as recording engineers, and it is not uncommon for studio engineers to moonlight in live settings. But the work and the life of the live sound engineer are very different than that of the studio engineer. Where the studio engineer may stay in one city for years, the live engineer may be in a different town each night. Where the studio engineer may place microphones and prepare for a recording, the live engineer may be found on a catwalk hanging speakers, running cables, unpacking gear, lugging boxes, and packing trucks. While the recording engineer can ask the band to lay down another take, the live sound engineer does not have that luxury.

From setting up the sound system, to testing the microphones, to checking the levels, to manning the mixing board during the show, the live sound engineer is responsible for all of it. This level of responsibility creates a considerable amount of pressure and while running live sound is an exhilarating experience, engineers need to be on top of their game at all times. Live sound engineers play an important role behind the scenes, and if they do their job well, the audience never notices them. But, if they make a mistake, everyone notices and the performance may be ruined. When most people go to a great sounding show or concert, they don't think about all the work that went into making sure that everything sounded great; they simply enjoy the performance. But if you are the kind of person who thinks about what it takes to make a show sound great, if you have the right music technology skills and experiences, if you enjoy traveling, love working hard, and can handle the pressure, you may be cut out for a career in live sound.

Sound Engineer for Live Concerts and Shows

Live concerts and shows entertain millions of people every year. These events range in size and scope from a few hundred people attending a high school musical production to hundreds of thousands in New York's Central Park. But whether you are entertaining thousands or a few dozen, the sound plays a critical role in making the event a success. Opportunities abound in this field, and experiences differ depending on if you are working for a traveling show, or if you have a job as the house engineer in a live theater or venue. Whether you are traveling or staying put, your job is to oversee all aspects of the sound before, during, and after the show.

Setup

Before the show, all sound equipment including speakers, amplifiers, microphones, soundboards, outboard audio gear, and sometimes computers need to be set up, wired up, and configured. If different shows are presented in your venue each night, you will need to make sure you have the right equipment a band or artist needs, selecting and placing microphones and working with their amps and instruments. Since each show is different, a keen familiarity with sound equipment at your venue is important for success. If you are working for a long-running show, such as a Broadway production, there may be few changes in setup from one night to the next and all you need to do is check wireless microphones for batteries.

Sound Check

A complete sound check is critical for success at show time. For these few precious moments the entire band or cast is required to attend and the live sound engineer takes charge. The engineer checks the levels and balance of microphones, instruments, effects, speakers, and front of house monitors. To become a successful live sound engineer, you will need to conduct sound checks quickly, deliberately, efficiently, and thoroughly.

Performance

During the performance, the live engineer oversees the mixing console. You are responsible for adjusting levels, enabling and muting microphones, playing sound cues, and being prepared in case something goes wrong. Programmable digital mixing boards have made it easier to manage a show by recording cues, levels, and settings in advance, thus making the engineer's job much less stressful.

After the Show

If you work in a live sound venue that features different acts each night, you will need to tear down the sound equipment and store it carefully for future shows. It is a good idea to carefully organize storage areas so that equipment is easily accessible. If you are working on a traveling show, at the end of the stay, you will need to pack up everything so that it can be loaded onto the truck. Careful attention must be given to this task, or expensive equipment can easily be left in a city.

Going on Tour

Working on a traveling show or tour can be a great way for a young engineer to get a lot of experience in the profession. Young people often have more flexibility and fewer family commitments, allowing them the freedom to be away from home for extended periods of time. They also have the stamina and strength required to perform the physical labor of unpacking, setting up, and packing up a show every time they are in a new city. Young people also seem to be better able to withstand the demands of travel, such as little sleep, lengthy bus rides, hotel beds, and fast food that keep many older engineers off the road.

Working at a Club

One place to start your career as a live sound engineer is in a local club that features live music. Running sound in a nightclub is a great way to learn the hardware, be exposed to lots of different musicians and a variety of genres, and really hone your audio skills and musical ears. Although the club scene offers lousy hours, less than ideal conditions, and some rowdy customers (sometimes the sound engineer has to double as one of the bouncers), working there can be a great résumé builder. As an engineer, you can begin working in a small club with just a few acts each week and if you do a good job and develop a reputation, move up to larger clubs with busy schedules, big crowds, and better pay. If you have experience playing in a band, this can be a real advantage as you will find it easy to talk to and work with the acts. This is one music technology setting where you will be working with musicians all the time, and if you don't speak their language, you simply won't be successful.

Working in a Church

Great opportunities for working with live sound can be found in churches. Compared to live sound venues, the hours and conditions are a lot more favorable, and rarely does the sound engineer need to throw an unruly patron out of a church! In many small churches, this job can be part-time, involving working only on Sunday mornings, and maybe one or two weeknights. A live sound engineer may work at a church to supplement their full-time job at a live venue, theater, or club. Many larger churches offer full-time jobs that pay good salaries and include benefits. So-called mega-churches may employ entire teams of sound engineers. These jobs can be found all over the country, but in some areas—such as the southeastern United States, which is sometimes referred to as the "Bible Belt"—the opportunities are even more abundant.

Specific Technology Skills Required

Hardware:

> Digital and Analog Mixing Consoles: able to route inputs and outputs through console, set levels, control panning, EQ, and onboard effects, record and edit automation, select and control output channels, mixes and submixes
>
> Preamps and Direct Boxes: able to connect, set levels, and use properly
>
> Outboard EQ, Compression, Reverb, and Delay units: able to manipulate settings to achieve desired effects
>
> Microphones: familiar with common models and brands, understand the distinction between and proper use of dynamic and condenser microphones and the use of phantom power, know effective microphone selection and placement techniques for all instruments and for amplifiers
>
> Speakers: familiar with common models and brands, able to route signal, adjust levels, and use effectively
>
> Monitors: familiar with models and brands, including on-stage as well as in-ear monitors, able to route signal, adjust levels, and use effectively
>
> Cables and connectors: able to run, connect, and properly care for required cables, cords, and wires, understanding differences and proper use of signal levels for speakers, microphones, and components

Software:

> Pro Tools: able to route audio signals, manage I/O and word clock settings, integrate with hardware devices, set up tracks, perform all recording and editing tasks
>
> Logic: able to route audio signals, manage I/O and word clock settings, integrate with hardware devices, set up tracks, perform all recording and editing tasks
>
> Audio Effects Plug-ins: able to effectively use effects processing, familiar with common settings for instruments and voice appropriate to various musical styles
>
> Console Software: able to use software and manipulate menus and options embedded in mixing consoles

Suggested Education and Training

> College Degree: BM, BA, BS, or BFA in music technology, audio engineering, or commercial music
>
> Experience working with live sound. This could include time at a college or university venue, a local theater, or in a recording studio
>
> Internship working in a live sound venue, club, or church

Interview with a Professional: Will Giuliani, Technical Director, Oak Mountain Church, Birmingham, Alabama

SP: I want to talk to you about your career as a recording engineer, as a live sound engineer, and as a music technologist. Can you tell me how your career evolved?

WG: When I was in college and I found out that there was a music technology program at the University of Alabama at Birmingham it really struck a chord in me. I've always enjoyed playing around with synthesizers, even when I was a little kid, playing with little keyboards. I've always enjoyed recording and coming up with sequences and tracking. I've always been into music. I play drums, and I was in the school band ever since I was in fourth grade, and I was in the marching band and jazz ensemble through college. But I didn't really want to be a music educator. That just wasn't my passion.

When I found out about music technology, it was just a no-brainer. There was the music theory that I was real interested in, but then there was this whole world of music technology and synthesis that really excited

PHOTO 6.1 Will Giuliani

me too. So it all started there. I didn't really have a job in mind. I was just kind of going on faith that there would be something there when I graduated. My approach in school was "I'm interested in this, I enjoy this, so I'm going to work as hard as I can and learn as much as I can and see what happens." I thought I might be able to get a studio job. I guess that was sort of what I had in the back of my mind, but I didn't really know.

So I graduated. I did my internship in a studio in town. That studio is no longer there, and that seems to be the story over the last few years. Big studios are having a hard time just because anybody can buy a laptop and do what a lot of their clients need, without all of the overhead. And so there wasn't really a studio job that I could find. I did some freelance recording and some other things to make money. I recorded bands for about a year.

About that time, my wife and I actually visited this church because a friend of ours went here. My wife saw a little blurb in the bulletin about a technical director position that they were looking to fill. I didn't know what a technical director at a church was. I didn't know anything about it at all, but I thought it was interesting. I got some information on it and sent a résumé in. Over the course of a couple months, I ended up getting the job. So that's how I ended up here.

SP: What kinds of things in your college training helped to prepare you for this job?

WG: If we are going to talk about the technical side of it, you know, understanding signal flow, understanding what music technology is and what you can do with it, that was a definite plus. When I first applied for the job and sent a résumé in, I was actually told, "Your résumé looks great but I'm looking for someone who has more live sound experience." I had plenty of recording experience through school and my internship, but not a whole lot of experience in live sound. And so I was a little disappointed, but I wasn't really sure about this job anyway.

But as time went on, it just kept eating at me. I just kept thinking about it, and I suddenly had an epiphany. I realized that while I didn't have a lot of live sound experience per se, I did understand signal flow. I knew that you have a microphone that plugs into a console that comes up on a fader that goes out through the sound system. I understood that, and I knew that there was a lot to be learned in running live sound, but I thought I had a good framework for coming into it. So with nothing to lose, I typed up a long email expressing all of that and sent it to the music minister here. I didn't really know if I would get a call or anything but a few days later, I got a call and he said, "let's go to lunch." That's ultimately how I ended up getting this job.

So I would say that in a music technology program, understanding signal flow and getting hands-on experience with equipment in an internship is vital. And in the school environment and in that internship, you're only going to learn as much as you put into it. That's really where it starts. If you start doing that in school, putting yourself fully into your work, when you try to get a job, I really believe you'll eventually be successful.

SP: Would you say that even though you had some skills, you developed additional skills on the job?

WG: Oh, I've developed a lot on the job. And I knew that I would. That's just the nature of the discipline, I think, because technology changes every day. What you learned in school, one year later, while it may not be outdated, and it's still useful, you have to continue to learn. I've really developed a lot and learned a ton here. My schooling was really the springboard that allowed me to come into a career like this and to evolve and continue to learn. And who knows where I'll go from here?

SP: In addition to the technical things, what other things did you learn in your college education that helped you?

WG: Let me start by talking about the musical aspects. Understanding how to read music has helped me to run tech for our big productions. When we do our Easter or Christmas productions, for example, there's a black binder full of music, all the charts that our music minister writes out and gives to the band. The week before we have the big rehearsals, we go through the charts and make lighting cues. I write down in my music where everything has to happen. I write in all lighting cues, microphone cues, and video cues that I need to call, and then I just follow the charts. If I wasn't able to do that, I don't know how I would be able to get through the entire show. So that's been a great asset.

Another important skill I learned is professionalism. In order to really do well in college, you have to be professional. You know, the way you relate to your professors, the way you collaborate with other students, that really helps prepare you for working in an environment with other people.

One more important thing, and something that I really liked about the program at UAB, was that in the music tech program, there was just sort of a creative atmosphere there. It was a combination of professionalism and creativity. It wasn't people just sitting around to see if anything strikes them, it was "I'm here to work on this project, and I need to be creative with it, but I need to get something done, and I need to be really motivated to do that." It was an environment where that was the norm and that was encouraged. You weren't just in there playing with synthesizers and trying to make cool sounds, you were actually focused on trying to get your work done for a project. That's really my day to day here. Week to week we have projects that need to get done and I get to come up with creative ways of doing things, but at the same time there's a deadline. So that was a huge carryover for me.

SP: Is it important to be able to work with people?

WG: Absolutely. It's very important. There were projects that we did in school where we worked with others and everything came together for the final project. You have to learn to be respectful of other people's creativity and other people's work. I don't know that you necessarily learn this in college, but it's definitely beneficial if you have a humble attitude rather than an attitude of, "Well I'm the best and everybody else's work is sub-par compared to mine." Learning to be respectful of other people is important.

You want to be the best, that's very healthy and there's nothing wrong with that. But in the environment at UAB, I was able to see what other people were doing, and I was able to aim higher. I would try to be more creative or try to be more successful in certain things. Instead of constantly trying to assert yourself as the best, or putting anybody else down, you actually want to appreciate people who are better than you. That way you can aim higher and try to do better. It's the same thing with people in the working world, or in a company, or in an organization like this. I look at what other churches do, any projects that they are doing or any recordings that they make. We are always looking at what others are doing and we're trying to do better. And I think that's also something that carried over from my schooling.

SP: So being able to work with people and being able to learn from other people are both important?

WG: Right. In college you may learn how to run a sound console but, in my opinion, you shouldn't view your time in school as the time where you're going to learn everything that you need to know about the job. That's just to whet your appetite. It's just your preparation. If you think about it, you're going to be in school, on average, for four years but you're going to be in your career for the rest of your life, 30 or 40 years. So it's really a primer that gets you going and gets you building those habits of being professional, being on time, working well with others, being humble, having a great attitude, and not putting other people down. Basically learning how to be the kind of person that other people like to work with and to work around. It's important to come into a working environment with a good attitude. No one wants to work with someone who's the best in the world, and knows it. I was able to show my boss that I was a go-getter kind of guy; that I had a basic understanding of live sound, but I was willing to learn and hungry to learn. He could see that I was the kind of guy that he could teach and he knew that this was what he wanted to have here.

SP: What is your schedule like, working as the technical director at a church like this?

WG: Our work is really impacted by the seasons and the holidays. Right now, we are in the summertime, and so we have some downtime. Some pastors go on vacation, and a lot of people go on vacation, so we don't really try to initialize a big production or anything. That gives us time to work on other things that we've wanted to get around to. For example, today we've been installing a new sound system in the gym. We've wanted to update it for a couple of years. During the summer I'll often take time in my schedule to learn a few new things. Recently I've found some online tutorials on synthesis. For the video work I do here, audio is everything. If you have great video but bad audio, then you don't really have great video. So I'm trying to take some time now to learn more about synthesis and some other things. In the summertime we kind of go around and clean out storage areas and do the kinds of things that we don't have time to do during other times of the year.

Now it's important to remember, that this is dependent on the seasons. Three weeks before Christmas we're having 50-60-hour workweeks. And it's the same thing with Easter. We also do one big video project each year here. We do little testimony videos here and there, and the weekly announcements video, but in November we do a big video. It scopes out who we are as a church, what we've done this year, what we want to do, what our vision is, and that sort of stuff. It's sort of a "vision" video. So there's a lot of work involved with that as well.

In addition to that we have children's programs. We do one in the spring and one around Christmas and we're heavily involved in that. We do set design and all kinds of other technical things for those productions. Last year, for example, we hung a giant mirror ball from the catwalk and we had light shining on that. We had to have that motorized and so we had to run all the wiring for that, and we had to get that thing rigged up so it wasn't going to fall. It was the kind of thing where it dropped down at a certain point and went back up. So it took us a couple of days to figure out how to do that. And that's the kind of thing that's a lot of fun to do.

SP: So what does your typical week look like?

WG: Even though it's the summer, we still do our video announcements every week. Generally on Mondays I'll come in and go through emails and learn from some online tutorials. Tuesday morning we'll shoot our announcement video. We also have a woman's Bible study that has worship in one of the classrooms there and so I set up the projector and sound system for them. On Tuesday I'll start editing the announcement video and maybe working on some new design projects. We have our rehearsals on Wednesdays, so I'll come in Wednesday morning and after checking emails I'll finish editing the announcement video, and then spend a lot of time in stage setup. That's a big part of what goes and it usually leads me into the rehearsal time on Wednesday evening.

SP: So Wednesday evening is when you rehearse for the Sunday morning services?

WG: That's right. And the stage setup changes from week to week. We have a worship ministry that is made up of mostly volunteers. We have four drummers, three or four electric guitar players, about half a dozen acoustic players, and maybe 50 or 60 vocalists. Everyone rotates in and out throughout the month or throughout the season, and so based on who is playing, I will move the stage around and get it all wired up, and then sound check everything. In Wednesday rehearsals we will have a volunteer to run the slides and our projection stuff, and a volunteer to run sound, and then I'll run lights in the middle of those two. I make sure that everyone's good to go.

Wednesday usually goes until about 9:00 or 9:30 PM and then Thursday I come in and usually tie up any loose ends. Throughout the week I'm working on other little projects like building computers, working on the sound systems in other parts of the church, helping set up technical things for meetings and so on. I'm also finishing all the video production that we need for Sunday. In addition to the weekly announcement videos there are other videos that we do, testimonial videos and other kinds of things. I make sure that everything is on the computer and good to go, so that I can come in a couple of hours early on Sunday and get everything up and running. So we have Fridays and Saturdays off because, of course, Sunday is a workday for us. We go Monday through Thursday and then Sunday.

On Sunday morning, I get in here a couple of hours early, before any of the volunteers get here for rehearsal. We get everything turned on, make sure it's sounding good, do any kind of lighting work such as changing out gels, or lamps that may have gone out. And then we do a run-through rehearsal, and then we have our service. In the summertime, we only have one service. We generally have two services, but during the summertime we combine them. It's just a packed out room, and it's cool. There's a lot of energy in the summertime when everyone's together for one service.

SP: How many people attend Oak Mountain Church?

WG: The church has around 2,500 members right now. And it has grown a good bit in the last six to ten years. When I came on staff, we were one year away from finishing construction on the new building. At that time, all of the conduit work was being put in place and all the wiring was being put in. From the very beginning, I was handed a stack of blueprints, and drawings from the consultants, and I had to make sure that the wiring was going in the right conduit and the proper distances were being maintained. I was introduced to all of that while I was in school. I was wiring up equipment in the studio and I learned that you need to keep your audio wiring separate from your power cables. I understood all those concepts and now I had all these drawings and I needed to go around and make sure that all of that was happening correctly. In school they didn't say, "This is how you read architectural drawings," but I still had the framework I needed to be able to look at those drawings and understand what they were saying. And

Google was helpful. I could go on Google and search for questions or look up anything that I needed to. I still do that.

SP: Is the music minister responsible for selecting music and programming all of the services?

WG: Yes he is. And our music minister has been a technical director at a much bigger church in another state. That was what he did before he became a worship minister. He's a bit of an anomaly because he's a music guy who does the programming and all that, but is also very technically minded. When he comes up with ideas for Easter or for Christmas, he knows the technical elements that are going to have to go in behind that show. We've worked together now for 6 1/2 years, and we work well together. He does all of the planning, as far as the worship is concerned and the people that are going to be involved, and then we work together at getting all the technical elements lined up.

SP: And all of the technical elements include?

WG: It's audio and video and lighting. Music technology, at least in the church and the worship environment, includes a lot. As I said before, great audio is essential to great video. If you can produce your own audio tracks for your video, then you can really have an advantage because you don't have to download stock stuff and you don't have to rip off other artists. It just makes your stuff a lot better.

SP: Do you think there are opportunities for young people who are interested in this work to go to a church and volunteer?

WG: Absolutely. A lot of churches these days are moving to a more technically demanding style of worship. There's lighting, and there's video, and they want to do great things with audio but they don't necessarily know how. There's a huge benefit to having a technically minded person on staff. We have a lot of churches that are smaller in our denomination that are coming by and asking us, "Hey, how are you doing this? How do you set up subs? How do you work the sound system? What equipment do you need to buy?" So there's a massive need for someone who has the know-how. A lot of churches have money to spend but they don't know how to spend it and they can waste a lot of money buying the wrong equipment. Knowing the right equipment to buy, that's a huge thing, because that's going to save a lot of money and going to get the job done efficiently.

You know, we're largely staffed by volunteers. The worship minister's philosophy here has always been that if someone has an inclination for getting involved in the worship ministry, we get them plugged in. We don't have any auditions or anything like that. So training is also a huge part of my job. And I love doing that. I love training people. It's kind of the way we've been set up here. Anyone that might be interested in running sound, I train them how to do it. They don't have to have a background in it. If you can be good at showing people what you're doing, that's a great skill to have in the working world.

SP: What would you say is the best part of your job?

WG: The best part about my job is that there is often something different every day. I don't come in and sit at the computer all day. There's creativity here. If you look at our church, our product is the Sunday morning service, and our clientele are the members of this church. So in the same way Apple sits around trying to figure out a better product that people are going to get excited about, that's what we do here in the worship ministry staff. We're always trying to discover new ways to get people excited about our product—our worship services. So my favorite thing is that there's variety and creativity in what we do.

Another one of the things I really love about my job is that I'm able to set my schedule. It's not a 40-hour a week job where you clock in, work your 40 hours and go home. I think those jobs are dwindling fast. And I wouldn't want one of those jobs. I would rather have a job that may range from 40 to 60 hours, but when my work is done, so am I. Being able to set my own schedule is nice.

SP: What would you say are some of the challenges for a person in your position?

WG: Well, sometimes deadlines are difficult. We have a hard deadline every week on Sunday morning. If I make a mistake on something that I'm building, or on a video that I'm putting together, and I get behind on it, if it takes 50 hours over the week, I've got to get it done for Sunday. Now that doesn't happen too often, and I've gotten better at being able to scope out my week over the last six years. On Monday I've got to look at the entire week and think about what are the things that might keep me up late on Thursday.

SP: What advice would you give to a young person who wants to be involved in this field?

WG: If you are interested in this field, find out how to do some of these things. The Internet has all kinds of videos and instructions that you can find and learn about these things. There are several audio programs that you can get for under a hundred bucks that can at least get you started at tracking audio and playing around. If you're passionate about it, just continue to learn, continue to play. As long as you're enjoying it, then that's going to drive your learning. I think it's easy to get discouraged. I get discouraged because there are all these things that I want to do as a part of my work. There are some programs that I want to learn to use better than I know how to use them now. Try not to get discouraged by looking ten years down the road at where you want to be and comparing that with where you are now. You just have to look at what you have today, and do something today. You know, I try to learn something new every single day. Continue learning.

SP: So this isn't a passive career?

WG: No. And I could sit back and just be happy with where things are today, and just continue to do the same things that I've been doing. But what's that going to do for me in ten years? Where am I going to be in ten years in my career? How will my skill set improve? How valuable of a resource will I be? If I sit back now and just try to go with the flow, I'm going to miss out on a lot and I'm going to kick myself in ten years' time. Always be driven, always be passionate, and always go after it.

It's also important to always have a good attitude, always be professional, and always be on time. When I was in the interview stage for this job, the church had three services, and our earliest service was at eight o'clock in the morning; our rehearsal time was at seven o'clock. So the call time for me and for my boss was six o'clock. After our first interview he said, "Hey, why don't you come by Sunday morning and show up at six o'clock and you'll get a feel for what we do." Well, six in the morning is early and I had to get up at five so I could get ready to go and get to work by six. That was difficult, but I thought this is something that I can do. So I showed up at six that Sunday, and I showed up every Sunday for the next month or so. Even though between interviews, there was no guarantee for a job, I just decided I was going to show up every Sunday morning at six o'clock because that is something that I can do to try to impress him and let him know that I'm passionate and driven about this job. Not everyone's going to want to do that, not everyone wants to get up that early on Sunday morning. If you can do the things other people aren't willing to do, that's going to help you out in any career.

SP: What opportunities do you see in this field?

WG: This is a growing field. Even among churches that are smaller, that may have historically been more traditional. They want to add new elements of video and sound. A person who is technically minded and is willing to learn, churches all over the nation are looking for someone like that. And don't be afraid of an entry-level salary. Focus on what you can learn on the job. The more you learn, the more marketable you will become. Don't let the small salary, whatever it may be, don't let that be a huge deterrent. Don't let it depress you, because if you continue to grow, the salary will jump up gradually with you. Try to put yourself in a position, starting out, where you don't have to have a high paying job at the beginning.

Get a job where you're passionate about it and you're enjoying what you're doing, and in the process you're developing more skills. If you're a young person, don't just play around and blow off your time at some job that's not very rewarding. Now is the perfect time for you to get serious about your career. Eventually, you may want to have a family. If you want to have a stable job where you can be creative, the time when you're young and fresh out of college is really the time to hit it hard and get started down that path.

SP: Thank you, Will.

WG: You're very welcome.

7

_____

Music Technologists in Film and Television

ON OCTOBER 6, 1927, *The Jazz Singer* first graced the silver screen. Al Jolson, widely considered the greatest American entertainer of his day, portrayed a young Jewish man who left his family's traditions to become a singer on the popular stage. While the audience watched the film, they heard several lines of spoken dialog and six songs performed by Jolson. The "talkie" was born, and from that time until now, recorded sound has played a central role in the movies. And whether it is for an independent documentary film, or a movie from one of Hollywood's famous studios, teams of people are responsible for recording, synchronizing, creating, composing, mixing, and performing the sounds and music that help bring drama, excitement, emotion, and realism to moving pictures.

Sound has always been a part of television broadcasts. Based on radio transmission technology, the world first became acquainted with the television at the 1939 World's Fair in New York, but World War II limited widespread manufacturing of the new device. It wasn't until 1948 that regular network programming began to be broadcast. The importance of sound to television programming is evidenced in the fact that musical programs were among the first to be regularly broadcast. In 1948 alone, the NBC Symphony Orchestra, under the direction of Arturo Toscanini, made ten broadcasts from their New York radio studios, which had been newly rebuilt for television. Today, just as with movies, sound is an integral part of television production.

While the audio personnel for a weekly TV show or news program may be focused on production, and the audio personnel working on a film may spend more time in the postproduction process, the jobs in television sound and music are similar. For this reason, film and television jobs will be considered together here. When referring to the film industry, the television industry is also implied.

If you watch the credits at the end of a movie, you will see that the number and types of jobs related to movie music and sound are many and varied. The following are titles of jobs usually seen in a film's sound credits:

Composer, music supervisor, music editor, scoring engineer, orchestrator, sound designer, supervising sound editor, sound mixer, recordist, boom operator, re-recordist, re-recording mixer, dialogue editor, ADR recordist, ADR editor, sound effects editor, Foley artist, Foley recordist, Foley editor.

Some of the job titles you may recognize, such as composer, editor, and mixer, but others may not be familiar, such as Foley artist, or ADR recordist. This chapter will discuss the kinds of jobs for music technologists in the film industry, and describe the skills and preparation necessary for success in these jobs.

Music Jobs

Music has always been a part of the movies. Even before recorded soundtracks were included with films, so-called "silent" films were never really silent. Theaters employed pianists and organists to perform live musical accompaniment for the action on the screen. Sometimes, simple musical scores were provided, but more often, familiar classical repertoire or theater music was played. In some cases, the music was improvised and musicians would follow a cue sheet that was provided with the film telling them when to play suspenseful, romantic, or scary music. Some movie house organs even mimicked the sounds of orchestral and percussion instruments and a few were capable of producing basic sound effects. As early as 1907, the first orchestral film scores were being produced for big-budget feature-length films. Live orchestras were hired to perform these scores in the theaters where the films played. In fact, music was such an integral part of films that during the height of the silent film era in the mid-1920s, movie theaters were the single largest source of employment for instrumental musicians in America.[1]

Music continues to be a critical element in filmmaking today. Many of the jobs related to the recording and preparation of music for films are similar to those in the recording studio. In fact, most original scores are recorded in large music recording studios. The London Philharmonic Orchestra, for example, has recorded scores for literally hundreds of films at the Abbey Road Studios in London. In these studios, audio engineers and mixers prepare the studio for the sessions, select and place microphones, verify inputs and outputs, balance levels, and mix tracks. But additional personnel working as music copyists, score supervisors, orchestrators, and arrangers are required in film music production to satisfy the demanding deadlines, intense work schedules, and time sensitive nature of the process.

Music Supervisor or Supervising Music Editor

The music supervisor is responsible for all musical aspects of the film. This includes selecting prerecorded songs and music to be part of the film and working with a composer to produce the original score. The music supervisor manages all of the details related to preparing the music, from scoring, to recording, to obtaining copyright permissions, to synchronizing the music in the final mix. Most music supervisors are experienced in the world of movie sound, and have worked on numerous projects as a recordist, editor, and mixer.

Composer

Perhaps the most recognizable name in the film's music is the composer of the original score. Names such as John Williams, Hans Zimmer, Danny Elfman, James Horner, and Howard Shore are familiar to most moviegoers. And while these big names have written scores for literally hundreds of films, and many of the most watched movies of all time, there are still thousands of other great composers writing music for movies. The composer works closely with the music supervisor and the supervising sound editor to realize the director's vision for the sound of the movie. The composer often creates musical themes that help identify characters, locations, emotions, and other elements in the film. These themes are then arranged and orchestrated, creating a musical tapestry that helps tell the story of the film.

Historically, film composers may not have needed any specific technical skills beyond the ability to use a pencil and staff paper. However, many modern composers use digital tools to write, orchestrate, and even realize their musical ideas. The speed and ease with which music can be created on the computer gives composers with technology skills a great advantage. While teams of orchestrators and arrangers may work on a *Star Wars*, *Lord of the Rings*, or *Twilight* film, most film composers will start out on much smaller projects that have significantly smaller budgets. A composer who can use technology to copy parts, produce demos, and even record the music can save a film a significant amount of time and money.

Arranger and Orchestrator

On large film projects, arrangers and orchestrators are hired to help composers realize their musical ideas. Writing out all of the parts of a large orchestral score can be tedious and time-consuming work, but in the world of film production, the score often needs to be created very quickly. As one of the last elements to be included in the film, the score often has to be created under extremely tight deadlines. Arrangers and orchestrators must have highly developed music theory and orchestration skills as well as the ability to effectively use modern music scoring software to produce the sheet music that the musicians will perform.

Sound Jobs

Sound Designer

The process of putting sound with pictures begins with the sound designer. This person works closely with the director and producers to determine the sonic character of the film. The sound designer is responsible for assembling all of the elements that will make up the final audio mix, including production dialogue and sounds, sound effects, Foley elements, atmospheres and ambiances, and music. On a small production, the sound designer may be personally responsible for all of these tasks, but on a larger production, they supervise teams of people who will provide these elements. Usually a sound designer is an experienced supervising sound editor, or re-recording mixer with years of experience in the film business. Often they have extensive audio recording, sound effects editing, and musical experience as part of their background.

Production Team

The production team consists of mixers, recordists, and boom operators whose jobs are to ensure that the sound on the set is properly recorded and prepared for later use in the postproduction process.

Recordists and Mixers

Recordists and mixers are responsible for operating sound recording equipment used in the movie studio, and on location with each shoot. They ensure that sound and film recordings are properly synchronized and cataloged so that audio elements can be found and edited after the live filming. They verify signal levels, direct the placement and selection of microphones, and control environmental factors where they can to achieve the best sound possible.

Boom Operators

Since actors can't wear microphones pinned to their lapels while filming a scene, boom operators use long poles with microphones attached to the ends (booms) to capture the dialogue. These recording specialists often use "shot-guns" or highly focused directional microphones that are carefully aimed at the actors during filming. The boom operator wears headphones with a feed from the recordist to make sure the mic is focused properly. They also need to be constantly aware of the camera shots and angles so that the boom and its shadow don't appear in the film. Boom operators can spend hours with a boom pole on their shoulders, crouched on the ground, or in other uncomfortable positions, trying to get the best angle for recording. The boom operator's job is not a glamorous one, but it is critically important.

Postproduction Team

The postproduction team includes editors, mixers, recordists, and artists who work to prepare the final elements of sound for the film. The term "postproduction" comes from the fact that this work is done after filming is completed. In many cases, postproduction work may not even be started until "picture lock" is achieved, meaning that the director or producers have given approval of the picture edit. Sound effects, ambient environments, Foley elements, replaced dialogue, and music are all combined at this point in the process in the "final mix." Depending on the genre, some films may require significantly more sound creation and editing than others. Science fiction and animated films are notoriously sound-intensive and teams of sound personnel can literally spend years in the postproduction process.

Supervising Sound Editor

The supervising sound editor's job is to collect, record, create, compile, process, and edit the sound elements required for the film. This may involve seeking out specific sounds to record, or using real sounds and a combination of synthesis and audio effects to create new sounds. The supervising sound editor works closely with the other sound editors to bring all elements to the re-recording process. The supervising sound editor also consults with the sound designer and director to create a cohesive sound environment for the film.

Sound Effects Editor

The sound effects editor creates or recreates all of the sounds that would naturally occur, or that the viewer would expect to occur in a film scene. This includes "hard" sound effects such as vehicles, doors opening and closing, impacts, machinery, office equipment, swords, guns, arrows, and knives.

It also includes "background" sound effects such as the outdoor environment of a city or park, or the woods, or the inside of a house, or an office, or a cave, or a crowded room. Many of these sounds are recorded live in their natural environment and then included in a film. Postproduction houses often own extensive databases with thousands of sounds carefully cataloged for easy retrieval. Some sounds that do not occur naturally, such as those used in science fiction films, must be designed and created by sound effects editors. These sounds can become recognizable and iconic in their own right. Ben Burtt, who has been designing sounds for the *Star Wars* movies since 1975, has created hundreds of these iconic sounds. One obvious example is the lightsaber; despite the fact that there is no such thing in real life, everyone knows what one sounds like.

Foley

Some sound effects, such as footsteps or other physical actions of an actor, like setting something on a table, the rustling of clothing, a kiss, and so forth, may be too specific to be found in an effects library, and would need to be tediously synchronized with the action in the film. The process to create these sound effects is known "Foley," and the people who create and record them are Foley artists, Foley recordists, and Foley mixers. Jack Donovan Foley (1891–1967) was a well-known sound editor in the 1950s who employed the live performance techniques used in the recording of radio plays to add sounds to movies. This new method of synchronizing sounds brought an added level of realism to films.

Foley artists usually employ a collection of props and materials and work in a specially designed studio where the film can be played on a large screen. The artists will watch the scene, select props, practice the performance, and then have their actions recorded by the Foley recordists. Foley mixers then prepare the sounds for inclusion in the final audio mix.

A careful ear, attention to detail, and a good bit of creativity are required for sound effects work. The recorded sound of an object may be very different from what the audience expects that object to sound like in a film.

ADR

In many instances, the dialogue recorded during filming is not usable for various reasons. There may be too much noise on the set, the signal is too weak, or the inflection of a line is not quite right. For this reason, dialogue is re-recorded in a studio environment and then added back into the film. This process is known as Automated Dialogue Replacement, or ADR. In early films, technicians had to create short loops of the movie's scenes that were then spooled onto projectors. Actors would take repeated attempts performing the lines until a good sync was achieved. Today's digital technology makes this process significantly less tedious, as video can be loaded into digital audio workstations and easily looped for repeated attempts. ADR recordists and mixers are responsible for preparing sections of the film and script that need to be recorded, then recording actors' performances and editing the clips to create a perfect alignment. ADR editors often use specialized digital editing tools in this process. The worldwide distribution of films has increased demand for ADR specialists because foreign language actors are required to record each line of a translated film's script.

Re-recording Mixer

The final step in the process of assembling the sound for a movie is performed by the re-recording mixers. During the final mix, the supervising sound editor, the music supervisor, the director, and others watch the film as the various sound and musical parts are combined. Decisions are made about what works and what doesn't work in the movie's sound and the re-recording mixers create a final soundtrack of the combined elements.

Geography

It has been pointed out in previous chapters that geography can have an impact on success in music technology and this is certainly true for jobs in the film industry. While movies are made in other areas, Los Angeles is the world capital of filmmaking and many LA-area schools have excellent programs that offer great career connections (see Box 7.1).

BOX 7.1

LA Schools

If your dream is to work in the music and sound of films, moving to the LA area to attend college can help you get a head start in the industry. And, while nonresident (out-of-state) tuition is very expensive in some places, tuition at colleges in the California system is among the most affordable in the US. Also, residency can be established in as little as one year. In the end, you can end up paying far less for a college education as a non-resident student in a California school than you might at most private colleges and universities.

The USC and UCLA film and music schools are well known for their successful degree and certificate programs, but there are many other schools in the area as well. One example is California State University, Dominguez Hills, whose digital media arts department features programs in audio recording and music technology. These programs are specifically focused on helping to prepare students for work in television and film. The school offers outstanding internships and boasts an impressive list of graduates who have successfully found work in area studios.

As you can see, there are many different opportunities in film music and sound, and each job requires some specific skills and techniques. However, for the purpose of listing required skills and education, we can group them into some larger categories consisting of jobs with similar skill sets. Here we will consider the necessary preparations for jobs as a composer, mixer, and editor.

Mixer (Music Mixer, Sound Mixer, ADR Mixer, Foley Mixer, Re-recording Mixer)

Specific Technology Skills Required

Hardware:

   Digital and Analog Mixing Consoles: able to route audio through console channels, set input and output levels, control panning, EQ, and onboard effects, record and edit automation, select and control playback monitors and talkback function, manipulate transport controls

   I/O, Sync, Word Clock, and Audio Interface units: able to set up and route audio and MIDI to these devices, manipulate settings, troubleshoot problems

   Patch Bays: able to manage signal flow with proper routing, understand normalled-through, and half-normalled configurations and the use of multi jacks

   Outboard EQ, Compression, Reverb, and Delay units: able to manipulate settings to achieve desired effects

Software:

> Pro Tools: able to route audio signals, manage settings, integrate with hardware devices, set up tracks, perform all recording and editing tasks
>
> Audio Effects Plug-ins: able to effectively use digital audio plug-ins for effects processing
>
> Film Editing Software: Familiar with AVID film products

Suggested Education and Training

> College Degree: BM, BA, BS, or BFA in music technology, audio engineering, or commercial music. Double major or minor in film helpful.
>
> Experience recording and working with video and sound projects.
>
> Internship working in a movie studio, with an independent filmmaker, in a professional recording studio, or in a live sound venue

Editor (production editor, music editor, supervising sound editor, sound effects, Foley, and ADR editors)

Specific Technology Skills Required

Hardware:

> Digital and Analog Mixing Consoles: able to route audio through console channels, set input and output levels, control panning, EQ, and onboard effects, record and edit automation, select and control playback monitors and talkback function, manipulate transport controls
>
> Analog Tape Machines: able to load, enable tracks, record, overdub, punch in and out, and scrub

Software:

> Pro Tools: able to route audio signals, manage I/O and word clock settings, integrate with hardware devices, set up tracks, perform all recording and editing tasks
>
> Logic: able to route audio signals, manage I/O and word clock settings, integrate with hardware devices, set up tracks, perform all recording and editing tasks
>
> Audio Effects Plug-ins: able to effectively use RTAS and AU plug-ins for effects processing, familiar with common settings for instruments and voice appropriate to various musical styles

Suggested Education and Training

College Degree: BM, BA, BS, or BFA in music technology, audio engineering, or commercial music. Double major or minor in film helpful.

Experience recording and working with video and sound projects.

Internship working in a movie studio, with an independent filmmaker, in a professional recording studio, or in a live sound venue

Composer (original score composer, arranger, orchestrator)

Specific Technology Skills Required

Hardware:

Mac and PC computers: able to save, manage, and transfer files, effectively use software (see below), connect to audio interfaces and hardware devices

Software:

Notation Software: Sibelius or Finale music notation software. Familiar with the use of hit points and other time-based plug-ins and utilities.

Software Instrument Plug-ins: able to effectively use software synths to produce high-quality mock ups and demo tracks.

Suggested Education and Training

College Degree: BM, BA, BS, or BFA in music technology, composition, or music theory.

Experience composing music for video projects and films. This could be a part of a student project, or an independent film or theater production.

Internship working in orchestration, score preparation and music production in a TV or movie studio.

Interview with a Professional: Robert Fernandez, Independent Film Scoring Mixer

SP: What is your job as the Scoring Mixer on a film?

RF: I record the music, mix the recordings down into what are called "stems," and then prepare the stems for delivery to the re-recording process.

PHOTO 7.1 Robert Fernandez

The object, as with any recording engineer, is to get the best recording possible.

SP: Where does your work take place and who works with you in this process?

RF: We work on what is called a music stage or a scoring stage. It's a large recording studio that will accommodate an orchestra and many instrumentalists, microphones, cameras, and equipment. In the control room, I work with the music editor, the composer and the composer's assistant, a Pro Tools operator, and a studio assistant. Out on the stage there are usually two additional crew members running headphone mixes, changing microphones, and standing by in case anything goes wrong. The film's music editor will take the mixes that we create to the re-recording stage and then he handles the music from there.

SP: Do you work for a particular studio or a scoring facility?

RF: I work independently now, and have for some time, but I was on the staff at Warner Bros. Studios for twenty-four years, and for sixteen of those years I was their chief engineer on the music stage. In total, I've worked on over six hundred films.

SP: Did you always want to work in the movies?

RF: Film scoring was my goal, always. I never wanted to work in the record business, although I've done quite a few records, and ended up with two Grammys. I've always had this attraction to film music and film scoring specifically. It was something I always wanted to do.

When I started to work at Warner's, I had to begin in the mailroom just to get my foot in the door and to be on the lot. Nearly every day on my mail route I would stop by the sound department secretary's office and ask for a job. Finally one Monday morning, before I could finish my sparring match with the secretary, I heard the words, "You're Hired! Come in here. I want to talk to you!" It was Al Green and he had just been promoted to the head of the Warner Bros. sound department on the previous Friday. I went into his office and he said, "I want anybody that's as persistent as you are working for me." All this time, he had been sitting in his little office off to the side overhearing my conversations with the sound department secretary. I learned that in this business, persistence pays off.

We sat down and talked about what I wanted to do and I said, "I want to record music for motion pictures." He said, "Oh, film scoring. I tell you what, you learn as much about film sound as you can." So I did, and he would quiz me every so often and give me little tests, and finally one day he said, "You're going over to the music stage." That was it. I started off on stage as an assistant working for Danny Wallin, who is probably in his mid-80s now and is still working. He was my mentor and is a phenomenal guy. I think he is probably the best there ever was. His music stands up today. His mixes were phenomenal.

SP: Is the world of scoring mixers a pretty small one?

RF: It used to be a very small world. I started at Warner Bros. when there were five major film studios. Each film studio had a staff scoring mixer. In the case of Warner Bros., we had two. I was the junior mixer for about eight years.

SP: Warner Bros. had only two scoring mixers?

RF: Yes. And that was because they had two stages. The other studios only had one scoring mixer on staff. So basically there were maybe six or seven people in town that worked for studios and did this. There were smaller studios around town that did some film work, and a lot of guys around town that did television stuff, but working on major films, it was just a small group.

Now it is totally different. Because the technology has changed, there are young composers coming in all the time that have a friend that they know, or that knows Pro Tools, and because they are really good at

PHOTO 7.2 A screen shot of the stem layout in Pro Tools for the film *Trouble with the Curve*.

working in the box, all of a sudden they come in and they are a scoring mixer. It doesn't upset me, but it saddens me because those of us who have been doing this for a while, we have a lot of practical acoustical experience working with orchestras, working with live musicians. I'm very good at Pro Tools, you adapt with the technology, but I still have the background to do all of that other stuff. You can put me in front of a hundred-piece orchestra and I won't blink. You can put me in front of a jazz group and it's the same thing.

I always encourage people interested in this to listen to as much live music as possible, but these guys are coming in now without that sort of background. You can't fault them, because that's the job and times have changed. I was fortunate enough to work as an assistant with some of the best producers and engineers ever. That was before I ever started mixing.

Working in the studio as a stage manager you really learned a lot. My duties included setting up the stage and control room for recording, aligning and running the tape machine on record dates and everything else the mixer passed down to me. Those kinds of opportunities don't exist anymore, I'm sad to say. All these young guys coming in would really benefit from that, from having the experience of actually going out there and learning how to set up microphones, learning about microphones, learning about acoustics, learning what the range of an instrument is and what microphone works best on it. I'm a firm believer that using the right microphone on the right instrument means less equalization and fewer problems in the mix. That just comes from knowing what the microphone does and how it sounds on a certain instrument. A lot of guys are not grasping that now. Maybe they are teaching a little bit of it in school, but these schools weren't around when I started. You can learn a lot in school, but there's the practical side when you get out there and you actually learn what to do in a session by watching people.

This is where being an assistant paid off for me. You get to work with a lot of people, you see how they react to situations, you see how they handle it when a problem arises and you see what they do. That can't be taught in school. You can talk about it, but you certainly can't teach a person how to react to various situations.

SP: How important is it to be a musician in your career? Are you a musician?

RF: Yes. I played for years. I finally stopped when I realized I wasn't going to make any money and I needed to eat. Truthfully it was never my goal to be a musician. I was like every other kid growing up who wanted to play in a band, and I did. I did a lot of that stuff. I was a bass player and played electric and upright. I studied with a couple of studio musicians in the area and was leaning towards the jazz/classical side but then played a lot of rock stuff as well. I played with several blues guys and toured around for a while. It was fun, but I never saw myself doing it for the rest of my life. I always wanted to do this. As far back as I can remember I've always been a cinema buff and when a friend told me that there was an opening at Warner's, I jumped at it.

SP: So how important has that musical background been to continuing your career?

RF: It really is very important because it helps you communicate with composers. Imagine trying to communicate with a composer without understanding what they're saying. I always have a score in front of me when I'm recording. You have to have that. I'm constantly making notes in it. I may have to raise something in the score or find a solo, or if they take something out, I circle that so that when I go back and do the mix I'm not looking for it. If we work for five days and record two hours of music, I'm not going to remember every cue, so that's why I have the scores with me. I think it's very important. You don't have to be the best sight-reader, you don't have to be the best musician, but you have to at least have a knowledge of the music and then have a knowledge of the technology. I totally immersed myself in Pro Tools when it came out because I knew where that was going. I have a Pro Tools room here at the house and I do a lot of film mixing here. It's not the biggest room, but it works really well. It is really important to know the music, know the technology, and stay current.

SP: What about these people who are assistants on the stage? Do they want to grow up to be who you are?

RF: Some do. Some don't. Some like being an assistant. When you're sitting in my chair you basically have a lot of pressure on you. When it's my session, if something goes wrong, it's on me. I'm in charge of the session. I always like to surround myself with people who are the best at what they do. I never have to think about what my crew is doing and working at the studios where I work, I'm fortunate to work with the best. The guy who operates Pro Tools for me, he's probably one of the best out there. When you get into my position, you have to surround yourself with people who you feel confident are good at what they do, and they allow you to do what you have to do. I need to deal with the director, deal with the producer, and deal with the composer. When the composer is on the podium, he has to feel totally comfortable and know that he has nothing to worry about because I have his back in there.

But students should get out there and try to find some sort of position in the studio. I did all the jobs that nobody else wanted. That was part of my agreement with the head of the sound department, to learn as much as I could possibly learn. I totally immersed myself in that. When I first started out on the scoring stage, after we would wrap everything up with Danny Wallin, I would stay in the studio and I would reload his tracks onto the tape machine and I would sit there until two o'clock or three o'clock in the morning and just practice. Almost every day I did this. You never know when that moment is going to come. When that moment came for me, I was ready for it.

SP: When did you start mixing?

RF: I was the stage manager at the time that happened. They called me in on Friday and said I wasn't on the stage anymore. I thought about it and I didn't remember doing anything wrong. But they said they wanted to see me in the office right away. So I went up to the office and Al Green, the head of the sound department, was there and Danny was there, and Al said, "Dan thinks it's time for you to become a scoring mixer. But we both feel that in order for you to understand what is required of a scoring mixer, you will need to know what the re-recording stage needs from the music stage. So on Monday you're going to dub stage one and you are going to be working with Walter Goss."

So I show up on Monday morning thinking we're going to have a class, but what they neglected to tell me was that it wasn't a class. Universal Studios had booked that stage for a year to do all of their mini-series' and some television shows. I showed up without any re-recording experience having to start a show that very morning. And it was sweaty palm time, but it turned out fine. Walter Goss sat there in the middle with the dialogue mix, and I was to his right with the music and the sound effects were on his left. He said, "I'll tell you what to do," and he would start shouting instructions to me and by the end of a month we were really good—we were doing a lot of work.

That lasted for about seven or eight months when my first feature film project as the scoring mixer came along. It was a film directed by Paul Schrader, starring George C. Scott and Peter Boyle. I was put on the film because it was not actually an orchestral score. The head of the sound department walks in with the head of music for Columbia Pictures and tells me he needs me on the music stage right away. Jack Nitzsche was the composer and he wasn't really happy with the sound he was getting and was threatening to pull the picture off the stage. He was a very rock-oriented guy. He had worked with The Rolling Stones and other groups like that. The score was very guitar oriented. At the time, I was a lot younger and thinner, and had long hair. They introduced me by the wrong name and told Jack I was the Rock and Roll mixer. You know when you get that feeling that you have been thrown to the lions? Well that was me.

So Jack and I exchanged niceties and shook hands and they left us alone. After we talked, being the former stage manager that I was, I went back to the microphone locker and started getting all the microphones I needed. I changed the microphones on all the drums, changed the microphones on the guitars, and started putting in compressors and equalizers. After the first rehearsal, he was in love with it. That was my first film, and I just stayed on the music stage from then on. During that time, not only would I record the score for the whole film, but then I would go to the re-recording stage and do that too. I went on to work on *Ghostbusters* and a lot of other really great projects. It was really fun. I even went on to work on three more films with Jack Nitzsche.

My first real serious orchestral score was a session that I walked into that Danny was starting. I had watched him record orchestras, and I'd assisted him on many orchestral sessions, but I never sat in that chair. So when I walked in that morning, from recording a solo guitar track for the *Dukes*

PHOTO 7.3 Robert Fernandez mixes the score of a Disney animated feature at the Warner Bros Studios in Burbank, CA.

of Hazard, he turned to the producer and said, "Do you mind if Bob does this session? I'm not feeling very well." And I said, "What?" And that was it. A fifty-piece orchestra right there and it went as smoothly as it could.

SP: Do you remember what the project was?

RF: It was a 1978 television mini-series called, "Little Mo."

SP: You've had quite a good run of it, haven't you?

RF: I have and I've enjoyed it. It's been a terrific ride. I always feel that I've been blessed to be in the position that I'm in; to have had the career— to still have the career that I have. I left Warner Bros. in 1994. The stage was being shut down for renovation. They had no idea how long it was going to take, but they thought maybe three to five years. Even with the retainer they offered me, I knew that if I sat there nobody would know who I was by the next day. I decided to go independent at that point. But on my way home from work that last day, I had this panic attack for about thirty seconds. For the first time in twenty-four years I had no place to go on Monday and I didn't have a steady paycheck. I thought, "Well, if the phone rings, great, and if it doesn't, I'll deal with it." Well the phone rang like crazy. In the first year, in 1995, I did so many projects I couldn't believe it. I was in London all of the time, and I was all over the place and I was just so busy it was amazing. I couldn't have asked for a better scenario. It turned out really well. I have kept my relationships up with the people I worked with at Warners, like Clint Eastwood, for example. I've worked on every film of his for the past thirty years.

SP: What are the greatest challenges in your line of work?

RF: You really have to get the recording and the mix right. That is the most difficult part. If you get the recording done right, then the mix is easier. Also, sometimes getting along with people is tricky, depending on who you are working with. Some people are difficult to please and you can mix something a hundred times for them. All you can do is make the mix sound as good as possible, and then let the composer make the final decision. Sometimes you aren't happy with it, but you didn't write the music.

SP: What advice do you have for young people interested in this field?

RF: I would encourage young people to get out there and listen to as much music as possible. Expose yourself to all that stuff and don't put blinders on yourself and say, "Well, I only listen to this." If you go downstairs in my room, there's got to be two or three thousand CDs down there and it pretty much covers everything from Jazz to Classical and beyond.

When I'm approached to do a film and the composer talks to me about what the music is going to be like, if I'm not familiar with that genre, I immediately go and I buy up all the CDs that I think I'll need, and I come home and sit there and immerse myself in that music just to get the feel and wrap my head around what that genre is all about. You need to do that. Listen to everything.

It's also a good idea to be an assistant or to come into the studio and find someone who will let you follow them around, to find someone who will mentor you. The entire film studio structure has changed. It's gone from being a few major studios to being so many independent companies now. Warner, Fox, Sony, those studios have guys on staff, and those jobs are highly prized, and there would be a thousand guys in line for that job if they heard it was opening up. But you can find a small studio somewhere, and get in there and learn as much as you can. When you're in that position, you listen to everybody, and listen to what's going on. I learned that when assisting other people to try to remember as much as I could. At some point in time you're going to need to call on that in order to get you through something. Find what you want to do and put yourself in that direction. You may find out while you're doing it that you don't really like it and you want to do something else.

Get out there and get yourself into the studio or follow somebody around that knows what they're doing. It's important that they know what they're doing because you don't want to pick up bad habits. When I was assisting and I was put in all these sessions with all these other engineers and producers, I learned what to do as well as what not to do. You can learn a lot from someone that's a jerk and doesn't know what they're doing, because you learn what you don't want to do.

SP: What is the process you go through when you are mixing the score for a film?

RF: When I get called to work on a film, whether it's with a composer that I've worked with in the past or it's someone new, what I like to do is to have a meeting with them and talk about what their approach to the score is. We'll look at the film, and we'll talk about the sound we want, and the approach to recording we will use. We decide if we're going to do it all live, or if we're going to have overdubs, and we talk about what's involved in the actual music for the film. We also discuss how the stems will be separated out. Once that's all decided, then we get the recording sessions set up, and we bring in any prerecorded tracks from the composer's studio that need to be added into the score. From there we head over to the music stage and we start recording.

You deliver music in stems to the re-recording studio; the dub stage. You may have an orchestra stem, a piano stem, a choir stem, a vocal solo, and so on. Once you determine what the number of stems is going to be, and what you want to separate out, you mix those stems for the dub stage.

SP: Can you explain more about what a stem is and how you and the composer decide what stems to create?

RF: Stems are audio files that contain groups of instruments that we have mixed together with their own effects, their own reverb, and their own sub-bass channel. My recommendation is that when mixing the score, you work with a group of instruments that create a certain sound and you put those together. You don't want to take a risk that the balance that you've created on the mix stage is lost. So you want to mix instrument groups in a stem. Each of the stems should be able to stand on their own. What happens on the dub stage is that the director will listen to the music and decide if there are parts of the sound that he may want to raise or lower, depending on the scene. The stems allow the re-recording mixer to re-balance around anything that they need. When you get the music to the dub stage, you're playing against dialogue, you're playing against sound effects, and that's where the fight between music and sound effects and dialogue plays out. Of course dialogue is king and always wins.

I personally don't like the music or effects too loud, because I don't think they serve a purpose that way. If you have a director who is really aware of this stuff and has great taste in this, you're going to get a really good mix where the music plays where it has to play, and the effects play where they have to play. Obviously, in a movie like *Transformers*, it's all effects. I just finished a Clint Eastwood film directed by Rob Lorenz called *Trouble with the Curve*. It's a really good story, but that's a film with a lot of dialogue and the music plays well with that. There are places where the music can really take off, there are these grand moments, but for the most part, the music just sits underneath as an underpinning to support the dialogue. You have to be very aware of the dialogue. No matter how great you might think the music mix is, dialogue is king. Music in a film is subservient to the dialogue and you have to keep that in mind.

A cue is a piece of music in a film that is written for a specific scene. If you're not in a time crunch, what I like to do is go through the score with the music editor and identify all the cues that are similar in terms of instrumentation or setup. They may not be in the same reel, but we will mix cues that are similar. Once I get that sound up on the console, then I don't have to do much tweaking on it but a little balance and EQ maybe. So we finish all that and then we go to the next group of cues that are similar in sound.

SP: Is there a challenge related to the fact that a lot of your work happens near the very end of the project?

RF: When we are up against the clock we don't have the luxury of arranging similar cues and we just start on reel one and go all the way to the end of the film in order. We'll have someone there running the mixes in to the dubbing stage as we finish them. We've had times when we had to stay up late that evening of the first day to prep for the second day, because of music coming in late. But we usually get that done and I've never missed a deadline. Sometimes we're there around the clock prepping for the session and getting it ready, but when ten o'clock comes the next day, we go in and nobody's the wiser that we were there until six o'clock in the morning. It all gets done. When I was working on *Spiderman 3*, we were at the Sony stage and they were dubbing in the theater next to us. As they were going late, although we had finished all of the music, the head of the music department wanted us to stay there because they weren't sure if they were going to have any changes. We basically sat there for two days without leaving just in case there was something that needed to be remixed.

SP: What is the best thing about what you do?

RF: The fact is that I get to work with the best musicians in the world. Something interesting about being in L.A. is that if you had a one hundred-piece orchestra session at Fox, Sony, and Warner's on the same day, you could fill them up with people who can play. You can't do that in Seattle and you can't even do that in New York. Maybe I'm prejudiced, but I think these guys are the best in the world at what they do. That's not to take away from anybody else, and those other areas have great musicians too, but L.A. has a much larger pool to draw from. These musicians come in and they see the music for the first time, and a lot of the film music can be very difficult. They come in and they can lay it down on the first take. They are phenomenal sight-readers. So to be able to be a session musician on a film date in L.A. you really have to be at the top of your game. I love these guys. People ask about my job, and I say, "What, are you kidding? I sit here and I listen to the best musicians in the world play music every day. What could be bad about that?" And I love the music. I just love film music.

SP: Do you have a favorite score?

RF: I can't really say. There are so many wonderful scores that I've done and it's like picking which of your children you love the most. I love what I do so much that when I'm working on a score, I immerse myself in that moment. There are some scores that are clearly better than others, but I adopt the attitude that the film I'm working on at that moment is the best film I've ever worked on.

SP: Thank you very much.

RF: You're welcome.

Note

1. Scott Eyman, *The Speed of Sound: Hollywood and the Talkie Revolution, 1926–1930* (New York: Simon & Schuster, 1997), 26.

8

Music Technologists in Digital Media

Digital: dig·it·al/'dijitl/
Adjective:

1. Relating to or using signals or information represented by discrete values (digits) of a physical quantity,
2. Involving or relating to the use of computer technology

We live in a digital world and whether we think about it or not, we almost always experience music using computers, MP3 players, handheld devices, cell phones, and game consoles. Even when one considers nondigital musical experiences, such as attending a live classical music concert or recital, digital technology has played an important part: from the sheet music that was digitally created, to the instruments that were built and calibrated using computer technology, to the performance being recorded digitally. Today, music is almost always created, recorded, performed, shared, and enjoyed through digital means. Music technologists are needed to write the codes and program the devices that make all of this possible.

Software Developer

Software development is a diverse field in which programmers, developers, and designers create the digital tools that we all use. The field has grown exponentially since the first computers were being built in the late 1950s. By the early 1960s, computer science pioneers such as Joseph F. Traub, George Forsythe, William F. Miller, and Allen Newell were fighting to create the country's first academic computer science programs at Stanford, Carnegie Mellon, Columbia, Berkeley, and MIT. They hoped to establish the computer science discipline, but it is unlikely they could have foreseen today's incredible demand for computer scientists. In an oral history recorded by the University of Minnesota's Charles Babbage Institute, Joseph F. Traub reflected on the incredible growth of these programs. He states, "Now practically every major university in the country has a computer science department."[1] That statement was made in 1985 and in the 27 years since, thousands of computer programmers have entered the workforce.

Today, some think that the demand for professionals with computer programming skills has weakened in the United States. They cite the collapse of the dot-com bubble in 2000 and the practice of widespread outsourcing by computer companies to programmers in foreign countries. However, the need for computer programmers in the US continues to grow. In 2010 there were 1.58 million jobs in software development, computer programming, and web design in the United States alone.[2] The latest report from the Bureau of Labor Statistics predicts that the number of these jobs will increase by more than 384,000 in the next eight years. The strongest sector of that growth is anticipated among software developers, with an expected increase of 30 percent by 2020.[3] And while music software and devices only make up a small portion of the digital world, programmers with musical skills are in high demand to create software, build websites, and provide media for an ever-expanding digital universe.

Computer programmers and software developers can find work in many different musical settings. Perhaps the most obvious job for a programmer is writing code for a software company. In music, software companies create and sell products for audio recording, sound design, audio effects, synthesis, sampling, live performance, notation, and education. But also, there is a world of digital audio hardware products from electric pianos, to sound consoles, to audio interfaces that require programming.

The line between software companies and hardware companies is becoming increasingly blurry. Many audio software companies now also sell hardware for music production. Native Instruments, for example, the German-based company whose Kontakt player is one of the most successful software samplers, has expanded its product line to include audio interfaces and control surfaces for DJing and live performance. Long-standing synthesizer manufacturers such as Yamaha and Korg also sell software synthesizers and with a digital audio workstation, musicians can play virtual versions of these popular keyboard instruments through a computer. Pro Tools, a pioneer in digital audio recording software and the industry standard, has been marketed with Digidesign's own proprietary audio interfaces. With the acquisition of

Digidesign by Avid, the products become part of one of the largest audio and video software and hardware conglomerates in the world. The company currently employs thousands of programmers to develop and expand their extensive line of audio and video products for the film, television, recording, and live sound industries.

Getting the Job

Box 8.1 contains a posting from the "Careers" page of Avid's website. This was one of over twenty open positions for software developers that appeared on the site during the month of July, 2012.

BOX 8.1

Job Posting

Market Title: Full Time Senior Software Engineer
Location: Daly City, California
Job Description: We are looking for a talented, creative, enthusiastic, Senior Software Engineer to join Digidesign's VENUE live sound engineering team. Since its launch six years ago, Digidesign's VENUE live sound environment has quickly become the new standard for major touring acts and installations around the globe. Artists including U2, Dave Matthews Band, Jay-Z, John Mayer, Paul McCartney, Tom Petty, Dixie Chicks, Barbra Streisand, and many others rely on VENUE to convey their live performances on a daily basis.

As a Senior Software Engineer, you will be responsible for creating, debugging, and maintaining C++ applications running on the Windows Embedded operating system. While your exact tasks will vary widely according to project requirements, typical tasks may include creating new features in our multi-threaded, real-time application, writing Windows UI code using our application framework, and contributing to the overall architectural design of future live sound products.

To join our high-performing team, you must have an in-depth understanding of software engineering and object-oriented design techniques, the ability to create, debug, and maintain bulletproof C++ code, an eye for detail, and extremely high standards with respect to software quality and reliability.

Specifically, we are looking for a person who meets the following requirements:

> BS degree and 5 years of experience, or MS degree and 3 year of experience.
> Degree in Electrical Engineering, Computer Engineering, or Computer Science.
> Experience programming multi-threaded Windows applications in C++.
> Experience designing and implementing object oriented software designs.
> Demonstrated ability to debug complex software systems.
> Excellent written and spoken English.

In addition, the strongest candidate will have one or more of the following:

> Experience in music and/or audio.
> Experience in system programming for audio, video, or multimedia applications.
> Experience programming real-time applications.
> Experience programming user interfaces with an industry standard GUI toolkits.

From the job description you will notice that Avid values musical and audio experience as well as software programming skill. This attitude is a major part of Avid's company philosophy. Notice the following statement on the "About Avid" page of their website: "Like our customers, we are artists and industry experts. Storytellers. Musicians. Composers. Filmmakers. Students. Videographers. Producers. Sound mixers. DJs. More than 50% of our employees have professional backgrounds in audio and video, and more than 70% use Avid products outside of the workplace. We draw on this knowledge to advance the development of digital audio and video technology in a way that helps our customers achieve their creative vision—however they define it."[4]

Suggested Education and Training

> College Degree: BA or BS in music technology with a computer science emphasis or a BA or BS in computer science with a music technology emphasis
> Experience working with digital audio tools, such as DAWs, software synthesizers, effects, and other programs. Experience programming using C++ to create, test, and debug software.
> Internship working in digital audio, sound design, software development

Video Game Sound Designer

One of the most exciting and rapidly expanding fields of software development is in the area of computer and video games. Here are some interesting facts about the gaming industry as reported by the Entertainment Software Association.[5]

America's entertainment software industry creates a wide array of computer and video games to meet the demands and tastes of audiences as diverse as our nation's population. Today's gamers include millions of Americans of all ages and backgrounds. This vast audience fuels the growth of this multi-billion dollar industry and helps bring jobs to communities across the nation. Below is a list of...entertainment software industry facts:

Consumers spent $24.75 billion on video games, hardware and accessories in 2011.

Purchases of digital content accounted for 31 percent of game sales in 2011, generating $7.3 billion in revenue.

The average U.S. household owns at least one dedicated game console, PC or smartphone.

The average game player is 30 years old and has been playing games for 12 years.

Sixty-two percent of gamers play games with others, either in-person or online.

Thirty-three percent of gamers play games on their smartphones, and 25 percent play games on their handheld device.

There can be no question that the gaming industry is a huge business employing thousands of computer programmers. And today's games rely on audio like never before. In the past, MIDI sounds were programmed on 8-bit systems to play in response to player actions and game events, but modern technology allows for the synchronization of high-quality audio samples. The sound design required for most games is similar in complexity and depth to that of a major motion picture and sound effects, Foley, ADR, and music mixing techniques are used (see Chapter 7 for definitions). In fact, it is not uncommon to see the names of film sound designers and special effects editors among the credits of popular video games.

In addition, there is an ever-expanding music game genre. Titles like Guitar Hero, Rock Band, and others have made music the subject of the game as well as part of the content. Some of the most cutting edge music technology is currently being developed for use in video games. For example, the game developer Ubisoft recently released Rocksmith, the first Guitar Hero-style game that allows the player to use a real guitar as the controller.

Getting the Job

Although sound designers for the games industry use many of the same skills and perform many of the same tasks as sound designers for film and television, the industry still relies on computer programmers to fill most of these positions. To land a job working in the audio department of one of the many video game companies, the successful candidate has to have a combination of sound design experience and computer programming skills and knowledge. The ability to write code and program in C++, as well as Wwise, FMOD, and Unreal are common requirements. Box 8.2 contains a listing for a job opening at LucasArts that is a good example.

BOX 8.2

Job Posting

Title: Full Time Audio Lead
Location: San Francisco, CA
Description: The Audio Lead is responsible for the delivery and quality of all in-game audio.

Lead the "audio vision" for an internal title and collaborate with the project's Creative Director to effectively execute on that vision. Lead your team in the creation and implementation of high quality audio content, ensuring all audio assets meet the creative and technical expectations of a LucasArts title.

Manage and direct your team to ensure their work is timely, on budget and of the highest quality.

Supervise the specification of the audio engine, the asset pipeline, and the integration of audio assets.

Coordinate with the Director of Audio and Production to create audio production schedules, budgetary projections and allocate resources to best meet the needs of your project and those of the studio.

Demonstrate positive working relationships within the department and with the development teams, emphasizing clear communication and disseminating your shared vision, both creatively and technically.

Participate in Audio Department operations as needed, such as equipment setup and troubleshooting, archiving sound effects, network and database maintenance, engineering recording sessions, etc.

Requirements

College degree in related field preferred. Musical and/or recording studio proficiency a plus.

Minimum 7 years experience leading an audio team on AAA titles.

Knowledge and expertise in professional Macintosh audio systems and applications, such as several of the following: Pro Tools, Digital Performer, Peak, etc. Excellent troubleshooting skills on Macintosh-based audio systems required.

Knowledge and expertise in Wwise, FMOD, and Unreal.

Knowledge of Windows based software, including pro audio software and the ability to learn proprietary game development applications.

Extensive knowledge and expertise in audio recording, field recording, processing, and mixing.

Excellent troubleshooting skills with pro audio hardware and computer-based audio systems required.

Excellent organization and communication skills. Proven ability to manage a large volume of audio data accurately and efficiently, and to work well as part of a team in a fast-paced, high pressure environment.

Knowledge of MS Word, MS Excel, MS Windows and at least one database application, such as FileMaker Pro or SoundMiner, required. Knowledge of batch processing tools and production tools such as Hansoft and Perforce very helpful.[6]

Suggested Education and Training

College Degree: BA or BS in music technology with a computer science emphasis or a BA or BS in computer science with a music technology emphasis

Experience working with digital audio tools, such as DAWs, software synthesizers, effects, and other programs. Experience programming using C++ to create, test and debug software.

Internship working in digital audio, sound design, software development

Interview with a Professional: Peter Lee, Cofounder and Co-owner, Rising Software, Melbourne, Australia

SP: What is Rising Software?

PL: Rising Software is a company that makes two software titles: *Auralia*, which is ear-training software, and *Musition*, which is music theory software.

SP: Can you give me a little history of how your company got started?

PL: Sure. I finished high school in 1993. I actually did two senior years of high school, and you can do that in Australia. It's not because I failed things, but because I wanted to hedge my bets as to whether I was going to do computer science or music. The structure in Victoria, which is the state of Australia where Melbourne is located, allows you to do subjects over a couple of years if you want. I did more subjects than most people so that I could do all of the math and science as well as the music subjects. The reason for that was that I had played piano since I was five, and I wasn't really that good at it, because I didn't practice like a lot of people, but I started singing when I was about 16. I enjoyed it and I thought I might do the music thing in college. The high school that I went to is significant, Blackburn High School. It's just a regular public school, but it had a very

PHOTO 8.1 Peter Lee

big music program. It was a beacon school for music so if you were a sax player and you lived 20 kilometers away, you could get special allowance to go to the school to be in the ensembles. Now I happened to go there just because I lived around the corner. I didn't do any music at school until my junior year of high school. So I didn't know if I wanted to study music or computer science and I decided to do both subjects in high school, and then I would make a decision somewhere down the track. As it turned out, I chose music, so I started a bachelor of music in 1994 at the University of Melbourne, in classical voice.

During my last year of high school, as part of one of the music subjects, there was a really difficult aural, or ear-training exam. It was so hard that it was like nothing else that they had ever had in the curriculum before. Teachers were stressed out and there were very few resources. This is back in the days when we had cassette tapes. If you wanted to practice aural skills, your teacher would go ahead and use their little recorder and put it up on the piano and play some intervals and record them. Then they would hand out these cassette tapes for everybody and you would take them home and then theoretically you could learn aural skills. So a friend of mine named Hamish, who is still one of the shareholders in the business, and myself, we thought we could write a computer program that would help people out. And so that is when we wrote Auralia version 1.

SP: Really?

PL: That's how it happened. And it was very primitive, but it did intervals and chords, and basic chord progressions, and it did rhythms. It still works in Windows 7 if you run it in administrative mode. So that's the only reason we actually did this. There was no sort of, genius idea that we're going to make millions of dollars, which we don't anyway. It was just out of personal need. So we sold it to our school, and we sold it to another couple of schools. Within about 12 months we got a distributor because there was a big need for it around the country. We got distribution with Intelliware in Australia. They were representing Passport Designs back then, the makers of "Encore" and "MusicTime" and "Master Tracks Pro." They took us on board and it was just a distribution arrangement. It was nothing fancy. They would buy it from us and sell it to resellers. That means that instead of us lugging around the computer, and literally we lugged around a computer and a monitor in my dad's car as we went to schools to demonstrate it. So, instead of doing that, we had resellers to do some of that for us. This happened in 1994–95. We were both at the University and Hamish was doing computer science and I was doing music. In 1997 we brought on

Tim Wilson. He's a jazz sax player, and he's one of the shareholders now and still works in the business. So that's how we started.

SP: Then you were very young when you created that first version.

PL: Yeah. We were in high school. We've been doing it a long time now.

SP: At what point did the distribution start to go outside of Australia?

PL: I think I attended the NAMM show for the first time in 1996. We went over there with Intelliware, and they introduced us to all the distributors of the Passport Designs products, so we just started to distribute via them in a lot of countries. Then there was a company called Thinkware that was more of a channel industry name, and they were a distributer for a lot of brands back then, Roland ended up owning them after they sold out. They represented us in the US for quite a while, up until 2003. So we probably started exporting in 1997.

SP: And at that point, you're a 22 or 23-year-old guy and you are distributing a music software title internationally. That's pretty remarkable.

PL: For whatever reason, we always knew that if we're going to do anything with the program, it had to go outside of Australia, because the market was just too small. And we really didn't imagine that it would turn into what we do today. It just kind of kept on going. And we went to universities in our hometown, so we had the luxury during that time of having our food paid for, and we didn't have rent. So it's not like the business itself was really sustainable, and we weren't drawing money out of it. It was just sort of trickling along and supporting itself. The decision whether it was going to be something more significant came a little bit later in 1999. When we were finishing at the university we had to ask, "What comes next?"

When I got to the university, I still wasn't sure about the whole music thing so I enrolled in three degrees. I enrolled in a double Bachelor of Arts/ Bachelor of Science so I could do my computer science in that, and I also enrolled in a Bachelor of Music. The university didn't care, they would let me do anything that I wanted to. As it turned out, it was just too much. I would've been there forever, and at the end of five years I was thinking that I need to get out of there. To finish the computer science degree, or the Bachelor of Arts degree as well, I would've just been there for too long. So I cashed out all of the credits from those degrees and put them in my music degree. I got credit for them and I ended up with a Bachelor of Music. In hindsight, I probably should have gotten the Bachelor of Science as well.

SP: Essentially what you did was you created for yourself a music technology degree. Today there are Bachelor of Science degrees that have courses in computer science and courses in music. You figured out how to get the skills and the training in both areas that you really wanted whether or not you graduated with all those degrees. Today, someone would hopefully be able to find a music technology program that would combine those two elements. There are degrees out there like that.

PL: I didn't have the time to do as many computer science or math subjects as I wanted to, because they were so time-consuming. Remember, we were trying to run the business at the same time. There was a bit of travel and other business, and you have to work really hard in those subjects.

SP: What is your role in the company now?

PL: To give you a little bit of context, we were distributing with those people all around the world until about 2003. At that time we came to an arrangement with Sibelius in the UK, who took over distribution of our products, and that was really good. We could travel a whole lot less and focus on development. It was just a much better arrangement overall. So that continued until Sibelius got purchased by Avid in 2006. Things remained in the status quo for a while, and then there was a huge reorganization at Avid, and things changed a little bit, but at the end of the day, we're still distributing with Sibelius. Once we started with Sibelius, we were able to focus a lot more on development. But that has changed in the last couple of years. I have to travel a lot more now, supporting dealers and going to shows and all that stuff, but there's only so much we can do.

So I run the company now, and we're not big. We're about four and a half to five people. It's not a mega operation. We don't all drive 7 Series BMWs or anything like that. Yes we're a global product, but it's a global product in a really niche market. So my current role now is a mix of things. It's a small business so I do all sorts of stuff. I do the accounts, which I probably shouldn't do. I should probably get someone else to do that, but there's not really enough to warrant someone else, so I do that. Between Tim and myself, Hamish is not involved so much right now, he's involved more on the back end of the server things, and has some other things that he is doing, but he does a little work for us, and that's fine, it's a completely amicable relationship.

All of the original shareholders after twenty years still get along, which is amazing. We socialize and it's all sort of fairly good, really. There are a lot of opportunities where things can go bad. So in terms of what I do, I do accounting stuff, and I handle some support cases. We have support people, but there is still some stuff, like the networking, that I understand better than anyone else, so I do that. Between Tim and myself, I guess the most important thing we do is product direction. We have to decide what features are going to be in, which features are going to be out. We probably have a pretty good track record of getting the feature set right. We aim for a major release every three to four years, which is a fairly long lifecycle. And we generally have an internal release that's a free upgrade in between. So we had version 3 in 2005, I think we added 3.5 in 2007. We had version 4 in 2010, which was a major exercise. We revamped everything for Mac and Windows, cross-platform code base, and that was an enormous change. And we've just released 4.5, which is our half-lifecycle free update for people. The major difference is that we've added the cloud feature, which is a separate license.

So in terms of product direction, that's probably the most important thing to do. I still write code, but I don't write nearly as much as I used to. We've got a long-term contractor who does a lot of that, but I'm still in there. I'm not the best programmer in the world but I'm okay. I have a fairly good understanding of how to structure things, but if you set me down in a room with a bunch of C++ gurus, I may come last. But that's not a big concern.

At the stage where we are at now, yes I can do all programming things, but it's really the direction of the product that's really important. The combined roles of the product design, and also the customer outreach, like doing shows, and visiting dealers and all that kind of stuff is immensely time-consuming and very expensive. It's not always about the results you get there on that day. You learn a lot of stuff at these things and understand how the market works, and also what the needs of the customer are. It's important for me to do that and to hear from them. I'm actually quite happy to go to shows and talk to people and understand what their day-to-day needs are. Also I do a whole mix of things including marketing and vision of what we're going to do. And we have stepped that up. It's always surprising to meet musicians who have never heard of our product. But unless you have limitless funds, you can't tell everybody. It's very, very hard.

SP: Where did you learn to program computers so that by 19 years old, you were creating software?

PL: My dad bought us a computer when I was in the eighth or ninth grade and I tinkered in QuickBasic 4.5, I think, which came on four floppy disks, if memory serves. And it was all just self-taught. If you look back at the original code, you can see that, and Hamish as well. None of that original code was very good, but it didn't really matter. It was the concept that mattered. The idea was good, the product was good, and in many respects, not under the surface but in terms of user interaction, the product still works very similarly to the very first version. It's not too different. We don't get very many complaints about how the product works. It's very clear, it's logical, it's simple to get in and out of things, and that design decision, for whatever reason, has worked out.

SP: So with all of these many roles, talk if you will about what your life is like.

PL: Well, there's some social information that's part of this. Now that I'm 37, I don't go to the pub three nights a week anymore. I have two kids, a two-and-a-half year-old, and a five-and-a-bit year-old. So my schedule is ridiculously busy, but it's probably no busier than anybody else who has two young kids and is trying to manage working and all that stuff. We all work from home. We don't have any need for offices, but having young kids and working at home is exceptionally difficult and I work a lot of late nights.

On an average day, I will get up at 6:30 or 7 o'clock with the kids. I muck around with the kids and do breakfast with them until about 8:30 or so, when it's time for me to go into my own little hole and start to work. In the morning, there's a lot of communication. I send a lot of emails and that's a real drag because a lot of the time, I feel that my real work should be working on the product. Thinking about the product and writing code. And it's really hard when you're multitasking. Multitasking small jobs is really quite easy; you have your list and you just tick things off. But writing code, it's not that easy to just jump into it for an hour. It doesn't work that way. And when you've got a whole lot of things on your plate, it's hard to get that stuff done. You can spend a lot of time keeping up with your email, and it's full of important correspondences, but sometimes, I just ignore it.

So the day continues. Now that we have the cloud solution, I'll check on the health of all of our cloud services, make sure that they're all up and running if I haven't got any text messages saying they're not working. There might be phone calls and people I need to talk to. I generally tend to have a pretty clear week in terms of meetings. I tend not to schedule a lot of that sort of thing because a lot of it can be a real waste of time. I try not to leave the house for silly things, because you get in the car and drive somewhere and it takes a half an hour to get there and another half an hour to do something and then half an hour to come back and there's an hour and a half gone, and it's all dead.

And then I'll probably have lunch about 12. Lunch is generally at the desk. I may read the newspaper, or something like that, but I'll work through until about five or so when it's dinnertime. I'll start again, or at least for the last eight to twelve months I have, at around 7 PM. I might watch an hour or so of television with my wife, but lately we've had so much to do that I just have to start working again. So realistically I'm working three hours the morning, and then I work in the afternoon, and I'll come back in the evening to do more. I don't know how many hours that is, and it's not all one hundred percent efficiency, don't get me wrong. I'm as susceptible as anyone else to reading an article about some gadget that I don't need. I think that's just normal life. But I try pretty hard to keep focused because we have a lot to do with a fairly small team. The business is growing and it's hard to juggle all of it. To compound things, there is often the need to stay up late because most of our customers are in America. Melbourne is fourteen hours ahead of New York and seventeen hours ahead of Los Angeles. If you want to chat with Americans you have to chat with them when it's convenient for them. That may be in the middle of the night here and I get that; it's reality.

SP: How much of your business is overseas?

PL: Most of our business is overseas—Australia is too small a market to survive in.

SP: That must involve a lot of traveling on your part.

PL: This trip is number three so far this year, and it's only July. I probably travel three to five times each year.

SP: When you go overseas, is it just flying to the United States? Or are you going to the United States, Great Britain, New Zealand, Asia and so forth?

PL: It depends on the trip. This trip is just in and out. I'm just in the US, talking with a few key customers, attending some meetings, and so forth. Inter-Asia is pretty easy, for an Australian anyway. It's not fourteen or fifteen hours, so you can do an overnight trip, and that works, and you don't eat up as much time. When you go to the US, you've got a day on either end of travel. When you have a family, it's not much fun being by yourself on the road. When I make trips, I usually stay in one region. Occasionally on the way back from the US, I might go to Hong Kong or something like that instead, but it really depends on what you need to achieve. Most trips are generally a combination of tradeshow appearances with other stuff. Occasionally, if we have some key customers, I might just go and see a key customer, for whatever reason.

SP: Is traveling like this pretty glamorous?

PL: No. Frequent travel is just very tiring and I don't think it matters what part of the plane you are in. Even if you sleep on the plane, it's still tiring.

And to avoid jet lag, you just don't go to sleep when it's daytime. When you arrive in the day, you just stay awake, push through, drink coffee and Coke, and you'll be alright. Some people might disagree with me, but it's just really tiring.

So like on this trip, for example, I went from Melbourne to LA, which is about eight hours or so, then from LA to Dallas and there was a three-hour wait. Then Dallas to Orlando, and I stayed two days in Orlando, and then flew to Boston for a couple of days there. Then down to New York City. I'll stay here for a couple of days and then fly home. It's not glamorous. It would be glamorous if you flew business-class once a year and stayed in really fancy hotels. That's glamorous, sure. And if you don't have that much to do it's not bad. Maybe you go to a conference and then go out to dinner and drinks and have fun. But when you're working the booth, it's really hard work. You're standing up all day smiling at people and talking. That's hard.

SP: What do you think is the best part of running your own company?

PL: The best part is having control over the product. It's really nice. And I don't have to answer to anyone, really. Our success has really been due to ourselves. And we've had a lot of help along the way, and a whole lot of luck. And I do enjoy seeing customers who use the product really well, and you see the results. It's really good to see that you've created something, and it does X, Y, and Z, and you've got it right, and they can use it, and it's really effective, and they enjoy using it. Sometimes you don't really hear about much of that. It's one of the good things about traveling and getting to see clients.

So having control of the product is great, and having the flexibility in my life is really nice, with the kids. A lot of people wouldn't have dinner with their kids every night. I do. I get to hang around during the day and that's nice 'cause the kids are great, and having that is good. But that's a very unique situation and I would be very reluctant to give that as an expectation to other people. That happens because I work from home. I don't know that I would recommend working from home, even if you do open your own business. I do it because I don't want to rent an office for twenty grand a year. And I don't want to commute all the time. But working at home has its challenges.

SP: What other challenges do you face with running your own company?

PL: All the usual stuff: money issues can be a challenge. We all invested like five dollars into this business at the start and everything has been generated out of that. We haven't had bank loans or anything. We're fairly stable. It's nice in the way that we don't owe the bank money, and we don't owe some venture capital guys money who don't care about us, but it does mean there's a lot of stress along the way. Which is fine when you're living at home and you're at the University, but when you have to buy a house and you've got dependents, it all gets a bit more serious.

SP: Can someone start their own software company today?

PL: I think it's absolutely possible for someone to get into it today. You've got to have a really good idea. There are all sorts of web start-up money and all that, where you have a great idea and you ask people to put money in. It's a very different situation than it was twenty years ago. But having said that, the market is a lot more global now than it was then. So if you do have a new idea, and you're not an established player, it may be hard to break in and compete. Things are moving so fast. Remember Myspace? It's kind of gone now. And Facebook? How many billions have they made, but I don't know if they'll be around in five years' time. They'll be around, in some way, shape, or form, but who knows if people will be interacting with their site in the same way that they do today?

SP: Could you have predicted, 20 years ago, what your career would be now, or what you would be doing?

PL: Not at all. We never planned for any of this. We seriously wrote the pro-gram for ourselves, and then it just kind of got bigger, and bigger, and bigger. And you know, we were lucky. We've worked with some good peo-ple along the way. Some of our resellers in Australia are very intelligent people; people that I still hang out with today. They helped nurture the product and actually gave us a chance. And the same is true with the peo-ple at Sibelius. Sure, the product's good, but there are a whole lot of things that go into it: timing, luck, and other things. And there are a lot of people who have provided good advice. Having said that, most of the decisions we've made have turned out pretty well. I don't think we've made a lot of bad decisions, and there's a lot of luck in that as well.

SP: What would you be looking for in someone who might join your company?

PL: It depends on their role. If looking for a developer, we're looking for someone with coding skills. We're looking for someone who can fit into a team. We've had people in the past, who lack the ability to take direc-tion and wanted to do things the wrong way. That's just a world of pain, especially in a small company. I would look for someone who's reasonably committed. We are happy to commit to somebody if they're happy to com-mit to us, and be a little dedicated to the product. I wouldn't expect them to work at the same rate that we do, because we have a vested interest. It's very hard to have your expectations in line with what you do personally as the owner of the company.

SP: How important is your musical experience in your work?

PL: I don't think I could work with the customers of my product if I didn't know what I was talking about. Now, I certainly can't sit down these days and write perfect four-part harmony; I could if I brushed up on it again. But I understand all of the musical aspects of our products. I understand the issues and concerns, and I've done this for 20 years.

SP: Do you have any last words of advice for young programmers or musicians?

PL: In terms of preparation for someone, they need to be realistic about what's possible for them to achieve. This may sound strange, but I always aim low and try to succeed high. I don't wake up every day like one of those morons that run those self-help seminars and say, "You just have to believe and you're going to be able to do this!" Well, no. That's not actually true. If 100 people wake up every day and say, "Today I'm going to invent Facebook version 2," that's not going to happen. So realistic expectations are important and so is a good general range of skills. It's important to have some skills you can apply in all sorts of areas.

In music, I think you've got to be a decent musician. I think that means you have to have some understanding of the underlying musical elements like chords and scales and all of the building blocks. If you go into music and think you're going to be a professional performer, you've probably got very little chance. But if you get creative and think about it, there are actually lots and lots of things that you can do with music that are not performance. It's very possible to have that musical skill and also do something else.

Last, if you get an opportunity while you're young, take the risk because it doesn't matter. When you get a bit older, you can't take those risks. Now that I'm older, well, it's not the age; it's the amount of responsibility you have in your life. Right now, I can't just change my life very easily. I could. I could take that risk, but the risk is very high, and there are a lot of people that it would affect. I have kids, and my family, I have a wife, and there are lots and lots of other things. I can't just say, "I'm going to go learn to play the alto saxophone, and I'm going to Juilliard. See you later." I just can't do that.

SP: And this is coming from someone who's done it. You took the risk when you were young.

PL: I could back then. So I recommend that people do it then, because it doesn't matter what happens. Even if you get your parents to chip in

$10,000 for some little adventure—I wouldn't ask them to mortgage the house—but, if they can afford $10,000 and it gets lost, it's not very much money. If it fails, you learn something from the failure; so I say just go for it. When you're young you've got the luxury in life to do those things. If you get some job offer that seems inconvenient, you should just go for it. You can always change in 12 months' time.

If an opportunity came up, in your second year of college, and you have to make a decision if you're going to put your university schooling on hold or not, do it. It's not going to matter. I've got no problem with University; it's important and you learn lots of stuff, and you need to finish it. But really, you learn how to learn at the University. That's what you take out of the university. Unless it's a very vocational course like medicine, or dentistry, or something like that, you're really getting general skills that you can apply in all sorts of areas. If you have a chance to take a break for a year because someone said they want you to help invent Pro Tools in Timbuktu, do it. Who cares? Go for it. You have much more to gain. And you can always come back to the university later on. You can't do that when you're 32 and you've got three kids and four wives. It's not going to happen. I don't recommend four wives, by the way.

SP: Thank you, Peter.

PL: You're most welcome.

Notes

1.   Joseph F. Traub, *Oral History Interview by William Aspray, OH 94* (New York: Charles Babbage Institute, University of Minnesota, Minneapolis, March 29, 1985), 3.

2.   United States Department of Labor: Bureau of Labor Statistics, "Occupational Outlook Handbook" [Online]. March 29, 2012. Available: http://www.bls.gov/ooh/computer-and-information-technology/home.htm.

3.   Department of Labor, "Outlook Handbook," March 29, 2012.

4.   Avid Technology, Inc., "About Avid" [Online]. Referenced August 4, 2012. Available: http://www.avid.com/US/about-avid.

5.   ESA Entertainment Software Association, "Industry Facts" [Online]. Referenced July 3, 2012. Available: http://www.theesa.com/facts/index.asp.

6.   Games Jobs Direct, Ltd., "Audio Lead" [Online]. Referenced July 22, 2012. Available: http://www.gamesjobsdirect.com/jobs/1058598/audio-lead.asp.

Music Technologists in Sales and Support

EVERY PRODUCT USED in the creation, performance, distribution, education, and enjoyment of music is bought and sold in a vast marketplace. For years, the storefront of this marketplace was the small, independently owned music store in everyone's hometown. Local musicians knew the owners on a first-name basis and the store employees knew their customers. Area music teachers would send their students there to buy instruments and music books, and the store kept a list of every piano teacher in town for referrals. But technology has had a major impact on this marketplace over the past two decades, and the impact has been felt in several ways.

First, technology has changed where people shop. Although many independent music stores still operate, a few large chain stores now dominate the music retail landscape. Guitar Center, the largest chain, operates 225 stores in forty-three states. They also own and operate many subsidiary brands. These include: Music & Arts Center, MusiciansFriend.com, GuitarCenter.com, LMI, Giardinelli, Musician.com, Private Reserve Guitars, Woodwind and Brasswind, and Harmony Central. In 2011 Guitar Center showed more than $2.08 billion in revenues.[1] Sam Ash, a music chain that is still family owned and operated, manages forty-five stores in seventeen states. Massive purchasing power and technologically advanced systems for managing inventory, storage, and distribution allow these chains to offer prices and selection that small music stores can't.

But chain stores are not the only place consumers are buying music technology. Online shopping has increased exponentially since its inception in the 1990s (see Box 9.1). Consumers often get better prices, have an unlimited selection, and enjoy the convenience of shopping from home or from the office. And since music technology products can be highly specialized and rather expensive, online stores can often sell products directly from the manufacturer without maintaining a vast and expensive on-site inventory.

BOX 9.1

Online Shopping:

The largest online retailer, amazon.com, which doesn't own a single physical store, reported $48.8 billion in sales in 2011. This number is more than double their sales in 2009, and is up from under $7 billion in 2004. In total, shoppers spent over $228 billion online in 2010.[2]

Today, most music retailers allow customers to purchase items in the store, or from their online catalogs. For some stores, such as Sweetwater Sound, in Fort Wayne, Indiana, or All Pro Sound, in Pensacola, Florida, online sales now account for the vast majority of their business. Websites such as zZounds. com, SonicElectronix.com, and Samedaymusic.com sell products exclusively online. Even iconic music store locations, such as the famous J&R Music and Computer World in midtown Manhattan, now devote a significant part of their business to online sales.

The second way technology has impacted the market is that it has changed what people buy. Consider this revealing statement from Guitar Center's 2011 Annual Report to the US Securities and Exchange Commission regarding music technology sales:

"The marketplace has changed materially since we opened in 1964…Over the past decade, technological advances in the music industry have resulted in dramatic changes in the nature of many music-related products. Manufacturers have combined computers and microprocessor technologies with musical equipment to create a new generation of products capable of high-grade sound processing and reproduction. Products featuring those technologies are available in a variety of forms and have broad application across most music product categories."[3]

In other words, music technology products have become big business. Hundreds of companies manufacture and distribute music technology products. Some have been around for a long time and are very familiar companies, such as Sony, Yamaha, Korg, Shure, Marshall and Gibson, but many have formed in the wake of the technological boom of the past twenty years. Box 9.2 contains a list of 550 music technology manufacturers. Some will be familiar to you, and many will not be, but all are making and selling music technology.

BOX 9.2

A Designs, Ableton, Access, Acoustica, AEA, Akai Professional, AKG, Alairex, Alesis Alfred, Allen & Heath, Alva, American DJ, Ampeg, Antares, Antelope Audio, APC, Aphex, API, Apogee, Apple, Applied Acoustics, Argosy, Arobas Music, Arriba Cases, ARS Nova, ART, Arturia, Ashly, Asus, Atlas Sound, Audient, Audio Ease, Audio-Technica, Audix, Auralex, Avalon, Avantone Audio, Avid, Aviom, BackBeat Books, Barcus Berry, BBE, Behringer, Belkin, Benchmark, Berklee Press, Beyerdynamic, BIAS, BigBends, Big Fish, BKE Tech, Blackstar, Blue Microphones, Blue Sky, Bock Audio, Bogner, Bomb Factory, Bose, Boss, Bricasti Design, BSS, Budda, Bugera, Burl Audio, Cable Nelson, CAIG Laboratories, Cakewalk, Cambridge Audio, Canare, Canon, Casio, Celemony, Celestion, CEntrance, Chameleon Labs, Chandler Limited, Charvel, Chase Case Co., Chauvet, Chicken Systems, Cinesamples, ClearSonic, Cleartone, Cloud Microphones, Coleman Audio, Contour, Cooperstand, Cordoba, Cory Care Products, Countryman, Crane, Crane Song, Creative Tunings, CreepNoMore, Crown, Cycling 74, D'Addario, D-Link, Da-Lite, Daking, dampit, Dan Dean Productions, Dangerous Music, Dave Hill Designs, Dave Smith Instruments, dbx, ddrum, Dean Markley, Denon, Digidesign, Digidesign ICON, Digidesign-Venue, DigiTech, DiMarzio, Direct Sound, Disc Makers, Dolby, DPA, DR Strings, Drawmer, Drobo, Dunlop, DW, Dynaudio, E-MU, Earthworks, East West, Ebow, EBS, Ebtech, ECS Media, Egnater, Electro Voice, electro-harmonix, Elektron, Elixir Strings, elysia, eMedia, EMG, Eminence, Empirical Labs, ENTTEC, EP Memory, Epiphone, Ernie Ball, Etymotic Research, Euphonix, Evans, Event, Eventide, EVH, F7 Sound and Vision, Fable Sounds, Feeltune, Fender, Fishman, Flux::, Focal, Focal Press, Focusrite, Fostex, Fretlight, Fulltone, Funk Logic, Furman, Future Sonics, FXpansion, G7th, Galaxy, Gallien Krueger, Gary Garritan, Gator, Gefen, Gen16, Genelec, Generic Audio, Gentner, George Ls, Get'm Get'm Wear, GForce, GHS, Gibraltar, Gibson, Glyph, GML, Godin, Grace Design, Granelli Audio Labs, Graph Tech, Grass Valley, Great River, Gretsch, Gretsch Drums, Griffin, Grimm Audio, Groove Tubes, Groove3, Grover, Gruv Gear, Guild, Hal Leonard, Hammond, Hand Held Sound, HardWire, Harmonic Vision, Hartke, Hear Technologies, Herco, Hercules Stands, Horita, Hosa, House of Troy, HQ Percussion, Humfrees, Ibanez, iConnectivity, IcyDock, IK Multimedia, Ilio, Image Line, Innovative Office Products, Intel, Intellitouch, IsoAcoustics,

ISP Technologies, isotope, Jackson, JamHub, JamStands, Jawbone, JBL, JDK Audio, JK Audio, JL Cooper, JoeCo, Joemeek, JVC, K&M, Kala, KAT Percussion, Kawai, Keeley, Keith McMillen Instruments, Kelly Concepts, Kemper, Kensington, Keyfax, KickPort International, KK Audio, Korg, KRK, Kurzweil, KuSh Audio, Kyser, LaChapell Audio, Lakland, Lanikai, Latch Lake, Latin Percussion, Lauten Audio, Lehle, Leslie, Levy's, Lexicon, Lifetime Memory, Line 6, Linksys, Listen Technologies, LittLite, Lizard Spit, LM Cases, LogicKeyboard, Loxx, LR Baggs, Lynx, M-Audio, Maag Audio, MacAudioLab, Mackie, Magma, MakeMusic, Malone Design Works, Manhasset, Manley, Marantz, Marshall, Martin, McDSP, MediaComplete LLC, Memorex, Mesa/Boogie, MIBAC Music Software, Microboards, Microsoft, Middle Atlantic Products, MIDI Solutions, Mighty Bright, Miktek, Millennia, Minnetonka, MIPRO, Misa Digital, Mission Engineering Inc., Mixed Logic, MODARTT, Mojave Audio, MonoPrice, Monster, Monster Power, Moog, Morley, Morpheus, Motion Sound, MOTU, Movek, Mu Technologies, Multi Platinum, Muse Research, Music Accessories, Music Games International, Music Pro Guides, MusicLab, MusicWorks, Musitek, MXR, Namba Gear, Native Instruments, Nektar, Neo Instruments, Netgear, Neumann, Neuratron, Neutrik, Neyrinck, Nord, NOTION Music, Novation, Numark, NZXT, Oasis, Ocean Beach Digital, Ocean Way Drums, Olsen Audio, Omnimount, On-Stage Stands, Orange, Ovation, Overloud, PACE, PageFlip, Panasonic Media, Parker, pArtScience, PDP, Peachpit Press, Pearl, Peavey, Pedaltrain, Pelonis, Peterson, PG Music, Pignose Amps, Pigtronix, Pioneer DJ, Planet Waves, Platinum Samples, pocketlabworks, Pomona Productions, PreSonus, Primacoustic, Primera, Princeton Digital, Pro Co, Pro-Mark, Professional, ProjectSAM, Propellerhead, Provider Series, PRS, Puresound, Pyware, QSC, QuikLok, Qwik Time, Radial, Rane, RapcoHorizon, Raxxess, Recordex USA, Red Witch, Remo, Rising Software, Rivera, RJM Music, RME, Road Toad Music, Rob Papen, Rock N Roller, RockStand, Rocktron, Rode, Roger Linn Design, Roland, Rotosound, Roxio, Royer, RTOM, Rupert Neve Designs, Sabian, Sabine, Sabra-Som, Sample Logic, Samson, Samsung, Sandisk, Sanyo, Savarez S.A., Schaller, Schecter, Schirmer Trade Books, Schoeps, Scratch Pad, sE Electronics, Seagate, Secrets of the Pros, Sennheiser, Serato, Seymour Duncan, Shadow Hills Industries, Shure, SIIG, Simon Systems, SKB, Slate Digital, Slate Pro Audio, Snark, Softube, Solid State Logic, Sonic Reality, Sonic Solutions, SONiVOX, Sonnet Technologies, Sonnox, Sonodyne, Sonoma Wire Works, sonuus, Sony, Sound Construction, Sound Devices, Sound On Sound, Sound.org, Soundcraft, SoundToys, Spectrasonics, Sperzel, Spirit, Squier, Stanton, Startech, Stedman Corporation, Steinberg, Steinberger, Sterling Modular, Steven Slate Drums, Stewart Audio, String Swing, Studio Projects, Studio Technologies, Studiologic, Summit Audio, Superscope, Supersonic Samples, SurgeX, Sweetwater, Switchcraft, SWR, Symetrix, Synchro Arts, Synth Tek, Synthogy, Takamine, Tama, Tannoy, Tapspace, TASCAM, Taylor, TC Electronic, TC-Helicon, Teac, Tech 21, Thermaltake, Thomson Course Technology, Timbral Research, Toby, Toft Audio, Tom Oberheim, Tone, Tone Gear, Tonelux, Toontrack, Town4Kids, Trace Elliot, Traveler Guitar, Trident Audio Developments, Trillium Lane Labs, Triple P Designs, Tripp Lite, True Systems, Tube-Tech, U&I Software, Ultimate Support, Ultra, Universal Audio, URS, UVI, V7, Ventura, Verbatim, Vestax, Vic Firth, Vienna Symphonic Library, Viewsonic, Vintech, Vir2, Visual Sound, Vital Arts, Vocalist, Voce, Voodoo Lab, Vox, Waldorf, WaveArts, WaveMachine Labs, Waves, Way Huge, Wechter Guitars, Western Digital, Westone, Whirlwind, WindTech, X-Tempo Designs, XILS-lab, XLN Audio, Yamaha, Z Systems, Zero-G, Zildjian, Zoom, ZPlane

Lastly, technology has changed the consumer. Again, from Guitar Center's annual report:

> The consumer landscape is more diverse, with each category of musician having different expectations, price sensitivities, purchasing habits and approaches to music. Customers are not satisfied with "one-size fits all" offerings and very few purchasing decisions are made solely on price. Further, musical instruments comprise a broad range of products each with their own underlying trends, including not only traditional products like guitars and drums, but also newer technology-intensive products like home recording equipment.[4]

All of these changes to the music marketplace mean new opportunities for careers in music technology sales and service. Manufacturing companies and retailers need to hire thousands of employees who understand the products, can talk about how they are used, can sell them to the customers, and can support the customers after the sale. This chapter will introduce you to three types of music technology jobs: retail sales, representing a manufacturer, and customer support.

Retail Sales

Guitar Center employs more than 9,500 people. Sam Ash employs 1,800, Sweetwater employs 430, and All Pro Sound has 80 employees. Online stores employ hundreds of people nationwide and local music stores hire music technologists to sell an ever-increasing number of products and to manage their online outlets. Consider the following information sent out in a press release[5] from Sweetwater Sound regarding six recently hired sales engineers. The employees' names have been removed, but their city of origin and professional and educational background are included here:

> Bridgeport, Michigan. Holds a bachelor degree in music industry management from Ferris State University. Has done freelance production of electronic and hip-hop music.
>
> Westerville, Ohio. Has a bachelor degree in music business from Full Sail in Orlando, and five years of retail sales experience working at Sherwin Williams.
>
> Columbus, Ohio. Holds a degree in audio production from Ohio University and has retail sales experience with Kohls.
>
> Fort Wayne, Indiana. Holds a bachelor degree in music technology from Ball State University. Ran live sound at the Interlochen Center for the Arts and had studio internships at Sweetwater and at the Chicago Recording Company studios.
>
> Fort Wayne, Indiana. Bachelor degree in music technology from the University of St. Francis and interned in the studios at Sweetwater.
>
> Danville, Kentucky. Attended the Conservatory for Recording Arts and Sciences in Tempe, Arizona, and has been an audio engineer for the past four years for the Pioneer Playhouse in Danville.

Clearly, there are jobs available for music technologists in retail sales. But many students shy away from, or don't even consider them. Perhaps working at a local music store seems too unimportant, or maybe it's the idea of working in sales in general that doesn't seem all that appealing. But selling music technology to customers can be a great way to break into the field. Retail sales engineers, as Sweetwater calls them, or sales clerks, or sales associates, work all day long with people in music. They get to talk about the things that they

---

BOX 9.3

Job Posting

Due to phenomenal growth, we are actively seeking sales professionals to join our outstanding team of sales engineers.

If you are a recent grad of a Music Technology program....

Have music industry experience in retail sales or as a manufacturer's rep, or work in a recording studio....

If you're someone who loves talking about the latest technology with people that share your passion, but are caught in what seems to be a dead-end job where your skills and knowledge are seriously undervalued....

Now might be the perfect time for a change. Imagine talking about your favorite subject while seated comfortably in front of a new computer. Then picture living in a community where it's safe to walk down the streets at night, where there are no traffic jams or smog, yet which has all the conveniences of the "big city." Finally, think about the great salary and excellent benefits package you'll be receiving while getting the immediate and long-term job satisfaction you've always wanted. Sound too good to be true? Well, the opportunity is here and the time is right. If you want to make a positive career move, please call immediately.[6]

---

enjoy and they have access to the latest information about the hottest music technology. Sweetwater, just as the other music technology retailers, continues to grow and hire new employees. Box 9.3 contains a job posting for additional sales engineers found on the "Careers" page of their website.

Within the large chain-store companies mentioned above, there are good opportunities for upward mobility inside the company. Sales clerks can be promoted to store managers, then to district management, and then to the corporate headquarters. Most corporate managers of retail companies have sales experience in their background.

But whether you are working at a large chain retailer or a small ma-and-pa store, a job as a retail sales clerk can be a great entry-level position. The work experience can be a valuable addition to a résumé and a great way to learn about and keep up with the latest technology. As a side bonus, retail employees usually receive a discount when purchasing gear. Also, music retailers interact with representatives from the manufactures whose brands they sell. These representatives form a behind-the-scenes network comprised of contacts in the music manufacturing industry. They can be a great source for learning about opportunities in manufacturing companies, and as a retail sales clerk, you will interact with them regularly.

Specific Technology Skills Required:

The sales associate needs to have a working knowledge of many music technology products; from guitars and amps to recording equipment and software programs. Reading music trade magazines, looking through catalogs, subscribing to online blogs, going to manufactures' websites and viewing YouTube videos are great ways to build up this familiarity. Successful retail clerks are real "gear-heads" who enjoy learning about the latest products and their features.

While it is difficult to have a commanding knowledge of all of the products a store offers, and some of this knowledge can be acquired on the job, familiarity with music technology hardware and software is critical. Simply put, the rate of technological development requires sales people to quickly learn the latest features of many products, and a solid background in music technology will lay the groundwork to allow this to happen.

The more familiar you are with products, the better able you will be to describe them to customers and to sell them. Successful retail outlets understand this, and often allow time for employees to work with demo products so that they can become familiar with them. These products are then sold to the customer, or store employees at considerable discounts. At a larger store, a sales clerk may focus on a specific area, such as recording, or synthesizers, but in a smaller store, you may be required to be generally familiar with the entire product line.

Suggested Education and Training

College Degree: BM, BA, BS, or BFA in music technology, audio engineering, music business, music industry, or commercial music. This is not necessarily required for entry-level positions, but will be necessary to move into management.

Experience playing musical instruments, performing in live bands, recording and working with live sound, and working with other audio-related products

An interest in, and affinity for, the latest music technology gear and products

Great communication and people skills
The ability to approach people, help people, work with people, and sell
to people

Company Sales Representative

Manufacturers create the products that retailers sell. But there are hundreds of manufacturers of music technology products, and retailers need to decide which items to offer. Each of these companies needs to make sure that retailers are familiar with, and want to sell, their products. For this purpose, manufacturers hire their own representatives and it is their job to make this happen. These company reps, sales reps, account managers, territory managers, or district managers usually represent only a specific line of products. Most customers will never meet these individuals, and are usually not aware of their role in the retail process. Yet they are key to making sure that a manufacturer is successful. Box 9.4 shows a job listing from Bose Corporation, the maker of high-end speakers, headphones, and sound systems.

BOX 9.4

Job Posting

Posting Title: Territory Manager
Category: Sales
Location: Western United States
Area: Field Sales

Scope of Responsibilities: Reporting to a Regional Business Manager, this individual will be responsible for the sales and services of Bose professional products in Montana, Wyoming, Utah, Colorado, Arizona, New Mexico, Las Vegas and El Paso, Texas. This person will be responsible for the selection, development and education of our dealers, integrators and consultants within the territory to support sales of our products into vertical markets. The network will be wide to cover our product focus into installed and portable applications. This person will be responsible for implementing new strategic initiatives as communicated by the regional business manager. This person will also manage key relationships in the region and develop new business opportunities within our target markets seeking new customers and dealers.

Specific Responsibilities:

Manage day-to-day activities in territory

Plan and manage the sales effort with the territory working with the regional business manager, field engineers and others

Launch new products and drive sales of these products to meet divisional goals

Drive regular reporting on results in territory to management

Distribution development and growth

Select, develop, and train distribution to cover portable, business music systems and engineered sound channels

In a team approach, develop relationships at all levels at larger dealers

Ensure that distribution is in line with the division's strategy

Set annual goals for each and monitor monthly, correct as needed

Select and develop a network of consultants who regularly specify our products

Develop relationships with other key influencers, such as architects, operators, and other influencers of vertical channels such as houses of worship, portable, and performing arts

Implement key strategic initiatives as directed by the regional business manager

Collaborate with other managers within APSG as needed to ensure that divisional goals are met. This includes coordinating their consultant efforts with the Consultant Liaison and make sure they have adequate (qualified) distribution in place to respond to consultant specifications with their regions

Perform business development with sales team to bring solid business to our partners

Attend key trade shows and customer meetings.

Must be able to establish and maintain solid relationship at executive, management, and sales rep engineering levels.

Skills:

Individual must be a very self-driven individual, who works well in both team and entrepreneurial environments. Experience in the Pro Industry a must. Excellent communication skills both verbal and written are required. Microsoft Office and CRM experience. About 50–75% travel is required. Position reports into Regional Business Manager.

Education:

Bachelor degree in technical discipline desirable with a minimum of 10 years in Operations, Sales, Finance or Management in an engineering driven organization.[7]

This job description gives a complete picture of the kind of person Bose is looking to hire, and most music technology companies have similar positions available. However, these job postings are not as easy to find as the retail jobs described earlier. Because of the great importance of these jobs, companies often try to hire people whose work they already know. Also, few people in music technology sales will start their careers at this level. Notice the amount of experience and expertise required for this position, not only in technology, but also in sales and task management.

For the company representative, educating and developing customers and clients is a time-consuming process based on the cultivation of relationships. As a result, successful company reps may stay in their jobs for years as they maintain the relationships they have fostered. Occasionally, reps will move from one company to another company within the industry, and sometimes company reps will move into corporate management, but often, the successful company representative can build an entire career.

Specific Technology Skills Required:

The company's sales representative needs to know the technical aspects of their line of products inside and out. They need to be up to date on the latest developments and newest features. They need to know how their products compare to others in the marketplace and how consumers use them. They must also be able to demonstrate their use, and teach others how to use them and demonstrate them. In short, the company sales rep needs to be the number one expert on their line of products to the retail outlets and dealers.

Suggested Education and Training

College Degree: BM, BA, BS, or BFA in music technology, audio engineering, music business, music industry or commercial music

BOX 9.5

A Day in the Life of Rick Naqvi, Vice President of Sales, PreSonus Audio Electronics:

6:30 a.m.: Wake up and grab coffee. Sit on the couch with my 2-year-old daughter. I crack open the laptop and start responding to emails (which right now are running about 150 per day). My daughter is trying to punch on the keys of the computer and my coffee will probably spill at any minute. After that I'll read my Bible for 20 minutes and then get ready for work.

8:15 a.m.: Leave to go to work. Put on the headset and make a few calls. Usually to my National Sales Director or a key sales rep. I almost always am on the phone when I'm commuting to work (30 minutes). I'm freshest at this time of the day (unless I had a gig or late recording session the night before) and it helps me focus on what I need to do as soon as I hit the office.

9:00 a.m.: Enter the office. Grab more coffee. Plow through a few more emails and make notes for things I need to knock out that day (examples might be putting together meeting agenda, people I need to contact that day, etc.). This is my quietest 30 minutes of the day in the office. From here it gets busier and more chaotic.

9:30 a.m.: Someone has barged into my office with the first fire of the day by this time. Topics range in intensity. It could be about a software bug that someone is shouting about on our forum. It could be about a manufacturing issue that we discovered in power supplies in Australia. It could be some joker on eBay that's posing as a PreSonus dealer, etc...I try to deal with these as they come.

10 a.m.: If today is Monday, then I typically have a meeting with the Executive Staff at this time. Each department head (Administration, Finance, Engineering, Product Management, Sales, and Marketing) will give a quick synopsis of what's going on in their particular department. We talk about recent problem issues, something cool that has happened, just whatever is relevant to the entire group. This invites discussion and the goal is to keep us on the same page. This meeting is supposed to last an hour but never does. My phone is buzzing like crazy during this meeting and I'm tempted to look at texts and emails but I try not to (or at least try not to get caught).

12 p.m.: The meeting finally ended and it's lunchtime. I usually grab one of my coworkers and leave for a quick bite. Since we live in Baton Rouge,

Louisiana, there are tons of great restaurants within about 3 miles so we pick one and usually talk about music, work or family stuff at lunch.

1 p.m.: Made it back to the office and another meeting is starting with some of the Marketing guys. Today we are discussing an upcoming trade-show; let's say Summer NAMM. Topics include: 1. Who will we be sending to the show? 2. What's the message we want to get across? 3. What will the demos be at the show? 4. Are we doing a webcast or something else in conjunction with the show? 5. Are we doing a rep meeting? 6. What type of materials do we need for our reps and dealers?

1:45 p.m.: If it's a Tuesday, then our weekly webcast is about to start. If I'm actually the guy doing the webcast, then I'm late because we usually start testing around 1pm. But if I'm not presenting, then I'm on the chat talking to customers and answering questions while the webcast is going on.

2:00 p.m.: Techtalk, our weekly webcast, is starting. It's typically a 30-minute presentation with Q&A following. It's a great time for us to connect with customers and actually use the products we sell in a live setting.

3 p.m.: Another meeting is about to start. This one is with the Product Management group. They are trying to fill out the Market Requirements Document for a new product we are designing. This meeting has to do with putting together initial sales projections and pricing. How much should this product cost to the customer? What will our domestic dealers pay for it? What will our International Distributors pay for it? How many will we sell in the first 6–12 months?

4 p.m.: Sales meeting to discuss upcoming promotions. We typically plan promotions 90–120 days in advance. Some of these are worldwide in nature. Others are in just specific countries. Still others are direct promotions that we might offer online to customers. I will typically meet with both of my sales guys (International Sales Director and National Sales Director) as well as our Marketing Communications Director to come up with these.

5 p.m.: Finishing up loose ends and trying to get ready for the next day's meetings.

6 p.m.: Leave to go home. Typically I'm on the phone for the entire drive home as well. It's amazing I haven't gotten in a wreck after all of these years. Since we are on Central Time, I typically am talking to people that are on the West Coast since it's only 4pm for them.

Real experience using the line of products being represented
Great communication and people skills
High-level task management skills
The ability to teach people, help people, work with people, and sell to
people

Customer Support

An extension of product sales is customer support and service. Most music technology retailers and manufacturers offer free technical support after the sale. Customers who are happy with the support they receive will become repeat customers and will refer their friends. Companies don't offer customer support out of the goodness of their hearts; it is simply good for business. And, the customer care department can be a great place for the aspiring music technologist to get a start on a music technology career. Many new hires by retailers or manufacturers of music technology are in the customer support, tech support, and customer relations areas. The following is a posting for a tech support job at PreSonus, a major manufacturer of digital recording consoles, audio hardware, and sequencing software.

BOX 9.6

Job Posting

PreSonus seeks a technically inclined person with experience in digital audio recording who enjoys resolving problems and helping people. Responsibilities include assisting callers in setting up our interface products and quickly diagnosing issues that can arise in a digital recording environment. Job Location: Baton Rouge, LA. Position: Full time

Required skills
General knowledge of audio recording, microphone preamps, signal processors, and Mac and PC platforms.

Familiarity with at least three or high level knowledge of at least one of the following DAW: Acid, Cubase, Digital Performer, Live, Logic, Samplitude, or Sonar.

Prior customer service, sales or technical support experience a plus.

Previous experience with PreSonus equipment a definite plus.[8]

Customer and tech support jobs may not seem like much fun. Representatives sit in a cubicle all day answering an endless stream of phone calls and emails. Sometimes the people on the other end are less than happy for reasons over which you have no control, and sometimes they are downright rude. Depending on the size of the company or retailer, you may need to support hundreds of products, or you may only support a few, and are required to address the same questions over and over again.

There is no question that customer support is a necessary evil. Certainly there is the opportunity to talk to people about great and interesting products, and there is the satisfaction that can come when you help someone solve a problem, but for the most part, tech support is tedious and painful.

This is wonderful news for you if you are looking for a way to break into the world of music technology. Customer support jobs are plentiful and they are a great way to get a job working with a company. They give you the chance to work with others in the industry while you are learning the intimate workings of the products you support. Think of it as getting paid to take lessons in music technology hardware and software. They give you the opportunity to show your employers that you are willing to work hard and will do whatever it takes to impress them. The best part about customer support is that a well-prepared, hard-working customer support representative won't be doing it for very long. Excellent customer support reps are often tapped to be company reps and sales managers. And if there are no positions available in your current company or retailer, the experience inside the business puts you ahead of other candidates when applying for other jobs.

Specific Technology Skills Required:

Customer support representatives need expertise in the technical aspects of the products they support. Much of this detailed knowledge is learned on the job, but experience in a music technology or commercial music program can help to provide a background so that learning details about specific products is easier. Also, the broader preparation that a college degree provides will prepare the customer support rep to move up in the company more quickly than others without that preparation.

Suggested Education and Training
College Degree: BM, BA, BS, or BFA in music technology, audio engineering, music business, music industry, or commercial music
Real experience using the line of products being supported

Great communication and people skills

The ability to be patient with people and help them to resolve problems

Interview with a Professional: James Frankel, Head of Digital Education for the Music Sales Group.

(At the time of this interview, Jim was Managing Director of SoundTree, the Educational Division of Korg, USA.)

SP: Hello, Jim. Thanks for speaking with me. Can you tell me about your career path?

JF: My career path was a traditional one, but not typical for someone in manufacturing and sales. I went into teaching first and technology actually was my hobby. Using technology made my teaching more interesting and more fulfilling for me, and gradually I realized that very few people were doing that. Eventually it took over my career and I went from being a band director to helping others with the technology. I left education to take over a company that's a reseller and manufacturer both tied into one. In the last four years that I've worked there, I've really gotten an inside view of the music business.

PHOTO 9.1 Jim Frankel

SP: Most people wouldn't think that if you go into music education you can find yourself involved in the music technology world, but actually a degree in music education can be a great preparation.

JF: I would argue that it's a fantastic career path. When I went to college in the late 80's and early 90's, the only music technology degrees around were audio engineering and maybe film scoring. But that wasn't technology, it was composition. I never even considered technology as a college major. It was my hobby, and I enjoyed playing with synthesizers and being a frustrated rock star keyboard player, but I never even considered it as an option for a career. The reason that I say that education is a great career path, is that, first of all, there's nothing like teaching what you love. I don't think there's any music technologist that is in it purely for the technology, or they really shouldn't be in the business. Music is the first love and then technology. Whether it's just a fascination with lights and knobs and sounds, or using technology to help you be a better musician. Everybody that I know is a musician first. And in my opinion, teaching other people about what you love is the coolest gig that there is.

And so while education may not be a traditional career path to music technology, it is a great one. A perfect example of different career paths is mine compared to my brother's. My brother went into the recording technology program at NYU. He's an amazing drummer, but got his degree in "Rec Tech," it was called. When he got out with an NYU degree, he got a job working at the Knitting Factory as an audio engineer. There were incredible acts he worked with and eventually he got promoted to being head of the recording studio at the Knitting Factory. Unfortunately, he didn't make a lot of money and he was working crazy hours so it was tough for him. The reason I point this out is that we're brothers, we're both musicians, both music lovers, but he didn't have any interest in teaching and I did.

I think a lot of young people think that they're just going to get out of college and get a job. It really doesn't work that way. You've really got to work hard to get a job. This is true in any field, but in music technology specifically. And then once you get that job, a lot of kids just assume they'll be able to have an apartment, go on vacations, pay their rent, buy food, have clothes, have a car. I think it's what my brother thought about that specific goal to be an audio engineer and be a recording studio guy. He was a top-level guy and he went out and became amazing. He was head of the recording studio at the Knitting Factory, which is a great gig, but he was making very little money.

He didn't think he could afford to do what he wanted to do the most, so he started his own company. He did location sound recording, and was working with some of the amazing artists he met at the Knitting Factory. He was doing that on the side and using that income to supplement his full-time job. After a while, he realized he was working 80 hours a week and still not making what he thought he could.

So he left both jobs and became a manufacture's rep for Sennheiser microphones. He worked in product management and went around to all the stores in Manhattan taking orders of Sennheiser, and Neumann and Schepps microphones, and sound boards. He did that for three or four years but he didn't like the sales aspect of it and to the horror of my parents, said, "I'm quitting. I'm going to be a professional drummer."

My brother is very similar, in my opinion, to what I think young people are like today. I was always thinking: I need money, I need a firm, stable job so that I can get married and then I can have a house and have kids. I need to know where my money is coming from. I'm very old-school that way. And my brother is only four years younger than me, but his thought was, "I'll just make it. Money's going to come my way. I'm not worried." I think a lot of young people today are like that, but once you turn 25 and you're off your parents' health insurance, the whole world becomes very real.

SP: So how did things work out for your brother?

JF: Well, now my brother is one of the Blue Men. He's pretty much set for life, or at least until that show closes. He's got an incredible job, everybody loves what he does, and he loves what he does. I think he's playing around for a living, and he's making a ton of money.

SP: So your brother's story is the realization of every young musician's dreams. They may say, "Yeah, it might be tough for a little while, but then I'll be famous." And your brother has made it as a performer; as a Blue Man in the Blue Man Group.

JF: But getting the job as a Blue Man was a total fluke. I want to make that very clear. He was one of 6,500 people that auditioned for that one spot. And you need to understand that my brother was a child prodigy on drums. When my brother was nine years old he was playing drums for the best drummers in the world like Gary Chester, and Dave Weckl. We have these pictures of my brother, this little child prodigy, with Dave Weckl. But even that good, he couldn't make it as a drummer with a rock band because he never got in *that* band. Even if you're the best, it's getting the break, getting in *that* band, meeting *that* person, and getting *that* connection. But it was his dream to be a performer and he's doing it now.

I think every kid needs a dream of what they would love to do. For me, it's kind of a dream to work for the keyboard company that I loved as a kid. I left the stable job that I had because I was going to work for Korg. I was going to work for a company I loved and where I had been a long-time customer. So that was a realization of a dream.

Recently someone asked me what my "special sauce" was, meaning how did I get there? I made it clear it was hard work. You have to be willing to work really hard, crazy hours, and work every day on bettering yourself, on getting your career going and being really motivated. You can't just sit around playing video games all day. I think a lot of people who have made careers in this are the hardest working people in show business, so to speak. You have to work your rear end off. And you balance your life, but we're hard workers, and I don't think there is any other way. Unless you get some crazy lucky thing that happens to you, the only way to get that dream is to work really, really hard. People always say to me, "I don't know how you do it." But it's my whole ethic—just work really hard.

SP: So even though you love your job, and you love what you do, and you're a musician, it's still work?

JF: It's work. Oh it's work. There are many days where I would much rather do something else. It's not like every day you have the most awesome day and you know this is what you were meant to do. There are 365 days in a year. You get about 10 of those, maybe 20 where you have this moment and you say, "I was born to do this." There are 340 days where you're getting out of bed thinking, "ugh!" It's so easy to get distracted in today's world. To fill the voids in your life with net surfing, Facebooking, video gaming, etc. But I am just hyper-focused on hard work, and it's gotten me where I am. I have this thing in my brain that to be successful you have to work hard; it doesn't just happen.

So, from the manufacturing side of things, a music technologist coming out of college today can absolutely find a job with a music manufacturer. And normally the entry-level position within a manufacturer is tech support. Starting immediately on phones and customer service. That's the entry-level gig. Or working in a shipping warehouse for a company. The young kids that I see working for Korg are all in customer support and customer service. Very few start out there selling or repping the product. Very rarely do they start with those as entry-level gigs. What I would say as career advice for those people is, when you get that job, it may seem like a grunt work crappy job, and it pretty much is, but work your rear end off in that job, because everyone notices when you don't. I think the

20-somethings, in my opinion, although this may come across as harsh, are the laziest generation of all time. Some of the ones I've seen, I just cannot believe. They want to show up at 9 and leave at 5.

SP: And so as a result, those who work stand out?

JF: No question about it. Those who get there early asking, "What can I do, how can I help, I'll volunteer, I'll come in on a Saturday when I'm not getting paid for it, I'll be there to help with inventory, I'll do this, I'll do that." Those go-getters are the ones who advance, absolutely. And the people who clock in and say, "Well, I have a job, you should be so thrilled that I'm here," never advance, and usually get fired. And I see two types of people, like a type A and type B. There's a leader and a follower. And it's the leaders who advance. The people who are happy clocking in at 9 and clocking out at 5, there's nothing wrong with it, but it's not going to work in this business. We have people in our accounting department, for example, who have been doing the exact same job for 25 years. They've gotten modest raises and have worked in the same cubicle the whole time. If you're happy doing that, go for it, but I could never do that.

I've hired graduates right out of the university to be tech support people, because they know the latest stuff and it's really fresh in their minds. But tech support is answering emails and phone calls all day. Answering questions about software and hardware. A perfect example is Brad Smith, who used to be our tech support guy. He was so incredible. Everybody loved him, the customers raved. He went way above and beyond what his job description was and he got promoted.

SP: And you hired him right out of a music technology program?

JF: Right out of Duquesne University. He graduated at 21 and four days later he had a job at SoundTree/Korg. And that's the other thing. If someone I trust recommends a kid, I will hire them, because I know they're not going to send me some lazy kid. With Brad, Bill Purse at Duquesne University said, "This kid is good." That's all I needed to know.

Another piece of career advice is that you never know who is going to be your boss some day and you never know who is going to be that one person that's going to get you that break. So always be so nice, and helpful, and put on that kind of persona of "I'm a hard worker and I'm here to help" to every single person you meet. At a trade show a few months ago, I saw this incredible musician, a music technology kid. I was sitting in the room and they were rehearsing. This kid had the foulest mouth and worst attitude I've seen in a long time. He thought he was God's gift to his instrument, just cursing and so on. He didn't know who I was, not that I am somebody, but you never know who is in the room. I thought, "I would never hire you. You are a piece of dirt." So the other thing that I think is really important as far as getting employed is that you never know who is going to be your boss. And in the music tech world, it's so small, you can't afford to upset someone with your cocky attitude or by thinking you're entitled to anything. It's about reverence and humility and respect.

SP: So getting the job is as much about hard work and attitude as it is about skills?

JF: I think those are the most important. I think attitude is probably number one, and part of that is the way you present yourself. In interviews I've had kids who come in with a three-piece suit and a résumé and they took it very seriously, and I've had kids who come in trying to look hip in their sweater and their jeans and their stocking hat on and I would never hire them. The outward persona that you give off is really, really important. That has to do with attitude because the attitude would inform you of how you should behave in an interview and how you should comport yourself in a professional atmosphere. The people who have this laid-back cool attitude, that doesn't impress me.

SP: No?

JF: No. Because fair, or unfair, it gives off the impression that they're lazy and they don't take it very seriously. They're not going to be a leader; they're just going to be a sheep.

SP: What are your working hours like?

JF: I literally start working at 6:00 am and stop working at 11:00 pm. That's every single day, seven days a week. And on the weekends, when I'm spending time with my family, I try to balance my work and my home-life, but my phone is never off. I never turn off. I never black out. What I try to do, and this will sound awful, but I'm working in the bathroom. Not to get graphic or anything, but what I'm saying is that I'll steal away a few minutes to answer email out of sight of my family. I have to because if I don't, when I get back on Monday, I'm not going to get my work done. So that's my day, and it's really every day.

I do my blue sky thinking on my ride home every day. I think about what I need to do next, what am I doing right, what am I doing wrong? An extremely important thing for anybody is to be very honest in their self-assessment. Make sure that you always know who you are and how you're doing in your job. Don't fool yourself by thinking you're so great. I'm very self-critical. I analyze if I could have handled something better, did I talk to that person correctly, was that email really necessary? I'm always thinking about that.

SP: Is there a lot of travel involved in running this company?

JF: A ton.

SP: Can you talk about how that plays into your schedule and if that takes a toll on you?

JF: Well, the reason you travel, and this applies to anyone in the music technology field, is that first, it's a lot of evangelism. You have to go and convince people that this is something that they want and need. So I'm constantly evangelizing. In order to do that, you have to get out on the road. I have become the public face of my company. I knew that when I took the job. For whatever it's worth, they wanted Jim Frankel to mean SoundTree and people to associate SoundTree with Jim Frankel. So I knew from day one that I was going to be traveling a lot. I do about 125,000 air miles a year; I'm on the road 100 to 125 nights a year. I've gained 30 pounds because you eat out all the time. Life on the road sounds really romantic, and for the first six months I really enjoyed it. I was seeing all these great places around America, and around the world, but after about a year, it becomes your job. So while I'm sitting here talking to you, and really enjoying the interview, part of me would much rather be home right now with my family.

SP: We're having this interview almost 1,000 miles from your home in New York, and it happens to be a Saturday morning.

JF: It's Saturday morning, and I'm not going to be home until Sunday at 3, and I have to be at the office on Monday. I remember asking my predecessor in this job if I got days off when I went to a conference or a trade show. And he laughed and he said, "Jim, you don't get any days off—it's 365." I can't say to my boss that I'm taking Monday off because I worked on Saturday. I'd be fired. When you run a company, you can't turn it off. You're always thinking about revenue coming in, and is everybody working as hard as they can, and all that stuff. Traveling a lot can seem very exciting, but when you're doing it as part of your job, and it's expected and it's constant, it's tough. For the next three months, for example, I'll probably be in hotels more than I'll be in my own bed. It is wearing and it is part of the job that you have to ask yourself if you are really cut out for it. On the other hand, there is a great community that I've built of friends and colleagues and people that I genuinely like. I like spending time with the people that I'm on the road with, or else I would quit.

SP: You live in New York, you're a New Yorker, and you talked about your brother working in the music scene in New York. There are some people who say that you have to make your way to New York, LA or Nashville if you are going to make it in the music technology industry. What do you think about that?

JF: You can make a living anywhere in music technology. But what I would suggest strongly to all people thinking about this as a career is to spend some time living in one of those areas; to cut your teeth and to get a real feel for it. Maybe that's unfair, and I'm a little geocentric and very much a New Yorker, but that's really where it is. New York, LA, Nashville and I would add Austin, Texas, to that list of cities. And each city has it's own reason for going there. If you want to do live sound, you go to Austin or New York, if you want to be a recording engineer in a certain genre of music, you go to Nashville, you want to do music production and use your skills for video game scoring or film scoring, you have to go to LA or New York.

A music technologist can do so many different things. I would strongly recommend that everyone going into music technology should be a Jack-of-all-trades. Do many things. Unless you're a phenom at a certain thing, you need to broaden what you can do and your skill set so you can work on a Tuesday making some music for a student film score, on a Wednesday doing live sound at a bar, Thursday, playing with your band in a club, and that's how people make it in these cities. And I'm sure there are other cities that people would argue need to be included in the list, but I think those are the four. It's important to be versatile, to be willing to work for free, be willing to do grunt work and to be a creative entrepreneur. If you're not getting work, make it for yourself. Figure out how you can create content or whatever you need to do to become a creative entrepreneur. Music technologists need all those chops. So whether it's giving lessons on software one day, or creating videos or whatever else, you need to make your own jobs too.

SP: What do you think about this statement? A career in music technology is one you can plan out from start to finish.

JF: Impossible. That's a ridiculous statement. Completely. I don't think anybody can. And that's one thing that's alluring about the whole field. You don't know, because music technology changes on an hourly basis. It's not a weekly, or monthly basis, it's pretty much hourly. I'd say it's a really exciting career path. Don't plan on getting rich unless you hit some quirky thing and it goes viral or whatever, and make sure that you absolutely love it and are passionate about what you are doing. There are so many things you can do. You can work retail. There is no shame in working in stores, like a Guitar Center, or Sam Ash, or wherever. It's a good gig, and a lot of young people can do that. If you want to be in music technology, you need to have six or seven jobs to start. You've got to figure out how to fill the income by doing all these different things. And most musicians are comfortable having many, many jobs. And music and technology are intrinsically linked. If you are a weak technologist, you won't get a job, and if you're a weak musician, eventually somebody's going to notice you're not going to work. You have to be a musician.

I think that if you have a solid work ethic, you have a great positive attitude and if you're versatile, you will make it. Don't think that anybody owes you anything. You're entitled to nothing. I think the people that go into it saying, "Yeah, that will be kind of cool," they'll find out really fast that they're not cut out for it. In any career there is a natural Darwinian where the strongest survive. You'll be weeded out quickly if you're not cut out for it, and that's a good thing. Because if you survive five years in it and you're still making money, then you're in. You will find a living in this business. You need to persevere and you'll do it.

SP: Thank you, Jim.

Notes

1.   United States Securities and Exchange Commission, *Guitar Center Holdings, Inc., Form 10K* (Filed March 26, 2012), 30.

2.   Statista, "Online Shopping—Statistics and Facts" [Online]. Referenced April 13, 2012. Available: http://www.statista.com/topics/871/online-shopping/.

3.   Securities and Exchange Commission, *Guitar Center*, 6.

4.   Securities and Exchange Commission, *Guitar Center*, 5–6.

5.   Christopher Guerin, "Press Release, Sweetwater Sound, June 26, 2012" [Online]. Available: http://www.sweetwater.com/about/press-releases/pr.php?id=00269.

6.   Sweetwater Sound, Inc. "Career Openings: Sales Engineer" [Online]. Referenced August 7, 2012. Available: http://www.sweetwater.com/careers/openings.php.

7.   Bose Corporation, "Careers at Bose" [Online]. Referenced June 12, 2012. Available: http://www.bose.com/controller?url=/about/careers/index.jsp .

8.   PreSonus Audio Electronics, Inc., "PreSonus Job Opportunities: Technical Support Representative" [Online]. Referenced July 3, 2012. Available: http://www.presonus.com/about-presonus/Careers.

10

Music Technologists in Education

EDUCATION IS ONE of the most rapidly expanding career fields for music technologists. The number of college bachelor degree programs in music technology is increasing at an amazing pace, and so are programs at community colleges, trade schools, and art schools. Additionally, more and more high schools and even middle schools are offering music technology classes as a part of their music programs. Experienced music technologists are needed to work in all of these educational settings.

Often, the teaching profession gets a bad rap. We hear that teachers are underpaid, and how challenging it can be to deal with young people these days. Stories in the news of violence in schools, teacher scandals, and state and local school board battles all contribute to the negative perceptions many people have of the teaching profession. These negative perceptions often lead people away from the profession before they ever find out if they would enjoy teaching or if they are good at it.

I didn't always know that I wanted to be an educator, but within a few weeks of taking my first teaching job, I realized that I loved it and really enjoyed working with young people. Over the course of my seventeen-year career as a professional educator, I have come to realize that education can be a great career choice. There is no question that teaching can be a challenging career that involves a lot of hard work, dedication, and education, but it also offers a great deal of security and stability for those who are successful. Also, while people grouse about how little public school teachers are paid, most work a strict eight-hour day, are often finished before 4 pm, never work on weekends, and have the summer off. The US department of Education reported in 2011 that the average salary for public school teachers in the US was $56,069,[1] and if a PE teacher coaches the golf team or the music teacher directs the marching band outside of school hours, they receive additional pay. Teaching at the university level also has its benefits. College teachers have a very flexible schedule, work with many highly motivated and focused students, and enjoy the intellectual and professional freedom to pursue areas of research and exploration that interest them. Most educators at any level have two full weeks off during the Christmas holiday season, another week off in the spring, three months off in the summer, and receive excellent health and retirement benefits. While you may not get rich as a music teacher, you can have a comfortable living, good benefits, job security, and a great schedule. And, teaching jobs can be found anywhere; there are no geographic restrictions. There is no question that teaching is a career that deserves a music technologist's serious consideration.

Public School Teacher

Middle school and high school music technology programs are becoming more common every year, and part of this has to do with the accessibility of computers in today's schools, and the permeation of technology into every aspect of American life. The simple fact of that matter is that computers are ubiquitous in elementary and secondary education. Every state in the country has added impressive technology standards to their curricula and billions of dollars have been and are being spent to ensure that every teacher and child in school has easy access to the latest computer technology. The most recent statistics from the Department of Education show that there was an average of one computer for every three children in American schools.[2]

Young people have more access than ever before to technology in their homes as well. Over 80 percent of American homes with school-aged children (parents between the ages of twenty-five and fifty-five) have more than one computer. And if one of the parents holds at least a bachelor's degree, the number shoots up to over 92 percent.[3] Today's young people have been exposed to computers for their entire lives. I often say that they are hardwired to work with technology, and for young people, technology and music go hand in hand. A recent Kaiser Family Foundation study found that kids between the ages of eight and eighteen spend an average of two hours and thirty-one minutes every day listening to music on computers, iPods, cell phones, and other forms of technology.[4]

With the prevalence of technology in schools, and the widespread use of technology by school-aged children, it seems natural that more and more school music programs are expanding their offerings to include music technology classes. These classes are not only popular with the students who already participate in traditional school music programs such as the choir, band, and orchestra, but they are also very popular with 80 percent of students who don't participate in school music electives.[5] Many of these students make their own music on home and personal computers and consider themselves musicians, despite the fact that they don't perform in a school-sponsored musical group.

Currently, most music technology classes are being created and taught by seasoned music teachers[6] who have gone back to school or taken advantage of considerable professional development programs to increase their technology skills. Just like at the college level, music teachers who have seen an interest from their students have started high school music technology programs (see Box 10.1). These teachers usually direct another music area, such as the band, orchestra, or chorus, but also teach music technology classes on the basics of

---

BOX 10.1

Technology Based Music Classes

In 2010 a nationwide research study was launched to determine the extent to which "Technology Based Music Classes," or TBMCs, were offered in American high schools.[7] The research, which surveyed high school principals and music teachers, found that approximately 14 percent of US high schools offer TBMCs. In some regions of the country, that percentage was found to be much higher. The Eastern United States reported the highest percentage, with 35 percent of schools offering TBMCs as compared with the southern US, where 6 percent of the high schools surveyed offered TBMCs. Of the high schools offering music technology classes, 19 percent reported that their classes were fed by a middle school that offered music technology classes as well. Additionally, the research reported that 75 percent of the classes had been started since 2000, and more than half had been started since 2005. When principals were asked if the TBMCs at their schools were a valuable part of the school's curriculum, 96 percent said that they were. Sixty percent of all principals reported that TBMCs would be a valuable addition to their school's programs and 56 percent said that offering such a course at their school in the future was a possibility. If there are approximately 25,000 high schools in the US, and up to 14 percent of them offer music technology classes, there could be more than 3,000 possible jobs for music technologists teaching in public schools today. And more jobs will become available every year.

music notation, audio and MIDI sequencing, recording, and live sound. In some cases, they may also teach music theory, AP music, or audio for broadcasting and theater. Often, these courses are very popular once offered, and it is not uncommon for the music technology courses at a school to expand quickly, until they fill a teacher's entire schedule. These teachers often serve as the music technology specialists at their schools and school districts and are called upon to help with sound reinforcement for live performances, to make recordings of ensembles and students, and to arrange music for various purposes. They become the "go to" people when purchasing decisions need to be made about music technology hardware and software for the school and district.

As more programs are created, and current teachers retire, many more new teachers will be needed who have the expertise to teach and assist students as they explore music technology and to help school music departments in their technology use (see Box 10.2). Fortunately, the expansion of college music technology programs means that more colleges are offering courses of study that prepare teachers with necessary skills to compete for these jobs.

Getting the Job

Since you can't get a bachelor's degree in music technology education (yet), you will want to get a degree in music education first. The entrance and audition requirements for a music education degree are almost identical to those for the music technology degrees discussed in Chapter 2. A major in music education may be a BS, BA, or BM degree and usually involves a considerable number of courses from the university's school or department

---

BOX 10.2

Technology Skills Can Lead to Job Security in Education

In some states, teacher salaries and teacher positions are being cut, while new initiatives like technology are well funded. I recently spoke with a high school music teacher who kept his job while the two other music teachers at the school lost theirs. One of the reasons he kept his job was that he had the skills to manage the new $60,000 music technology lab that the school had just purchased as part of a technology initiative.

of education in addition to music courses. After successful completion of a music education degree, most students are certified to be public school teachers in the state in which they studied. If you can get your degree from a school that also offers music technology, you can take electives in music technology, get a minor in music technology, or consider a double major. A master's degree in music technology is often a great addition to a teacher's education and experience, and there are several master's in music technology programs around the country that are specifically focused on helping current teachers become skilled in music technology. Appendix C contains a listing of graduate programs in music technology in the United States. Some of these programs are even offered online so teachers can participate in them from anywhere in the country. The online master's degree at Indiana University-Purdue University Indianapolis (IUPUI) is an example of this type of program.

Specific Technology Skills Required

Hardware

Mac and PC computers: able to save, manage, and transfer files, effectively use software (see below), connect to audio interfaces and hardware devices

Synthesizers and MIDI controllers: familiar with common models and brands, especially those owned by the school, able to select and modify patches and programs, able to run through an amplifier or route through a computer

Microphones: familiar with common models and brands, especially those owned by the school, understand the distinction between and proper use of dynamic and condenser mics, know effective mic selection and placement techniques for various instruments and especially for various musical groups such as concert choir, show choir, concert band, jazz band, and orchestra in both live performance and for recording

Recording equipment: able to record ensembles and individuals for rehearsal, performances, auditions, and other purposes, able to use analog and digital recorders, CD burners, computers and other equipment available at the school

Live sound hardware: able to run live sound for various types of performances and venues, using analog and digital mixing boards, microphones, and speakers.

Lab maintenance and management: able to set up, manage, and maintain the music technology lab, whether it be a few old Macs borrowed from the school library, or an extensive lab and studio costing hundreds of thousands of dollars

Software:

Music Notation software: able to use and teach students to use Finale or Sibelius to create musical scores and arrangements, transpose parts, create practice accompaniments, compose original music

Instructional software: familiar with various programs for teaching music theory, exploring musical elements, and for practicing and preparing music

Recording software: able to use GarageBand, Logic, Pro Tools, Studio One, or other sequencing and recording software to record and mix performances and auditions and to create CDs, DVDs, and MP3s

Suggested Education and Training

College Degree: BM, BA, BS, or BFA in music education with a minor or additional coursework in music technology or audio engineering

Possible master's degree in music technology or music education with an emphasis in technology

Experience managing or working in an educational music lab setting. This could be as a part-time assistant in a university lab or as part of a student teaching experience

Experience recording and working with live sound. This could include time at a college or university studio, a home studio, or a professional studio

College or University Music Technology Professor

Teaching music technology at the college level can be a great career path for the experienced music technologist with the right combination of interests, skills, experience, and education. Someone pursuing this path needs to be a seasoned musician who also enjoys teaching, reading, researching, and writing. They need to be able to work with students at various ages and levels of experience. They should have experience working in the professional world of music production, music education, composition, or performance.

For full-time and long-term employment, most colleges require teachers to have what academics call the "terminal degree" (see Box 10.3), but there are many part-time and some full-time positions for music technologists with only a master's, or even a bachelor's degree, as illustrated in Figures 10.1 and 10.2.

BOX 10.3

The Terminal Degree in Music Technology

In music, the terminal degree is a doctorate of philosophy (PhD) or doctorate of musical arts (DMA). However, there are only a small number of PhD programs in music technology offered in the United States, and no DMA programs. This has led some to question if the master's degree should be considered the terminal degree in music technology. Does the fact that the master's degree is the highest academic degree readily available in music technology make it the terminal degree? Unfortunately, there isn't a consensus on this point, and while Graph 10.1 illustrates that a significant percentage of full-time music technology teachers hold only a master's or bachelor's degree, fewer and fewer universities will hire a full-time tenure-track faculty member unless they hold the doctorate degree.

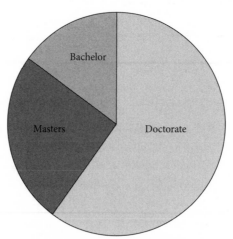

GRAPH 10.1 Highest Degree Held by Full-time Professors Teaching Music Technology

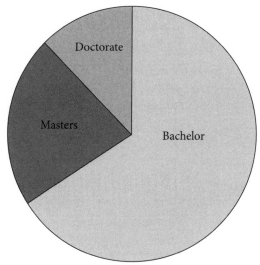

GRAPH 10.2 Highest Degree Held by Part-time Professors Teaching Music Technology

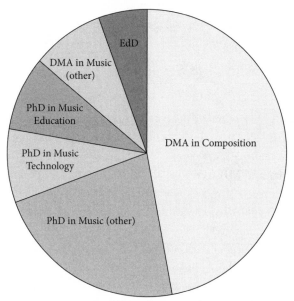

GRAPH 10.3 Doctorate Degrees Held by Full-time Professors Teaching Music Technology

Currently, professors with degrees in areas other than music technology are hired to direct most university music technology programs. Often these faculty members will teach technology as well as other courses in the areas of their expertise. Figure 10.3 shows the degrees held by tenure earning music technology faculty at universities offering bachelor degrees in music technology.

Hiring part-time or adjunct faculty to teach some music technology classes is common at many universities. Professionals with experience working in a studio, or running live sound at a performance venue, can often be recruited to support the university's full-time faculty by teaching music technology classes. While they lack the academic credentials of most college teachers, these professionals possess the necessary technical skills to teach music technology.

Although the number of jobs teaching college is significantly less than in public school teaching, there are also fewer qualified candidates for these positions. The level of experience needed and the combination of skills and interests required limits the applicant pool significantly. And, the lack of graduate programs, and especially doctoral programs, in music technology means that the academic world is producing few qualified candidates to teach music technology at the college level (see Box 10.4). These factors, combined with the expanding number of undergraduate music technology programs, create a significant demand for college music technology teachers.

Specific Technology Skills Required

Hardware:

  Mac and PC computers: able to save, manage, and transfer files, effectively use software (see below), connect to audio interfaces and hardware devices

  Synthesizers and MIDI controllers: familiar with common models and brands, especially those owned by the school, able to select and modify patches and programs, able to run through an amplifier or route through a computer

  Microphones: familiar with common models and brands, especially those owned by the school, understand the distinction between and proper use of dynamic and condenser mics, know effective mic selection and placement techniques for various instruments and especially for various musical groups such as concert choir, show choir, concert band, jazz band, and orchestra in both live performance and for recording

  Recording equipment: able to record ensembles and individuals for rehearsal, performances, auditions, and other purposes, able to use analog and digital recorders, CD burners, computers, and other equipment available at the school

---

BOX 10.4

The Need for More Doctoral Programs in Music Technology

More doctoral programs are needed to give music technologists the academic skills and credentials required to ensure the future of music technology as an independent academic discipline. It is in doctoral programs that academic research is conducted. Not only do students in doctoral programs conduct research, but universities that offer advanced degree programs have more strenuous research requirements for their faculty as well. Graduate students often teach undergraduate classes as part of an assistantship, which allows full-time faculty to spend time in research activities. All academic disciplines require a healthy research base to advance the philosophy, standards, and legitimacy of that discipline. More doctorate programs in music technology are needed to increase the amount of research and research-based publications that can help to establish the discipline.

The lack of candidates with a terminal degree forces some universities to rely on part-time faculty to direct music technology programs. Part-time teachers generally don't attend faculty meetings, participate in university functions, or sit on university committees. Simply put, adjunct faculty members don't have the necessary engagement with the university to be able to build and support the music technology programs in which they teach. In university music departments, all areas must constantly work to publicize their activities and the accomplishments of their students, and to recruit new students. If the music technology area has no one to advocate for it, it can be difficult for that area to grow and expand.

Until there are more doctorate programs in music technology, and thus more music technologists with advanced degrees, universities may struggle to build up and maintain the kinds of undergraduate programs needed to train today's music technologists.

Live sound hardware: able to run live sound for various types of performances and venues, using analog and digital mixing boards, microphones, and speakers.

Lab maintenance and management: able to set up, manage, and maintain the music technology lab

Software:

> Music Notation software: able to use and teach students to use Finale or Sibelius to create musical scores and arrangements, transpose parts, create practice accompaniments, compose original music
>
> Instructional software: familiar with various programs for teaching music theory, exploring musical elements, and for practicing and preparing music
>
> Recording software: able to use GarageBand, Logic, Pro Tools, Studio One, or other sequencing and recording software to record and mix performances and auditions and to create CDs, DVDs, and MP3s

Suggested Education and Training

> College Degrees: PhD in music technology or music education, or DMA in composition, master's and bachelor's in music technology, music business, music education, composition, or performance with significant coursework in music technology, music business, or audio engineering
>
> Experience managing or working in an educational music lab setting. This could be through public school teaching experience, experience as a professional composer, or in a teaching assistantship in a master's or doctoral program
>
> Experience recording audio and working with live sound. This could include previous professional experience in a recording studio, live sound venue, church, or other setting

Interview with a Professional: Barbara Freedman, Electronic Music Teacher, Grades 9–12, Greenwich High School, Greenwich, Connecticut

SP: Can you start by telling me a little bit about your job?

BF: Yes. I teach music technology, or what our school calls Electronic Music. Back in 1969, a former teacher here started a course called Electronic Music. It became what other schools would call General Music or Music Appreciation. So, the idea was to take a Music Appreciation course and turn it into a hands-on applied learning course using technology. That has been the name of the course since 1969, and it's been offered every year since. I teach four levels of Electronic Music now.

PHOTO 10.1 Barbara Freedman

SP: What kinds of things do you teach in those classes?

BF: I teach music content strictly, especially in my introductory course. It is not about teaching technology, it's about teaching music, and using technology as a way to save, edit, manipulate, and produce music. Instead of writing it down with pen and paper, we use a computer.

SP: So you are teaching music composition?

BF: I teach music through composition using technology.

SP: Please tell me how your career evolved. How did you end up teaching music technology?

BF: I went into teaching late in life. I was 33 years old when I went into teaching and I taught in New York City. I did not have an education degree. I had three degrees in music performance, and I had started my doctorate in orchestral conducting. In the program I attended, at the Hartt School of Music, there were a lot of teachers. They were saying to me, "You'd be a great teacher, you'd be a great teacher." At the time, I was working part-time as a business manager and doing sales and business and all of that stuff, and freelancing, and freelancing, and freelancing. My stepdaughter was going to college and I needed more steady work, and a better career.

So I looked around at schools and sent my résumé out and one of the places called me. I landed a teaching job in New York City at a very good school. I was really only interested in teaching general music, as opposed to band or orchestra or chorus, but they said, "If you're going to teach general music, you're going to have to teach one chorus class." I said, "Sure, why not?" I had no idea what I was doing, and I was probably horrible the first year or two, but I just studied a lot and got better. I was on the technology committee of the school, which was a group of teachers and the principal, and we talked about different ideas for the school. For example, they were putting in a big room with a T1 line and videoconferencing, which was a really big deal 15 years ago. So I was on this technology committee.

After four years of working in New York City public schools, I was looking to get out. I had sent my résumé around, and there was an opening in Greenwich schools for a band teacher, a part-time band teacher, which was not a job I wanted, but I thought, "Hey, I'll send them my résumé anyway." In my cover letter it said I was on the technology committee at my old school. So I got a call just a week later. Their electronic music teacher was leaving to take a job as a choir director and they asked if I would interview for the electronic music job. I had, when I was in graduate school, done a work-study doing recordings of the music school. We did stereo recordings, and maybe I worked the soundboard with one microphone. So in response, I said, "Yeah, yeah, no problem, I know that. Yeah, yeah, I can teach that." That's what I said in the interview, but I had no clue. The truth is, I really had no clue. So it was the same thing as when I took the job teaching chorus.

But I'll tell you what I discovered. The truth is that I had everything I needed. Because what you teach is music. I'm teaching kids music. They didn't want to know what an XLR cable was, or a ¼ inch cable, or an RCA cable. They didn't really care about signal flow. We had a little computer lab with old PC computers, keyboards, and soundcards and SCSI cables. We had mixing boards that went back into the computer, and into a Yamaha MU 50 sound module, because there was no such thing as software synthesizers at the time, it was all sound modules. So you had to do this whole MIDI configuration through the mixing board and back into the computers. And every 20 minutes the PCs would crash so you had to restart them. And we were using Freestyle by Mark of the Unicorn, MOTU, which is a fantastic program and not difficult at all to learn.

So what I realized was that the kids just wanted to get on the computers and make music and compose. So I thought, "Okay." So they would compose. And I would go around, and I would listen and I'd say, "You know what? You have no clue how to quantize because you don't know what quarters, eighths and sixteenths are, and how they fit together. I can teach you that. You guys don't know anything about how to compose a melody. I can teach you that. You guys don't know anything about scales and chords. I can teach you chords and inversions and how to extrapolate a baseline. I can teach you that." So I began to teach them music, and they would teach me the software.

SP: And at the time, they were just using MIDI, right?

BF: Totally MIDI. And mostly, in my first two class levels we still do only MIDI. I don't do any audio until Level II. There's the introduction course, then Level I, Level II, and Level III with an honors section. So I don't do any audio until we get to Level II. I do this because you have to know about music to work with MIDI, if you're playing on piano keyboards. I use piano keyboards as MIDI controllers. Why do I choose a piano keyboard? Because it is based on the foundation of Western music theory: white keys and black keys. And that's what I want engraved in their brains, the foundation of Western music theory.

SP: You discovered that despite your own concerns about your technology background, what you were teaching them was music, and there you had a lot to offer.

BF: A lot. I had a ton to offer. And as a musician, I have a different way of listening to music, which is also something we explored.

SP: Can you tell me some more about your musical background?

BF: I have a bachelor's degree and a master of music degree from the City University of New York, the Conservatory at Brooklyn College.

SP: What is your primary instrument?

BF: I'm a percussionist. And I still play. I play with the Ridgefield Symphony, and the Bridgeport Symphony, and sometimes the Greenwich Symphony. I freelance all around. And I teach private lessons on beginning drums after school. I have a handful of students. So I still play a lot, during the year. Timpani is my main instrument. So I have a bachelor's and master's from Brooklyn and I have a professional performance diploma from the Mannes College of Music, and I started my doctorate in orchestral conducting at Hartt, which is the University of Hartford, the Hartt School of Music. So I have a lot of paper. And then I went back to school to get my education degree once I started teaching.

SP: How important is your musical background to what you're doing?

BF: Well, I think teachers need to be extremely proficient in their content. I think the very first thing for a teacher to have is their love of kids, and their desire to teach them. That is the number one most important thing for a teacher to have. The second most important thing for a teacher to have is a great deal of content knowledge. The third thing is to have a skill, or at least the ability to develop a skill for content delivery. And to be able to, almost dance with the particular group of kids, or the people you have in the room, and to adjust your content delivery so that they get the content. You have to have the ability to do that. I guess the education world is calling that differentiation now. So I think that my music background as a performer is hugely important to be able to deliver content.

SP: What's your feeling about the atmosphere for music technology in high schools?

BF: I think any concerns people may have about a new music technology program coming to a school building are based on the fear that it will undermine current programs. However, in my experience, that isn't the case at all. Only in rare instances has that happened at my school; maybe only a handful of kids. I can honestly only think of two or three kids in eleven years that have dropped the performance ensemble to take my course.

SP: So you're not stealing kids from other music areas, but you are providing a new music area for a whole new crop of kids.

BF: That is exactly right. And current music teachers would do well to go into technology. They would do well to go into technology to save their jobs. And here's why: you have to expand your client base. It's true in any business. If you want to keep your business open, you have to make sure that your customer base is broad enough. People need to come in to your business and pay, as it were. The truth is, we are elective teachers. If kids aren't asking for our course, we don't teach it. If they're not knocking on your door, your shop is closed. Now, bands will always be around, in certain parts of this country, because they also serve the football team. This country has a very deep cultural and philosophical commitment to this event called the halftime show, and the marching band. The football parents and the community expect the halftime show. So we have to do that, and make sure that the band is uniformed well, and they perform well, and they sound good, and they're given all the resources they need, because it supports the general community culture of this thing called football. I mean, that's fantastic; I don't have an issue with that. I think it's perfectly fine. In certain parts of this country that will be the norm and it isn't going anywhere. But I live in the Northeast and here, that's not necessarily the case. The school I used to teach at in New York City, we didn't have football, and football doesn't exist in Great Britain, and it doesn't exist in other parts of the world. It really doesn't exist in the Northeast in the way that it does in other parts of the country. Where football isn't the driving force behind school music, there need to be good reasons to justify music programs.

The state of Connecticut is changing its high school graduation requirements in 2014. The requirements currently state that you have to take one music, or art, or technology course to graduate. Technology can be science technology, good old-fashioned shop courses, or anything defined as a technology course, including something having to do with computers. This is important, because now they're changing the verbiage. Because of the new technology requirements, because of the Race to the Top funding, because of the new STEMs funding, Science Technology Engineering and Math, they are making this change. There is the Common Core Standards, which is really based mostly in English and Math and the other content areas, and there are the STEMs areas. But where is music and art in any of this? Nowhere to be found. So how do we make music part of the STEMs curriculum so that it is a required, viable content area? In Connecticut, the change will make it so that you have one credit in music or art and one credit in technology. Music technology classes will serve for both. This is how you make yourself pertinent. The other way you make yourself pertinent is to make sure that more kids are asking for your class than any other class in the building. Part of that is offering music technology courses and part of that has to do with teacher personality, available equipment, and other things.

SP: But music technology classes can be the draw that helps music teachers keep their jobs.

BF: Absolutely.

SP: In your own case, you are filling all your classes. And now they're hiring a new teacher to teach more sections of music technology at your school. You basically can't teach enough music technology classes. The students are clamoring for these classes.

BF: I will teach five or six sections of intro classes in a semester. That's 120 kids. And then, the next semester, I'll teach another 120 kids. Next year, I'll be teaching three sections of Level I. That's an additional 60 kids. I'm also teaching one section of Level II, which is 20 students and one section of Level III, which is 20 students. And the new teacher is teaching additional sections. Administrators love this because this is a business. If people don't understand the business of how a school runs, they can't keep their job. They say, "Isn't music great?" Yeah, music is great, but no one cares when it comes to the bottom line.

SP: So music technology is a great way, in a very pragmatic sense, to explain to the administrator that you are worth the money; that beyond the wonderful benefits of learning music, these courses are extremely valuable to the school for financial reasons?

BF: Absolutely.

SP: How have your diverse experiences helped you to be better at what you do?

BF: I think what's important for musicians and students of music in college to understand, is that musicians make a living the same way Bach made a living. And they have for all those hundreds of years since Bach, and for hundreds of years before Bach.

SP: And how is that?

BF: We do everything we can related to music to make a living. Think about this: My teacher played with the New York Philharmonic for 45 years. There were three contracted percussionists with the New York Philharmonic and they all had their jobs for that long or longer. So every 45 or 50 years, there's an opening in the New York Philharmonic. New York City has five major conservatories of music and every year they each graduate between nine and twelve percussionists. That's how many people want the New York Philharmonic job. Every year. So how do you make a living, because those are the jobs that give you a really great living? You do several things. You play for regional orchestras, which I do, you play in every freelance job you can, at a certain level, you teach privately, you teach in schools, you compose, you perform, you create, you do everything around music just like Bach. He wrote, he taught, he composed, he performed, he built organs. He did everything he could around music to make a living. That's what we do. So you have to be diverse. And music teachers would do well to be just as diverse in their schools.

SP: Explain what you mean by that.

BF: Bands are great, and orchestras are great, and choruses are great, and I don't ever want to see them leave education. But, they only reach a small percentage of the students. We have to reach the rest. And just like in Connecticut, other states are going to require some music course of all students. I think all music teachers should ask themselves this question: "Do you really want to teach music appreciation as a lecture-based history course? Do you really? Do you think your kids care?" They don't. But if you have a way to have a music appreciation course that is really cool and wonderful and incorporates technology, and you can teach them about Bach and Beethoven, if you can pull that off, you're going to find success. Because you have a customer over there. It's called a 15-year-old boy. What do you want to sell to a 15-year-old boy? Because if those 15-year-old boys aren't buying your product, you are out of work.

SP: And you think music technology is attractive to 15-year-old boys?

BF: Yes. And I have empirical evidence to back it up.

SP: So what's the best part about being a teacher?

BF: The best part, for me, about being a teacher, is being around my students. That's the best part. And that has nothing to do with music technology. When I was leaving my job in the New York City public school, I was really upset. I had this sadness about leaving the school. I love my kids. But the truth is, you're going to love the kids wherever you go. They're going to change every year, or every four years anyway. But you do it because you love kids.

I was in business, and I did a lot in sales also, and I have never worked harder, psychologically, emotionally, and physically harder, in a single day than I have worked while being a teacher. Ever. I do four or five performances a day. I stand up and perform in front of people. If you're not performing, and putting it out there, and doing your song and dance when they're in the room, you lose them. I can't just say I'm not feeling good or I think I'm going to have a cup of coffee, or I'm going to go to the bathroom. So it's hard work.

But it's also very gratifying. On average, 35% of the seniors in my two most advanced classes go on to study music in college. That translates into something between six and twelve kids a year going into music; music composition, music technology, music production, and music business. One third of those kids never studied music before my class. And I find that when you are opening your doors to the other 80%, you get a different kind of kid. There are kids that go to college for music technology that would never have thought of going to college before.

I tell kids right away, early on, if you have any thoughts of going into music technology or audio engineering for college, you need to go and learn an instrument. Learn guitar or piano. Piano is preferable, and I can give them names of private teachers to go to, or put yourself in the choirs here at our school. Why? Because who says you can't do a vocal audition when you go to college? 95% of my students are boys and our choir teacher loves it when I send him those boys. This is a college-tracked course. I teach four levels because I can take a kid, when they're a freshman, and they've never had any experience in music, and I can send them to college in this subject. And a lot of these kids never would have thought of doing this before. I'm talking about college. I'm not talking about going to trade schools. I rarely send high school kids to trade schools. I don't believe in trade schools until you are at least 25 years old, and you've tried college. That's my philosophy. Whether it's a two-year college and you're starting with an associates degree, or a four-year degree, you're going to college. That's just my philosophy. And they go to college.

College is not about really training you for a career. It can be, and you will learn useful things. But college is really about feeding your brain. It's about working this muscle while it's developing, until you're around 25, and experienced with different people, and different things. You don't get that at a trade school. You missed out completely on the opportunity, the social, emotional learning that college is. Which is another reason that I think online education is great, but for that age, get yourself in and around with your peers.

SP: One last question. How important is networking to what you do?

BF: Because music technology teachers find themselves in the position of being the only ones in their district, having connections to other music technology teachers is very important. It's good to have feedback, or to get ideas, or if I get stuck with something, it's good to know about the resources that are available. I get a lot of Internet feeds that give me content information on technology, and not just from music educators, but also from other professionals and web resources that deliver content. I can't sit there and go through all of the resources that are available, so when people around the world who are picking up on various resources, when they tweet it, or they put on the music PLN, or they put it on a Facebook page, this network of people that I have gathered in this community becomes the aggregator of information for me. And from that I can draw what I need. So I think that the availability of social media and participation in it becomes your own learning network and that is very important.

How do you keep track of what's new? How do you stay fresh? This is my eleventh year teaching music technology here. It's my eleventh year and you do get into a rut where you know what works and you just keep going. But you need to stay fresh. Plus, the technology is changing a lot, and changing very quickly. So how do you stay fresh? I think it's important for music technology teachers to get themselves to the TI:ME conference. I really do. It's the best technology conference for music teachers around. I think the TI:ME conference offers the best, most cutting-edge information, and that's where the best, most cutting edge people are so get yourself there. If there's one conference you go to every year as a teacher of music technology, go to the TI:ME conference.

SP: Thank you very much.

BF: You're welcome.

Notes

1. National Center for Education Statistics, "Table 83: Estimated Average Annual Salary of Teacher in Public Elementary and Secondary Schools: Selected Years, 1959–60 through 2010–11," *Digest of Education Statistics*, Prepared May 2011, [Online]. Available: http://nces.ed.gov/programs/digest/d11/tables/dt11_083.asp.
2. Steve Henderson, "More than 75 Percent of American Households Own Computers," *Focus on Prices and Spending, Consumer Expenditures: 2008*, 1:4, May 2010. [Online]. Available: http://bls.gov/opub/focus/volume1_number4/cex_1_4.htm.
3. Henderson, "Computers," 1:4.
4. Victoria J. Rideout, Ulla G. Foehr, and Donald F. Roberts, *Generation M2: Media in the Lives of 8- to 18-Year-Olds* (Menlo Park, CA, Henry J. Kaiser Family Foundation, 2010), 28.
5. Rick Dammers, *"Technology Based Music Classes in High Schools in the United States"* (Minneapolis, MN: Paper presented at the Association for Technology in Music Instruction National Conference, 2010).
6. Dammers, "Technology Based Music Classes," 2010.
7. Dammers, "Technology Based Music Classes," 2010.

11

Conclusion

Be Ready for Anything

The previous chapters have described careers in six broad areas of music technology: the recording studio, the live sound venue, the film and television industry, computers, retail sales and manufacturing, and education. Hopefully by reading about the types of jobs that are available, the musical and technological skills required for each, and the interviews with professionals working in those fields, you have started to gain the perspective to help you decide which area of music technology you would like to pursue.

But some music technologists, especially in the beginning of their careers, find that to be successful, they need to work in many of the areas described in the book. While Chapters 6 through 10 are presented as if each area of music technology is discreet and separate, there exists considerable overlap in the skills required for all of them.

The following interview with Doug Siebum illustrates that a music technologist with varied skills, a strong work ethic, and personal initiative can succeed working in several aspects of music technology. Doug Siebum is a recent graduate of the Digital Media Arts program at California State, Dominguez Hills that was highlighted in Chapter 7. In the following interview, he talks about his diverse career and experiences while successfully working as a music technologist in one of the most competitive entertainment markets in the world: Los Angeles.

Interview with a Professional: Doug Siebum, Freelance Audio Engineer

SP: Can you tell me a little about how your career got started?

DS: I guess my career in audio really started back when I was in high school. I had friends who were in punk bands. I would go to their shows and help them carry their equipment, and I think that was my first introduction

PHOTO 11.1 Doug Siebum

to working around musicians. As I got a little bit older, I had friends who were in recording studios all the time. They suggested that I learn how to run some of the equipment since I was hanging around the recording studio. I started taking classes at Sacramento City College in the Audio Production program and I went there for a few years as I was trying to figure out what I wanted to do, but recording and audio production really stood out to me. So I got an associate's degree in audio production. While I was doing that, I ran sound at a local theater called the Studio Theatre in Sacramento. It was probably about a 100-seat theater and I did sound there for about nine months. Eventually I transferred to Cal State Dominguez Hills because I thought it would be good to get a bachelor's degree. So I went into their Digital Media Arts program and got my degree with an emphasis in Audio Recording.

SP: You decided to move from Sacramento to the LA area. How did you learn about that program?

DS: I learned about it online. I was looking for schools in California that had audio programs and it was one of the ones I found. I figured that moving to LA was a good move because I figured that if you learn to swim in the deep end of the pool, you can swim anywhere. It really was quite an experience. It was a big adjustment. Because the entertainment industry is largely based in Los Angeles, there is a lot of opportunity. But there is also a lot of competition; especially in the movie industry. I was interning at a postproduction house called Hacienda Post, and I created sound effects for cartoons. That's where I learned a lot about cutting sound effects. Some of the effects I cut were used on cartoons.

SP: What does that mean, that you were cutting sound effects?

DS: When you're watching a movie, or a TV show, or a cartoon and something happens, any sound that you hear that's not production sound comes from Foley and sound effects libraries. And when you hear a sound effect, it's not that they just took one sound effect and put it there. When you're cutting sound effects, you're taking sound effects from the library and you're layering them and splicing them together. To make one sound effect for one incident that happened, say the sound of someone falling down, you may have seven or eight different effects from the library layered to make that sound. It's a lot more involved than most people think. When we were in school doing it, we were on the very introductory level. We didn't know any better and we would just take one sound effect and put it in the movie and say, "Oh yeah, this is great." But when you see these professional sound effects editors, their hands are just flying and they're cutting these effects really fast, and layering them, and it's really amazing to see them work. Because LA is so competitive, the quality of work is very high. There are just so many great people you can choose from.

SP: And only the best survive?

DS: Exactly.

SP: What other things did you do in your internship?

DS: I worked a little with dialogue, but didn't like that very much. I did a lot of backgrounds or BGs. I would take the sound effects library and put wind and whatever city noises you would hear like cars going by, or whatever was needed to make it sound like you were there. Cutting BGs was a big part of what I did. I also cut some hard effects. Hard effects would be, depending on the movie, a spaceship being shot down or something else big happening in the movie. I also did some Foley editing; synchronizing footstep in the cartoons.

SP: Can you talk about how your career evolved?

DS: While I was in school, I also started working for an online radio station. I had been working at the campus radio station, and the station coordinator started an online station that he sold to a bigger company.

PHOTO II.2   Doug Siebum behind the microphone at the Home Depot Center

He gave me a job there, at the station called perreoradio.com. The guy that owned the radio station was Jay Rifkin. He is a big film and music producer who started Mojo Records in the late 1990s. He was involved with *The Lion King* and produced "Hakuna Matata." This guy is a giant in the industry and I was working for him at his radio station doing basic sound editing. I was cleaning up podcasts, and commercials and so forth.

That was one of my first paid sound editing gigs. I worked there for about a year after school and while I was there, I started working at the Home Depot Center, which is where the LA Galaxy and Chivas USA play. I was working in the broadcast department, and they base what they do in stadium broadcasts on a broadcast TV model. So if you can do stadium sound and broadcast, it's very similar to doing broadcast TV. That gave me the skills necessary to pick up some broadcast TV jobs. So if you can get a job at a stadium, it can be a good way to get into broadcast TV sound.

Someone told me early in my career, "You are going to end up working somewhere totally different than where you think you are going to be." I thought I was going to be in recording studios with bands. But what I fell into was working in broadcast TV, and doing some sound effects editing, and I still work at the stadium; I've been there about five years now. In the evening, I mix audio for clubs and bands and I also do music festivals. I'm pretty diverse in the kinds of jobs that I pick up. In addition to all of that, I've worked on three films, two independent features and one documentary. For the documentary I was the music recordist, for one of the indie films I was the sound effects editor, and I was a re-recording mixer for the other.

SP: How did you land the film jobs?

DS: It was kind of a coincidence. You know, your classmates and your teachers are great connections. It's really what going to college is all about. It's about the networking. It keeps coming up throughout your career. One of my professors had asked me to come back and speak to his class. After giving the lecture, I saw another one of my former teachers. He was having a guest give a lecture in his class. He said, "Hey, there's someone I want you to meet." It was producer and director Charles Unger and he was making a movie called *Come Together*. We exchanged information and he ended up hiring me to work on his film as a re-recordist.

SP: Had you ever done re-recording before?

DS: I had done a little bit on student projects, but nothing like this. Tackling a feature film, after I had only done a few small things, was a big project. It really opened my eyes to how much needs to be done. The other re-recording mixer and the sound effects supervisor for the film was James Morioka. He's a top-notch sound effects editor and has worked on a lot of big films. I learned a lot from him. I still stay in touch with him and to have him as a resource is really great.

SP: So you really learned a lot on the job?

DS: You always have to learn on the job. In school you're going to get a lot of technical information, but you really have to do internships and learn on the job because you'll be learning from professionals. It's one thing to try learning at home, or in your garage, or by yourself, and maybe you'll do ok. But learning from professionals who do this for a living, every single day of their lives is different. They're going to teach you the right way to do it and you'll learn a lot of shortcuts. They know ways to avoid problems, and things you're not going to see if you are doing it on your own. Working with professionals and getting in that environment, whether it's on the job training and you're being paid, or through unpaid internships, you can really learn from people who know what they're doing.

SP: Would you say that the skills required are similar if you're running live sound at a major sporting venue, or if you're in a studio working with a band, or if you're in a television setting, or if you're working on a movie?

DS: Yes, and no. The basic skills are very similar and a lot of things will apply across the board. For example, learning frequencies of common sounds and instruments, and knowing what things sound like, and should sound like. But the environments are very different. Postproduction is done very much in Pro Tools. It's almost all inside the box—on the computer. In the case of live sound, you're setting up amps and speakers and running cables and making sure there's no radio interference with the wireless gear and so on.

SP: Can a person with your skills find themselves working in various aspects of all of those environments?

DS: That's how it has worked out for me. Some people will get into something and they will just fall into a niche and that's what they do. Sometimes an internship will turn into a job, and that's what they do for their career. There were no openings when I finished my internship and so I had to find work in other places. I think that is why I'm so diverse, and I think it's important because I can step into different roles. I can do broadcast TV, or I can do sound effects for movies, or I can do live sound for a concert.

For example, I met Tony Newton at a party held at 4th Street Recording Studios. Tony was one of the original Motown bass players. He played and toured with Smokey Robinson, Stevie Wonder, Michael Jackson, Diana Ross, Marvin Gaye, and many others. We just started talking and he needed someone to record sound for this documentary he was shooting at Alvas Showroom in San Pedro. He wanted to have that live-show sound for the music he was doing so he wanted someone who was a live sound engineer to do the recording and to run sound for the event and the movie shoot. Because of my experience with live sound at the stadium and at clubs, and my film experience, he asked me to do it. In other words, I can be where I need to be depending on where the money is.

That's just very much how I work. I'm all freelance, even though I have the stadium and certain clubs and sound rental companies that I'm a regular for. But it's all on a freelance basis. I work all the time. I'm so busy right now that if I want a day off, I literally have to book myself for a day off. Because otherwise I can go three weeks working without a day off. I actually have to write on my calendar, "Day off. Do not accept work."

SP: That's got to be a good thing, right?

DS: It is. But the hours are crazy. I'll do sound at a club that closes at two a.m. and I'll get out of there and be driving home at three or three thirty. I may have a job at the stadium that starts at nine a.m. or even six a.m. I have to be careful when I set my schedule because the hours are all over the place. But when the work is there, I'm working.

SP: What do you suggest for getting your foot in the door? How does a young person get started?

DS: My opportunities have come largely from connections at school. The position at the radio station came from people I met while I was working at the radio station at school. The job at the stadium came from one of my former classmates in school. The director of broadcasting at the stadium had hired him, and after about six months he asked him if he knew anyone else that he would recommend. I think he reached out to about five people, but I was the one who jumped on it. As a side note, my friend was working at Guitar Center when he was hired by the stadium. I actually know several people who were discovered, as it were, while working at Guitar Center, so that's not a bad place to start out either. In terms of live sound for clubs and music festivals, I have former school mates who are all over. One of my former classmates is the senior sound guy at Whiskey a Go Go, one of the most famous clubs in L.A. He writes the schedule over there, so I work there every once in a while. Now I find that I'm the person throwing work to my former classmates. In the evenings and on weekends I work at a blues club called Harvelle's. They're in Long Beach and Santa Monica and most of the sound guys there are people that I helped them find from CSU Dominguez Hills.

SP: Once you break into this business, how do you move up?

DS: Don't give up. You have to be extra-ambitious, extra-determined and you just have to work harder than everyone else. No matter how hard people thought they were going to have to work in this industry, they need to multiply it a hundred times. You have to be willing to go in there and have really rough days and just keep coming back with a smile on your face.

And I also recommend that you dress and act professionally. There certainly isn't a dress code and you will see those guys that come in with the holes in their jeans and a Mohawk. But for me, it's about being able to pick up a variety of jobs. I can be doing a rock concert one day, but running sound at a corporate event the next. So I always dress and act professionally.

Building your career is something that just comes with time. Once you're in the business for a little while, you're going to start making more and more connections. People are going to know you, and you'll get offered jobs. It just starts to happen. And over time, you build your skills to the point where people know that you're not the new guy anymore. When you walk into the room, stuff starts happening. Things go right when you're there. People can see the value in that and it gets you work.

SP: Thanks, Doug.

DS: You're welcome.

College Programs by School

Table A.1: American Colleges and Universities Offering Bachelor
Degree Programs in Music Technology, Audio Recording,
Music Industry, and Music Business

College or University	City	State	Degree(s)	Program
Albright College	Reading	PA	B.A.	Music Business
American InterContinental University	Weston	FL	B.F.A.	Audio Recording & Sound Design
American InterContinental University	Atlanta	GA	B.F.A.	Audio Recording & Sound Design
American University	Washington	DC	B.A., B.S.	Audio Production, Audio Technology, Business and Music
Anderson University	Anderson	IN	B.A.	Music Business
Appalachian State University	Boone	NC	B.S.	Music Industry
Art Institute of Atlanta	Atlanta	GA	B.A.	Audio Production

(*Continued*)

Table A.1　(Continued)

College or University	City	State	Degree(s)	Program
Art Institute of Nashville	Nashville	TN	B.A.	Audio Production
Augsburg College	Minneapolis	MN	B.A.	Music Business
Ball State University	Muncie	IN	B.S.	Music Media Production and Industry
Barton College	Wilson	NC	B.S.	Audio Engineering
Bay State College	Boston	MA	B.S.	Music Industry
Belmont University	Nashville	TN	B.A., B.S. B.B.A.	Music Industry and Audio Engineering, Music Business
Berklee College of Music	Boston	MA	B.M.	Music Business, Music Technology
Bloomfield College	Bloomfield	NJ	B.A.	Music Technology
Brigham Young University	Provo	UT	B.M.	Media Music, Sound Recording Technology
Brown University	Providence	RI	B.A.	Computer Music & Multimedia Track
Butler University	Indianapolis	IN	B.A.	Recording Industry
California Institute of the Arts	Valencia	CA	B.F.A.	Music Technology: Intelligence, Interaction, and Design

(*Continued*)

Table A.1 (Continued)

College or University	City	State	Degree(s)	Program
California State Polytechnic University	Pomona	CA	B.A.	Music Industry
California State University, Chico	Chico	CA	B.A.	Music Industry and Technology/ Recording Arts
California State University, Dominguez Hills	Carson	CA	B.A.	Music Technology, Audio Recording
California State University, Northridge	Northridge	CA	B.A.	Music Industry
California State University, San Bernardino	S. Bernardino	CA	B.A.	Music Technology
California University of Pennsylvania	California	PA	B.S.	Commercial Music Technology
Capital University Conservatory of Music	Columbus	OH	B.A., B.M.	Music Technology
Carnegie Mellon	Pittsburgh	PA	B.S.	Music Technology
Chowan University	Murfreesboro	NC	B.A.	Music Industry
City College of New York	New York	NY	B.F.A.	Music and Audio Technology
Clemson University	Clemson	SC	B.A.	Audio Technology
College of Saint Rose	Albany	NY	B.S.	Music Industry
Colorado Christian University	Lakewood	CO	B.A.	Sound Recording Technology emphasis
Columbia College	Chicago	IL	B.A., B.S.	Audio Arts, Acoustics

(*Continued*)

Table A.1 (Continued)

College or University	City	State	Degree(s)	Program
Dallas Baptist University	Dallas	TX	B.A., B.S.	Music Business
Delta State University	Cleveland	MS	B.A., B.S.	Sound Recording Technology, Music Industry
DePaul University	Chicago	IL	B.M.	Sound Recording Technology
Drexel University	Philadelphia	PA	B.S.	Music Industry
Duquesne University	Pittsburgh	PA	B.M.	Music Technology
Elmhurst College	Elmhurst	IL	B.M., B.S.	Music Business
Elon University	Elon	NC	B.S.	Music Technology
Evangel University	Springfield	MS	B.S.	Emphasis in Recording Technology
Ex'pressions College for Digital Arts	Emeryville	CA	B.A.	Sound Arts, Interactive Audio
Ferris State University	Big Rapids	MI	B.S.	Music Industry Management
Five Towns College	Dix Hills	NY	B.M.	Audio Recording Technology, Music Business
Florida A&M University	Tallahassee	FL	B.S.	Music Industry
Florida Atlantic University	Boca Raton	FL	B.M.	Commercial Music
Florida State University	Tallahassee	FL	B.A.	Commercial Music
Fort Hays State University	Hays	KS	B.A.	Music Technology

(*Continued*)

Table A.1 (Continued)

College or University	City	State	Degree(s)	Program
Francis Marion University	Florence	SC	B.S.	Music Industry
Full Sail University	Winter Park	FL	B.S.	Music Business, Recording Arts
Georgia State University	Atlanta	GA	B.M., B.S.	Music Recording Technology, Music Management
Globe University	Woodbury	MN	B.S.	Music Business
Hampton University	Hampton	VA	B.S.	Music Recording Technology
Houghton College	Houghton	NY	B.M.	Audio Technology & Production
Illinois State University	Normal	IL	B.A., B.S.	Arts Technology
Indiana State University	Terre Haute	IN	B.A., B.S.	Music Business
Indiana University	Bloomington	IN	B.S.	Recording Arts
Indiana University-Purdue University Indianapolis	Indianapolis	IN	B.S.	Music Technology
International Academy of Design and Technology	Tampa	FL	B.F.A.	Audio Engineering
International Academy of Design and Technology	Las Vegas	NV	B.F.A.	Audio Engineering
Ithaca College	Ithaca	NY	B.M.	Sound Recording Technology
Jackson State University	Jackson	MS	B.M.	Music Technology
James Madison University	Harrisonburg	VA	B.M.	Music Industry
Johns Hopkins University	Baltimore	MD	B.M.	Recording Arts and Sciences

(*Continued*)

Table A.1 (Continued)

College or University	City	State	Degree(s)	Program
Keene State College	Keene	NH	B.A.	Music Technology
Kent State University—Stark	Stark	OH	B.S.	Music Technology
La Sierra University	Riverside	CA	B.S.	Music Technology
Lebanon Valley College	Annville	PA	B.M.	Sound Recording Technology
Lehigh University	Bethlehem	PA	B.A.	Music Business
Living Arts College	Raleigh	NC	B.S.	Audio Engineering
Lyndon State College	Lyndonville	VT	B.S.	Music Business
Madison Media Institute	Madison	WI	B.S.	Entertainment & Media Business
Mansfield University	Mansfield	PA	B.M.	Music Technology
McNally Smith College of Music	St. Paul	MN	B.A., B.S.	Music Business, Music Production
Mercy College	Dobbs Ferry	NY	B.S.	Music Industry
Middle Tennessee State University	Murfreesboro	TN	B.S.	Music Industry
Millikin University	Decatur	IL	B.M.	Music Business, Commercial Music
Minnesota State University	Moorhead	MN	B.M., B.S.	Music Industry
Missouri State University	Springfield	MO	B.S.	Music Business
Missouri Western State University	Saint Joseph	MO	B.M.	Music Technology

(Continued)

Table A.1 (Continued)

College or University	City	State	Degree(s)	Program
Montana State University	Bozeman	MT	B.A.	Music Technology
Montclair University	Montclair	NJ	B.A.	Media Arts with Audio Concentration
Murray State University	Murray	KY	B.A., B.S.	Music Business
Nazareth College	Rochester	NY	B.S.	Music Business
New England Institute of Art	Brookline	MA	B.S.	Audio & Media Technology
New England School of Communications	Bangor	ME	B.S.	Audio Engineering, Live Sound Technology
New York University	New York	NY	B.M.	Music Technology, Music Business
Northeastern University	Boston	MA	B.S.	Music Industry, Music Technology
NYU—Tisch School of the Arts	New York	NY	B.F.A.	Music Business
Oberlin College	Oberlin	OH	B.M.	Music Technology
Ohio University	Athens	OH	B.S.	Music Production & Recording Industry
Plymouth State University	Plymouth	NH	B.A.	Music Technology
Point Park University	Pittsburgh	PA	B.S.	Music Business
Radford University	Radford	VA	B.A., B.M.	Music Technology, Music Business

(*Continued*)

Table A.1 (Continued)

College or University	City	State	Degree(s)	Program
Saint Mary's University of Minnesota	Winona	MN	B.A.	Music Industry—Business or Technology Track
Salisbury University	Salisbury	MD	B.A.	Music Technology
San Francisco State	San Francisco	CA	B.A.	Music Technology
Savannah College of Art and Design	Savannah	GA	B.F.A.	Audio Engineering
Shenandoah University	Winchester	VA	B.M.	Music Production & Recording Technology
South Carolina State University	Orangeburg	SC	B.A., B.S.	Music Industry
Southeastern University	Lakeland	FL	B.S.	Music Business
Southern Illinois University	Carbondale	IL	B.A.	Audio Production
State University of New York, Fredonia	Fredonia	NY	B.S.	Sound Recording Technology
State University of New York, Potsdam	Potsdam	NY	B.M., B.S.	Music Business
Stephen F. Austin State University	Nacogdoches	TX	B.M.	Sound Recording Technology
Stetson University	Deland	FL	B.A., B.M.	Music Technology
Stevens Institute of Technology	Hoboken	NJ	B.S.	Production/ Recording/ Sound Design
Syracuse University	Syracuse	NY	B.S.	Music Industry

(*Continued*)

Table A.1 (Continued)

College or University	City	State	Degree(s)	Program
Texas State	San Marcos	TX	B.S.	Sound Recording Technology
Towson University	Towson	MD	B.S.	Audio/Radio Concentration
Transylvania University	Lexington	KY	B.A.	Music Technology
Trevecca Nazarene University	Nashville	TN	B.A.	Music Technology
Troy State University	Troy	AL	B.S.	Music Industry
University of Alabama at Birmingham	Birmingham	AL	B.A.	Music Technology
University of Alabama at Huntsville	Huntsville	AL	B.A.	Music Technology
University of Albany	Albany	NY	B.A.	Electronic Music & Media
University of Central Missouri	Warrensburg	MO	B.M.	Music Technology
University of Colorado at Denver	Denver	CO	B.A., B.S.	Music Business, Music Industry, Recording Arts
University of Denver	Denver	CO	B.M.	Audio Production
University of Hartford	W. Hartford	CT	B.S., B.M.	Music Production, Audio Engineering Technology
University of Maine at Augusta	Augusta	ME	B.M.	Audio Technology
University of Massachusetts—Lowell	Lowell	MA	B.M.	Sound Recording Technology, Music Business

(Continued)

Table A.1 (Continued)

College or University	City	State	Degree(s)	Program
University of Memphis	Memphis	TN	B.M.	Sound Recording Technology
University of Miami	Coral Gables	FL	B.M., B.S.	Music Engineering, Music Business and Entertainment Industries
University of Michigan	Ann Arbor	MI	B.M., B.S., B.F.A.	Music Technology, Sound Engineering, Performing Arts Technology,
University of Montana	Missoula	MT	B.A., B.M.	Music Technology
University of Nebraska at Omaha	Omaha	NE	B.M.	Music Technology
University of New Haven	West Haven	CT	B.A., B.S.	Music Industry, Music and Sound Recording
University of North Alabama	Florence	AL	B.A., B.S., B.B.A.	Music Industry
University of North Carolina, Asheville	Asheville	NC	B.S.	Music Technology
University of Oregon	Eugene	OR	B.S.	Music Technology
University of Southern California	Los Angeles	CA	B.M., B. S.	Music Industry, Music Technology
University of Southern Mississippi	Hattiesburg	MS	B.S.	Music Industry
University of St. Francis	Joliet	IL	B.A.	Digital Audio Recording Arts

(*Continued*)

Table A.1 (Continued)

College or University	City	State	Degree(s)	Program
University of Texas at Arlington	Arlington	TX	B.M.	Music Media—Audio Production, Music Business
University of Texas at El Paso	El Paso	TX	B.M.	Commercial Music
University of the Incarnate Word	San Antonio	TX	B.A.	Music Industry
University of the Pacific	Stockton	CA	B.A., B.M., B.S.	Music Business
University of Wisconsin	Oshkosh	WI	B.M.	Recording Technology
Valparaiso University	Valparaiso	IN	B.M.	Music Industry
Virginia Polytechnic Institute	Blacksburg	VA	B.A.	Music Technology
Wayne State University	Detroit	MI	B.M.	Music Technology
Webster University	St. Louis	MO	B.S.	Audio Production
Western Illinois University	Macomb	IL	B.M.	Music Business
William Paterson University	Wayne	NJ	B.M.	Sound Engineering Arts
York College of Pennsylvania	York	PA	B.S.	Music Industry, Recording Technology

College Programs by State

Table B.1: American Colleges and Universities Offering Bachelor Degree Programs in Music Technology, Audio Recording, Music Industry, and Music Business, Ordered by State

College or University	City	State	Degree(s)	Program
Troy State University	Troy	AL	B.S.	Music Industry
University of Alabama at Birmingham	Birmingham	AL	B.A.	Music Technology
University of Alabama at Huntsville	Huntsville	AL	B.A.	Music Technology
University of North Alabama	Florence	AL	B.A., B.S., B.B.A.	Music Industry
California Institute of the Arts	Valencia	CA	B.F.A.	Music Technology: Intelligence, Interaction, and Design
California State Polytechnic University	Pomona	CA	B.A.	Music Industry
California State University, Chico	Chico	CA	B.A.	Music Industry and Technology/ Recording Arts

(*Continued*)

Table B.1 (Continued)

College or University	City	State	Degree(s)	Program
California State Univ., Dominguez Hills	Carson	CA	B.A.	Audio Recording, Music Technology
California State University, Northridge	Northridge	CA	B.A.	Music Industry
California State University, San Bernardino	S. Bernardino	CA	B.A.	Music Technology
Ex'pressions College for Digital Arts	Emeryville	CA	B.A.	Sound Arts, Interactive Audio
La Sierra University	Riverside	CA	B.S.	Music Technology
San Francisco State	San Francisco	CA	B.A.	Music Technology
University of Southern California	Los Angeles	CA	B.M., B.S.	Music Industry, Music Technology
University of the Pacific	Stockton	CA	B.A., B.M., B.S.	Music Business
Colorado Christian University	Lakewood	CO	B.A.	Sound Recording Technology emphasis
University of Colorado at Denver	Denver	CO	B.A., B.S.	Music Business, Music Industry, Recording Arts
University of Denver	Denver	CO	B.M.	Audio Production
University of Hartford	W. Hartford	CT	B.S., B.M.	Music Production, Audio Engineering Technology
University of New Haven	West Haven	CT	B.A., B.S.	Music Industry, Music and Sound Recording
American University	Washington	DC	B.A., B.S.	Audio Production, Audio Technology, Business and Music

(*Continued*)

Table B.1 (Continued)

College or University	City	State	Degree(s)	Program
American InterContinental University	Weston	FL	B.F.A.	Audio Recording & Sound Design
Florida A&M University	Tallahassee	FL	B.S.	Music Industry
Florida Atlantic University	Boca Raton	FL	B.M.	Commercial Music
Florida State University	Tallahassee	FL	B.A.	Commercial Music
Full Sail University	Winter Park	FL	B.S.	Music Business, Recording Arts
International Academy of Design and Technology	Tampa	FL	B.F.A.	Audio Engineering
Southeastern University	Lakeland	FL	B.S.	Music Business
Stetson University	Deland	FL	B.A., B.M.	Music Technology
University of Miami	Coral Gables	FL	B.M., B.S.	Music Engineering, Music Business and Entertainment Industries
American InterContinental University	Atlanta	GA	B.F.A.	Audio Recording & Sound Design
Art Institute of Atlanta	Atlanta	GA	B.A.	Audio Production
Georgia State University	Atlanta	GA	B.M., B.S.	Music Recording Technology, Music Management
Savannah College of Art and Design	Savannah	GA	B.F.A.	Audio Engineering
Columbia College	Chicago	IL	B.A., B.S.	Audio Arts, Acoustics

(Continued)

Table B.1 (Continued)

College or University	City	State	Degree(s)	Program
DePaul University	Chicago	IL	B.M.	Sound Recording Technology
Elmhurst College	Elmhurst	IL	B.M., B.S.	Music Business
Illinois State University	Normal	IL	B.A., B.S.	Arts Technology
Millikin University	Decatur	IL	B.M.	Music Business, Commercial Music
Southern Illinois University	Carbondale	IL	B.A.	Audio Production
University of St. Francis	Joliet	IL	B.A.	Digital Audio Recording Arts
Western Illinois University	Macomb	IL	B.M.	Music Business
Anderson University	Anderson	IN	B.A.	Music Business
Ball State University	Muncie	IN	B.S.	Music Media Production and Industry
Butler University	Indianapolis	IN	B.A.	Recording Industry
Indiana State University	Terre Haute	IN	B.A., B.S.	Music Business
Indiana University	Bloomington	IN	B.S.	Recording Arts
Indiana University-Purdue University Indianapolis	Indianapolis	IN	B.S.	Music Technology
Valparaiso University	Valparaiso	IN	B.M.	Music Industry
Fort Hays State University	Hays	KS	B.A.	Music Technology
Murray State University	Murray	KY	B.A., B.S.	Music Business
Transylvania University	Lexington	KY	B.A.	Music Technology
Bay State College	Boston	MA	B.S.	Music Industry

(*Continued*)

Table B.1 (Continued)

College or University	City	State	Degree(s)	Program
Berklee College of Music	Boston	MA	B.M.	Music Business, Music Technology
New England Institute of Art	Brookline	MA	B.S.	Audio & Media Technology
Northeastern University	Boston	MA	B.S.	Music Industry, Music Technology
University of Massachusetts—Lowell	Lowell	MA	B.M.	Sound Recording Technology, Music Business
Johns Hopkins University	Baltimore	MD	B.M.	Recording Arts and Sciences
Salisbury University	Salisbury	MD	B.A.	Music Technology
Towson University	Towson	MD	B.S.	Audio/Radio Concentration
New England School of Communications	Bangor	ME	B.S.	Audio Engineering, Live Sound Technology
University of Maine at Augusta	Augusta	ME	B.M.	Audio Technology
Ferris State University	Big Rapids	MI	B.S.	Music Industry Management
University of Michigan	Ann Arbor	MI	B.M., B.S., B.F.A.	Music Technology, Sound Engineering, Performing Arts Technology,
Wayne State University	Detroit	MI	B.M.	Music Technology
Augsburg College	Minneapolis	MN	B.A.	Music Business
Globe University	Woodbury	MN	B.S.	Music Business
McNally Smith College of Music	St. Paul	MN	B.A., B.S.	Music Business, Music Production
Minnesota State University	Moorhead	MN	B.M., B.S.	Music Industry

(*Continued*)

Table B.1 (Continued)

College or University	City	State	Degree(s)	Program
Saint Mary's University of Minnesota	Winona	MN	B.A.	Music Industry—Business or Technology Track
Missouri State University	Springfield	MO	B.S.	Music Business
Missouri Western State University	Saint Joseph	MO	B.M.	Music Technology
University of Central Missouri	Warrensburg	MO	B.M.	Music Technology
Webster University	St. Louis	MO	B.S.	Audio Production
Delta State University	Cleveland	MS	B.A., B.S.	Sound Recording Technology, Music Industry
Evangel University	Springfield	MS	B.S.	Emphasis in Recording Technology
Jackson State University	Jackson	MS	B.M.	Music Technology
University of Southern Mississippi	Hattiesburg	MS	B.S.	Music Industry
Montana State University	Bozeman	MT	B.A.	Music Technology
University of Montana	Missoula	MT	B.A., B.M.	Music Technology
Appalachian State University	Boone	NC	B.S.	Music Industry
Barton College	Wilson	NC	B.S.	Audio Engineering
Chowan University	Murfreesboro	NC	B.A.	Music Industry
Elon University	Elon	NC	B.S.	Music Technology
Living Arts College	Raleigh	NC	B.S.	Audio Engineering
University of North Carolina, Asheville	Asheville	NC	B.S.	Music Technology

(*Continued*)

Table B.1 (Continued)

College or University	City	State	Degree(s)	Program
University of Nebraska at Omaha	Omaha	NE	B.M.	Music Technology
Keene State College	Keene	NH	B.A.	Music Technology
Plymouth State University	Plymouth	NH	B.A.	Music Technology
Bloomfield College	Bloomfield	NJ	B.A.	Music Technology
Montclair University	Montclair	NJ	B.A.	Media Arts with Audio Concentration
Stevens Institute of Technology	Hoboken	NJ	B.S.	Production/ Recording/Sound Design
William Paterson University	Wayne	NJ	B.M.	Sound Engineering Arts
International Academy of Design and Technology	Las Vegas	NV	B.F.A.	Audio Engineering
City College of New York	New York	NY	B.F.A.	Music and Audio Technology
College of Saint Rose	Albany	NY	B.S.	Music Industry
Five Towns College	Dix Hills	NY	B.M.	Audio Recording Technology, Music Business
Houghton College	Houghton	NY	B.M.	Audio Technology & Production
Ithaca College	Ithaca	NY	B.M.	Sound Recording Technology
Mercy College	Dobbs Ferry	NY	B.S.	Music Industry
Nazareth College	Rochester	NY	B.S.	Music Business

(*Continued*)

Table B.1 (Continued)

College or University	City	State	Degree(s)	Program
New York University	New York	NY	B.M.	Music Technology, Music Business
NYU—Tisch School of the Arts	New York	NY	B.F.A.	Music Business
State University of New York, Fredonia	Fredonia	NY	B.S.	Sound Recording Technology
State University of New York, Potsdam	Potsdam	NY	B.M., B.S.	Music Business
Syracuse University	Syracuse	NY	B.S.	Music Industry
University of Albany	Albany	NY	B.A.	Electronic Music & Media
Capital University Conservatory of Music	Columbus	OH	B.A., B.M.	Music Technology
Kent State University—Stark	Stark	OH	B.S.	Music Technology
Oberlin College	Oberlin	OH	B.M.	Music Technology
Ohio University	Athens	OH	B.S.	Music Production & Recording Industry
University of Oregon	Eugene	OR	B.S.	Music Technology
Albright College	Reading	PA	B.A.	Music Business
California University of Pennsylvania	California	PA	B.S.	Commercial Music Technology
Carnegie Mellon	Pittsburgh	PA	B.S.	Music Technology
Drexel University	Philadelphia	PA	B.S.	Music Industry
Duquesne University	Pittsburgh	PA	B.M.	Music Technology
Lebanon Valley College	Annville	PA	B.M.	Sound Recording Technology
Lehigh University	Bethlehem	PA	B.A.	Music Business

(*Continued*)

Table B.1 (Continued)

College or University	City	State	Degree(s)	Program
Mansfield University	Mansfield	PA	B.M.	Music Technology
Point Park University	Pittsburgh	PA	B.S.	Music Business
York College of Pennsylvania	York	PA	B.S.	Music Industry, Recording Technology
Brown University	Providence	RI	B.A.	Computer Music & Multimedia Track
Clemson University	Clemson	SC	B.A.	Audio Technology
Francis Marion University	Florence	SC	B.S.	Music Industry
South Carolina State University	Orangeburg	SC	B.A., B.S.	Music Industry
Art Institute of Nashville	Nashville	TN	B.A.	Audio Production
Belmont University	Nashville	TN	B.A., B.S., B.B.A.	Music Industry and Audio Engineering, Music Business
Middle Tennessee State University	Murfreesboro	TN	B.S.	Music Industry
Trevecca Nazarene University	Nashville	TN	B.A.	Music Technology
University of Memphis	Memphis	TN	B.M.	Sound Recording Technology
Dallas Baptist University	Dallas	TX	B.A., B.S.	Music Business
Stephen F. Austin State University	Nacogdoches	TX	B.M.	Sound Recording Technology
Texas State	San Marcos	TX	B.S.	Sound Recording Technology

(*Continued*)

Table B.1 (Continued)

College or University	City	State	Degree(s)	Program
University of Texas at Arlington	Arlington	TX	B.M.	Music Media—Audio Production, Music Business
University of Texas at El Paso	El Paso	TX	B.M.	Commercial Music
University of the Incarnate Word	San Antonio	TX	B.A.	Music Industry
Brigham Young University	Provo	UT	B.M.	Media Music, Sound Recording Technology
Hampton University	Hampton	VA	B.S.	Music Recording Technology
James Madison University	Harrisonburg	VA	B.M.	Music Industry
Radford University	Radford	VA	B.A., B.M.	Music Technology, Music Business
Shenandoah University	Winchester	VA	B.M.	Music Production & Recording Technology
Virginia Polytechnic Institute	Blacksburg	VA	B.A.	Music Technology
Lyndon State College	Lyndonville	VT	B.S.	Music Business
Madison Media Institute	Madison	WI	B.S.	Entertainment & Media Business
University of Wisconsin	Oshkosh	WI	B.M.	Recording Technology

Graduate Programs by School

Table C.1: American Colleges and Universities Offering Graduate Degree Programs in Music Technology, Audio Recording, Music Industry, and Music Business

College or University	City	State	Degree(s)	Program
American University	Washington	DC	M.A.	Audio Technology
Belmont University	Nashville	TN	M.B.A.	Entertainment & Music Business
Brown University	Providence	RI	Ph.D.	Computer Music and Multimedia
Carnegie Mellon University	Pittsburgh	PA	M.S.	Music Engineering Technology
Dallas Baptist University	Dallas	TX	M.B.A.	Music Business
Duquesne University	Pittsburgh	PA	M.M.	Music Technology
Florida International University	Miami	FL	M.M.	Music Technology
Full Sail University	Winter Park	FL	M.S.	Entertainment Business

(Continued)

Table C.1 (Continued)

College or University	City	State	Degree(s)	Program
Georgia Southern University	Statesboro	GA	M.M.	Music Technology
Georgia Institute of Technology	Atlanta	GA	M.S., Ph.D.	Music Technology
Illinois State University	Normal	IL	M.S.	Arts Technology
Indiana University-Purdue University Indianapolis	Indianapolis	IN	M.S.	Music Technology
Johns Hopkins University	Baltimore	MD	M.A., M.M.	Audio Sciences, Music Technology
McGill University	Montreal	CAN	M.M.	Music Technology
University of Michigan	Ann Arbor	MI	M.A.	Media Arts
Middle Tennessee State University	Murfreesboro	TN	M.F.A.	Recording Arts and Technologies
Mills College	Oakland	CA	M.F.A	Electronic Music & Recording Media
Missouri Western	St. Joseph	MO	M.A.A.	Digital Media
New York University	New York	NY	M.M., Ph.D.	Music Technology
Northwestern University	Evanston	IL	M.M.	Intermedia Music Technology
Savannah College of Art and Design	Savannah	GA	M.A., M.F.A.	Sound Design
University of Massachusetts— Lowell	Lowell	MA	M.M.	Sound Recording Technology

(*Continued*)

Table C.1 (Continued)

College or University	City	State	Degree(s)	Program
University of Akron	Akron	OH	M.M.	Music Technology
University of California at Santa Barbara	Santa Barbara	CA	M.A.	Electronic Music and Sound Design
University of Colorado at Denver	Denver	CO	M.S.	Recording Arts and Technologies
University of Miami	Coral Gables	FL	J.D., M.M. M.S.M.E.T.	Joint Degree in Law and Music Business, Electronic Music, Music Business and Entertainment Industries, Music Engineering
University of Oregon	Eugene	OR	M.M., Ph.D.	Intermedia Music Technology
University of South Florida	Tampa	FL	M.M.	Electro-Acoustic Music
West Chester University	West Chester	PA	M.M.	Music Technology
Yale University	New Haven	CT	M.F.A.	Sound Design

Notes

Chapter 1: The Professional Music Technologist

1. Christoph Wolff, *The New Bach Reader: A Life of Johann Sebastian Bach in Letters and Documents* (New York: W. W. Norton and Company, 1998), 365–366.

2. Andre Millard, *America on Record: A History of Recorded Sound* (New York: Cambridge University Press, 2005), 132–134.

3. Clayton M. Christensen, *The Innovators Dilemma* (New York: HarperCollins Publishers, 2003), 64.

4. Philip Elmer-Dewitt, "iTunes Store: 5 Billion Songs; 50,000 Movies per Day," *Fortune Magazine* [Online]. June 19, 2008. Available: http://tech.fortune.cnn.com/2008/06/19/itunes-store-5-billion-songs-50000-movies-per-day/.

5. Jim Turley, "The Two Percent Solution," *EE Times* [Online]. December 18, 2002. Available: http://www.eetimes.com/discussion/other/4024488/The-Two-Percent-Solution.

6. Thomas Fine, "The Dawn of Commercial Digital Recording," *ARSC Journal*, 39:1, 7.

7. Fine, "Commercial Digital Recording," 13.

Chapter 2: Preparing to Be a Music Technologist

1. Malcolm Gladwell, *Outliers: The Story of Success* (New York: Little, Brown and Company, 2008).

2. Ken Scott and Bobby Owsinski, *Abbey Road to Ziggy Stardust* (Los Angeles: Alfred Music Publishing, 2012), 3.

3. Scott and Owsinski, *Abbey Road*, 28.

4. Scott L. Phillips, *"Contributing Factors to Music Attitude in Sixth-, Seventh-, and Eighth-Grade Students,"* (Ph.D. diss., University of Iowa, 2003, Iowa City, IA).

5. Peter Webster and David Williams, *"Music Technology Skills and Conceptual Understanding for Undergraduate Music Students: A National Survey"* (Richmond, VA: Paper presented at the Association for Technology in Music Instruction National Conference, 2011).

Chapter 3: Studying to Be a Music Technologist

1. Southern Association of Colleges and Schools, *Mission Statement of the Commission* [Online]. Available: http://www.sacscoc.org/documents/Mission-Statement.pdf.
2. Belmont University College of Business Administration, *"Accreditation"* [Online]. Available: http://www.belmont.edu/business/accreditation.html.
3. Paul Clark, "The Sound of Science" *UNC Asheville Magazine* [Online], 3:2 (Fall/Winter 2011). Available: http://www3.unca.edu/magazine/archives/vol4no1/feature1.html.
4. Scott L. Phillips, *"A Survey of Music Technology Programs in the United States"* (Portland, OR: Paper presented at the Association for Technology in Music Instruction National Conference, 2009).
5. Association of American Colleges and Universities, "What is a 21st Century Liberal Education?" [Online]. Referenced March 23, 2012. Available: http://www.aacu.org/leap/what_is_liberal_Education.cfm.

Chapter 4: Starting Your Career as a Music Technologist

1. Costa Lakoumentas, "A Must-attend Trade Show," *The NAMM Show* [Online]. Available: http://www.namm.org/thenammshow/2013.
2. Robert K. Oermann, "Grand Ole Opry: The Show that Made Country Music Famous," *Official Website of the Grand Ole Opry* [Online]. Available: http://www.opry.com/about/WhatIsTheOpry.html.
3. Paul Mackun and Steven Wilson, "Population Distribution and Change: 2000 to 2010," *2010 Census Briefs* (March 2011). Volume C2010BR-01, pp. 1–12.
4. Austin City Limits, "History of ACL" [Online]. Referenced July 7, 2012. Available: http://acltv.com/history-of-acl/
5. Branson/Lakes Area Convention and Visitors Bureau, "A Branson History" [Online]. Referenced July 5, 2012. Available: http://www.explorebranson.com/about/branson-history.
6. Rick Dammers, *"Technology Based Music Classes in High Schools in the United States"* (Minneapolis, MN: Paper presented at the Association for Technology in Music Instruction National Conference, 2010).

Chapter 5: Music Technologists in the Recording Studio

1. Recorded January 5, 2012, Louisville, KY.

Chapter 6: Music Technologists in Live Sound

1. Recorded July 19, 2012, Birmingham, AL.

Chapter 7: Music Technologists in Film and Television

1. Scott Eyman, *The Speed of Sound: Hollywood and the Talkie Revolution, 1926–1930* (New York: Simon & Schuster, 1997), 26.
2. Recorded August 24, 2012.

Chapter 8: Music Technologists in Digital Media

1. Joseph F. Traub, *Oral History Interview by William Aspray, OH 94* (New York: Charles Babbage Institute, University of Minnesota, Minneapolis, March 29, 1985), 3.
2. United States Department of Labor: Bureau of Labor Statistics, "Occupational Outlook Handbook" [Online]. March 29, 2012. Available: http://www.bls.gov/ooh/computer-and-information-technology/home.htm.
3. Department of Labor, "Outlook Handbook," March 29, 2012.
4. Avid Technology, Inc., "About Avid" [Online]. Referenced August 4, 2012. Available: http://www.avid.com/US/about-avid.
5. ESA Entertainment Software Association, "Industry Facts" [Online]. Referenced July 3, 2012. Available: http://www.theesa.com/facts/index.asp.
6. Games Jobs Direct, Ltd., "Audio Lead" [Online]. Referenced July 22, 2012. Available: http://www.gamesjobsdirect.com/jobs/1058598/audio-lead.asp.
7. Recorded July 24, 2012, Birmingham, AL, Via Skype.

Chapter 9: Music Technologists in Sales and Support

1. United States Securities and Exchange Commission, *Guitar Center Holdings, Inc., Form 10K* (Filed March 26, 2012), 30.
2. Statista, "Online Shopping—Statistics and Facts" [Online]. Referenced April 13, 2012. Available: http://www.statista.com/topics/871/online-shopping/.
3. Securities and Exchange Commission, *Guitar Center*, 6.
4. Securities and Exchange Commission, *Guitar Center*, 5–6.

5. Christopher Guerin, "Press Release, Sweetwater Sound, June 26, 2012" [Online]. Available: http://www.sweetwater.com/about/press-releases/pr.php?id=00269.

6. Sweetwater Sound, Inc. "Career Openings: Sales Engineer" [Online]. Referenced August 7, 2012. Available: http://www.sweetwater.com/careers/openings.php.

7. Bose Corporation, "Careers at Bose" [Online]. Referenced June 12, 2012. Available: http://www.bose.com/controller?url=/about/careers/index.jsp .

8. PreSonus Audio Electronics, Inc., "PreSonus Job Opportunities: Technical Support Representative" [Online]. Referenced July 3, 2012. Available: http://www.presonus.com/about-presonus/Careers.

9. Recorded January 7, 2012, Louisville, KY.

Chapter 10: Music Technologists in Education

1. National Center for Education Statistics, "Table 83: Estimated Average Annual Salary of Teacher in Public Elementary and Secondary Schools: Selected Years, 1959–60 through 2010–11," *Digest of Education Statistics*, Prepared May 2011, [Online]. Available: http://nces.ed.gov/programs/digest/d11/tables/dt11_083.asp.

2. Steve Henderson, "More than 75 Percent of American Households Own Computers," *Focus on Prices and Spending, Consumer Expenditures: 2008*, 1:4, May 2010. [Online]. Available: http://bls.gov/opub/focus/volume1_number4/cex_1_4.htm.

3. Henderson, "Computers," 1:4.

4. Victoria J. Rideout, Ulla G. Foehr, and Donald F. Roberts, *Generation M2: Media in the Lives of 8- to 18-Year-Olds* (Menlo Park, CA, Henry J. Kaiser Family Foundation, 2010), 28.

5. Rick Dammers, *"Technology Based Music Classes in High Schools in the United States"* (Minneapolis, MN: Paper presented at the Association for Technology in Music Instruction National Conference, 2010).

6. Dammers, "Technology Based Music Classes," 2010.

7. Dammers, "Technology Based Music Classes," 2010.

8. Recorded July 19, 2012.

Chapter 11: Conclusion

1. Recorded August 3, 2012.

Index

FASKEN LEARNING RESOURCE CENTER
9000084259